ABOUT THE AUTHOR

Nigel Goodall is one of the most respected celebrity biographers in the UK, with more than 20 books on the movie and pop worlds to his credit. He has written about some of the biggest names in showbusiness including Elton John, Kylie Minogue, Ray Winstone, David Tennant and Winona Ryder, which combined have sold over a million copies and won him a literary prize nomination. Formerly a graphic designer with over 300 record sleeves to his name, a brief spell as a pop manager, voice-over artist and disc jockey, and the co-producer of the syndicated 1978 *Elvis Gospel* radio special, he has also contributed to various album, video and television projects for over a decade, including most recently, the *A&E Biographies* of Demi Moore and Christian Slater.

Nigel, who first wrote about Johnny Depp in 1997 and has followed his amazing career ever since, lives in Sussex, England, from where he travels occasionally to New York, San Francisco and Los Angeles for research and author interviews.

www.nigelgoodall.co.uk

D1394315

The Secret World of

JOHNNY DEPP

NIGEL GOODALL

JB

JOHN BLAKE

Published by John Blake Publishing Ltd,
3 Bramber Court, 2 Bramber Road,
London W14 9PB, England

www.johnblakepublishing.co.uk

First published in paperback in 2007
This edition published in 2010

ISBN: 978-1-84358-258-8

British Library Cataloguing-in-Publication Data:

A catalogue record for this book is available from the British Library.

Design by www.envydesign.co.uk

Printed in Great Britain by CPI Bookmarque, Croydon CR0 4TD

1 3 5 7 9 10 8 6 4 2

Papers used by John Blake Publishing are natural, recyclable products made
from wood grown in sustainable forests. The manufacturing processes conform
to the environmental regulations of the country of origin.

Every attempt has been made to contact the relevant copyright-holders, but
some were unobtainable. We would be grateful if the appropriate people could
contact us.

To the memory of Edy Wynhamer Samson.
An irreplaceable, spirited, joyful and loving woman.

CONTENTS

AUTHOR'S ACKNOWLEDGEMENTS

Thanks to everyone who has helped with this book and made it such fun to do. They include Vicki McKay, Mette Vesterdal, Neil Milner, Scott Coldwell, Michael Wilson, Eric Harshbarger, Cheryl Newman, Adam Parfitt, Ceri Parsons, Charlotte Heylar and Laurie Bratone. Keith Hayward was an enormous help and did some invaluable research. I would also like to mention two excellent websites devoted to all things Johnny – johnnydeppfan.com and Everything Johnny – both of which were of great help to me, and earned me my own Johnny and Winona pages on their sites. Thanks are also due to James Steven at Consolidated Communications, Georgina O'Neil at Entertainment Films, Charlotte Day at Sony Pictures, Vicky Lewis at Buena Vista International, the Louis B Mayer Library at the American Film Institute in Los Angeles, Sean

Delaney at the British Film Institute for all his help with film productions notes, scripts and articles, and the American Indian College Fund in New York for their generous help. Thanks too, to Mark Barker for the US box office information in the filmography. I am also indebted to Charlotte Rasmussen for the informative film glossary at the end of this book.

At Blake Publishing, my thanks to John Blake for commissioning the book, my editors Mark Hanks and Allie Collins for their enthusiasm and sharp eyes, and Graeme Andrew for excelling with the design and setting of the book, the stunning cover and picture sections.

I would also like to acknowledge the many magazines and newspapers that were consulted during my research: *Rolling Stone, Vogue, US, Now, GQ, Interview, Advocate, Vanity Fair, Icon, Harpers Bazaar, People, Hello, The Face, the Guardian, the Observer, The Times, Heat, The Sunday Times, FHM, People Weekly, TV Guide, Studio, Movieline, Newsweek, Eva, Flicks, Daily Star, Sky, Chat, Chicago Sun-Times, the Mirror, Los Angeles magazine, Total Film, Winona Fanzine, Planet Winona, Daily Mail, the Sun, Cowboys & Indians, Shout, the Detroit News.*

Finally, I am indebted to two books in particular: *Johnny Depp: A Modern Rebel* by Brian J Robb (Plexus, 1996) and *Winona Ryder* by Dave Thompson (Taylor, 1997).

INTRODUCTION

'I DON'T WANT TO KNOW WHO'S HOT,
WHO'S NOT, WHO'S RICH, WHO'S POOR,
WHO'S SUCCESSFUL, WHO'S JUST, YOU KNOW,
TAKEN A DUMP. I DON'T CARE.
I DON'T WANT TO KNOW ANY OF IT.'

The English writer Richard Holmes described the meaning of 'biography' as: 'A kind of pursuit, a tracking down of the physical trail of someone's path through the past, a following in the footsteps, of someone you would never quite catch. But maybe if you were lucky you might write about the pursuit of that fleeting figure in such a way as to bring it alive into the present.'

Looking back, that analogy seems apt to best describe my aim ever since I first wrote about Johnny Depp in 1997, in my biography of Winona Ryder, Johnny's highest profile girlfriend before Kate Moss. His three-year engagement to Winona was essential to my writing of her story. If I have succeeded in my aim, then I hope I have given the reader the correct tools to create his or her own portrait of one of Hollywood's most respected actors.

Back then, of course, if you had tossed a rock in Hollywood, the odds were reasonably high you would have hit some pretty boy haunted by his teen idol status and moaning about getting his due respect as a serious actor. Precisely the kind of teen pin-up star Johnny Depp used to be. In the years that have passed, of course, since he fronted every teen magazine at every newspaper stall, the *21 Jump Street* star has made a concerted effort to leave his teen idol years behind and attain artistic credibility in its stead. And in so doing, he has created a body of work that stands proud in its integrity.

He passed on the *Speed* role that catapulted Keanu Reeves to stardom, declined offers to play *Interview With the Vampire*'s Lestat, and *Bram Stoker's Dracula* (plum parts snatched up by Tom Cruise and Gary Oldman), rejected the mythic *Legends of the Fall* and the *Thelma and Louise* hustler assignments later taken by Brad Pitt, and chose to bequeath the roles of Robin Hood and Charlie Chaplin to Kevin Costner and Robert Downey Jnr.

Instead Johnny cemented his reputation in Hollywood by brilliantly portraying such *outré* souls as the lonesome, freakish protagonist of *Edward Scissorhands*, and the independent, cross-dressing *Plan Nine From Outer Space* director Ed Wood. As Johnny once explained, being a 'blockbuster boy' was never on his agenda, so isn't it ironic that today, he is now the number one box office star in Hollywood, simply for doing what he usually does, playing a role that interests him. Except on this occasion, portraying a roguish pirate gentleman, in Jerry Bruckheimer's action adventure *Pirates of the Caribbean*, earned him his first Oscar nomination for Best Actor. As Johnny told Chris

Connelly on the red carpet outside the Kodak Theater along Hollywood Boulevard during the arrivals for the 76th Annual Academy Awards ceremony, 'This is a horse of a different colour.'

The product of a small-town, blue-collar upbringing, Johnny was born to an engineer father and a homemaker mother in Owensboro, Kentucky. As a young boy, he spent as much time as possible visiting his beloved grandfather, who died shortly after Johnny's seventh birthday. That same year, Johnny's family moved to Florida, where his father found employment as director of public works in the coastal town of Miramar. Distraught over the death of his grandfather, and feeling displaced by the loss of the only permanent home he had known (the family lived in a dozen different houses after relocating to Florida), Johnny had become a surly and disinterested student by the time he reached high school.

Matters were made worse when his parents divorced shortly after he turned fifteen, and the contentious teen experimented widely with drugs and ultimately dropped out of school. Quite improbably, he discovered his next direction in life through an uncle who was fundamentalist minister. After watching his cousins perform gospel numbers at his uncle's church, Johnny took a shine to the electric guitar. His mother bought him a used instrument for 25 dollars, and soon the self-taught Johnny had become an accomplished garage-band guitarist.

Axe in hand, so to speak, Johnny set out to make his fortune playing rock music. He hooked up with a band called Flame, and though he was still legally a minor, the neophyte rocker began earning twenty-five dollars a night playing gigs at Florida nightclubs. But because he was underage, Johnny had to enter the clubs through the back door, and was allowed to remain inside for the first set only.

Shortly after changing its name to The Kids, the band toured as the opening act for punk rocker Iggy Pop. Two years later, Johnny and company relocated to Los Angeles, where they found the club scene so saturated with hopeful bands that they were forced to take day jobs to stay afloat. But that didn't help either. Not even Johnny selling telephone ads for what he still attributes as his first training as an actor. Even if it was fun, as Johnny says, without gigs or money, The Kids eventually disbanded.

During that same period, Johnny had met and briefly married make-up artist Lori Allison, who in turn introduced him to actor Nicholas Cage, who was so taken with Johnny's scruffy rocker look that he arranged an interview between Johnny and his agent.

That meeting resulted in Johnny's feature film debut in the role of a spiky-haired youth who becomes a midnight snack for a ravenous bed in director Wes Craven's *Nightmare on Elm Street*. 'It was really exciting,' Johnny exclaims today. 'I was shocked at Wes Craven and Annette Benson, the casting director, for taking such a chance on this guy who was totally green. I mean I had no idea. I didn't know [anything about] lights, marks, camera, position. I was clueless.'

Although Johnny's next role in the teen sex romp *Private Resort* made his *Nightmare* role look like a coup by comparison, and without much else on the horizon at the time, the newly aspiring actor enrolled into the Los Angeles

Loft Studio for what he considered was some much needed drama coaching.

But despite such reservations, and fresh out of acting school, Johnny won a small role in Oliver Stone's Oscar-winning Vietnam epic *Platoon*. Thereafter, his acting fortunes improved appreciably through a small assortment of television roles and he filled his free hours by playing in a new band called the Rock City Angels.

Johnny was originally offered his *21 Jump Street* role – that of Detective Tommy Hanson – shortly after filming wrapped on *Platoon*, but at that time, he did not want to stoop to small screen work, and refused even to look at the script. The producers hired another actor to play the role, but complications eventually caused them to solicit Johnny's services once more.

Johnny's agent finally persuaded her reluctant client to take the part by convincing him that the series stood an excellent chance of being cancelled after only one season, thereby freeing him to pursue other acting interests. To Johnny's lasting trepidation, the series was an instant hit, and he became the most popular cast member during his three seasons as Hanson. Despite his dislike for the show, he was quick to realise that 'if you want to go down this road where you are going for a quick career, lots of money, assembly line, kind of bang 'em out trash sort of stuff, you can do that. It's accessible and then there is the other thing where you try to do stuff that you want to do and have some semblance of integrity. I swore that when I got off the series, I was going to do only the things that I want to do and do interesting things that stimulate me.'

Determined to break from his teen boy image, and that

'bang 'em out trash', Johnny parodied his own dreamboat rep in his first post *Jump Street* film assignment, a role in maverick director John Waters' ruthlessly satirical *Cry Baby*. Though he was consistently high-minded in his choice of roles from then on, Johnny's quest for professional respectability took a few well-publicised detours.

In 1993, actor River Phoenix died of an apparent drug overdose at Johnny's Los Angeles nightclub, The Viper Room, and Johnny and his partners were subjected to no small amount of unflattering tabloid scrutiny following the tragic incident.

A hotel habitué, he made headlines in 1994 when he was arrested for trashing the presidential suite at Manhattan's Mark Hotel, although all charges against him were dropped after he agreed to pay for over two thousand dollars' worth of damages.

Another distraction, without doubt, was the 1993 break-up of his three-year engagement to his *Edward Scissorhands* co-star, Winona Ryder, in the wake of which Johnny had to have his 'Winona Forever' tattoo removed.

But perhaps the most distracting incident of all came in 1999. As I readied my manuscript for the first edition of this book, Johnny was arrested for chasing paparazzi photographers with a plank of wood through the streets of Mayfair in London's West End, which seemed to make him even less interested in co-operating with a biography about himself.

Since then, there has been more controversy. Most contentious were his misunderstood remarks to a German magazine about America being 'a dumb puppy' during the height of the US war with Iraq.

In spite of the continual upheavals in his personal life, however, Johnny delivered particularly excellent performances in *What's Eating Gilbert Grape?* and *Benny and Joon*. His stunning turn as a deep-cover FBI agent alongside Al Pacino's mob wise guy in *Donnie Brasco*, playing his pal Hunter S Thompson in the drug-inspired pseudo-memoir *Fear and Loathing in Las Vegas*, and the scientific Constable Crane in *Sleepy Hollow*, merely confirmed his reputation as one of the most gifted actors of his generation.

No stranger to the realm of celebrity romance – he has broken engagements to actresses Sherilyn Fenn and Jennifer Grey, in addition to his failed tryst with Winona – Johnny was sporadically involved with ultra-svelte supermodel Kate Moss for some years after the two first met at New York's trendy Cafe Tabac in 1994. He is now in a long-term relationship with French singer and actress Vanessa Paradis, to whom his bond is their first and second child together, and a spectacular villa they share in the south of France.

Perhaps as a result of his Winona fiasco, Johnny has yet to adorn himself with a 'Vanessa' tattoo; the 'Betty Sue' stencilled on his left bicep is in honour of his mother, and another tattoo on his right arm, a Native American chief's head, is in tribute to his Cherokee heritage. In 1996, he purchased a lavish Hollywood Hills mansion that once housed famed Dracula portrayer Bela Lugosi; the manor now houses Johnny, anytime he is in Los Angeles, and his collections of insects, rare books and guns.

Always one step ahead of the typecasting spectre, Johnny's most surprising big-screen successes came in the true-life story of US cocaine baron George Jung in *Blow*, as a troubled clairvoyant police detective on the trail of Jack the Ripper in *From Hell*, playing a romantic interest, albeit briefly for seventeen minutes of screen time, opposite Juliette Binoche in *Chocolate*, and as a corrupt CIA agent in *Once Upon A Time in Mexico*, the continuing story of El Mariachi.

He then appeared trapped in seventeenth-century England as the Earl of Rochester in *The Libertine* and reunited with Tim Burton, for a fourth and fifth time, firstly for a new version of the Roald Dahl classic *Charlie and The Chocolate Factory*, and secondly in Burton's animated masterpiece *Corpse Bride*. He has also reprised the role he made so famous, Captain Jack Sparrow, in the *Pirates of the Caribbean* sequels *Dead Man's Chest* and *At World's End*, and after that, he played the title role in Tim Burton's *Sweeney Todd*, and the Mad Hatter in *Alice in Wonderland*, another Burton collaboration. In 2009, Johnny took on the role of John Dillinger in *Public Enemies*. In 2011, he is expected to appear in Indian director Mira Nair's latest film, *Shantaram*, to which he seems to have been attached for ages. There is also talk of Johnny exec producing *The Rum Diary*, in which he will play his late pal, Hunter S Thompson, for a second time, in an adaptation of the gonzo journalist's first novel of the same name.

Not that long ago, shortly before we were treated to Johnny's remarkable portrayal of infamous outlaw John Dillinger in *Public Enemies*, the American journalist Johanna Schneller commented that Hollywood '...probably wishes that Johnny would do more mainstream movies and capitalise on his looks and play more conventional heroes, but he's never going to be that guy'. With work recently completed on *The Tourist* with Angelina Jolie, and now with a string of box-office smashes behind and in front of him, it is questionable whether that prophecy will turn out to be true or not. As Schneller concludes, '...you got a bunch of people in Hollywood who say Johnny Depp is now box office, which is hilarious because Johnny at any point could have chosen movies that had box office written all over them, and went in other directions deliberately and on purpose.'

It is a remarkable attitude to find in someone who works in a field that actively discourages such individuality. But that, however, may be the key to his success. With or without his star on the Hollywood Walk of Fame (interestingly enough, just two places up from Winona's) Johnny Depp has already proven that he can rise above the profit margin, and in so doing, has risen above the coins in the box-office coffers, and the stars as well.

CHAPTER 1

*'MOST OF THE FILMS I'VE BEEN INVOLVED WITH
HAVE BEEN OUTSIDE THE HOLLYWOOD STRUCTURE.
I HAVEN'T DONE MANY WITH LOTS OF ACTION AND
EXPLOSIONS AND PEOPLE IN JEOPARDY.
USUALLY I JUST MAKE FILMS THAT I THINK ARE
RIGHT FOR ME AND THAT I HOPE THE AUDIENCE
WILL FIND INTERESTING.'*

SWASH BUCK HERO

Vanessa Paradis loved spending Oscar night with Johnny Depp. At long last, the man she says she wants to spend the rest of her life with was finally achieving the kind of achievement that all Hollywood was applauding. If he hadn't played the role that had won him such acclaim, if he wasn't attending as a nominee, then perhaps there was no way that he and Vanessa would have come out for the big night in February 2004, the earliest in the year that the Academy Award rituals had ever been staged.

Nor would he and Vanessa have been hobnobbing with Johnny's celebrity peers. They would have probably preferred to stay home. As Johnny is quick to point out, 'I'm happy to say that I know nothing at all about who's in or out, or anything about the Hollywood scene. I don't watch contemporary films and I don't read trade magazines, I just don't know who's doing what, or who's a failure and who's a success.'

All the same, he was completely shocked 'that a movie which I was part of made a whole lot of money, and that thousands of kids went to see it. When a little kid approaches me on the street and screams "Hey, you're that Captain Jack Sparrow!" then I am always deeply touched.'

'That Captain Jack Sparrow,' as the kids called him, was the lead character in Jerry Bruckheimer's surprise summer hit of 2003, *Pirates Of The Caribbean: The Curse of The Black Pearl*. A film that was based on one of the top attractions in Disneyworld's Magic Kingdom.

Even though Roger Ebert, writing his review in the *Chicago Sun-Times*, couldn't quite understand the point of it, and called it 'a movie that charms the audience and then outstays it welcome.' With a $305 million gross in America and another £27 million in Britain, where it ran second only to *The Matrix Re-Loaded* as the biggest box office hit of the year, one could hardly say that it had outstayed its welcome.

Perhaps another point that Ebert had overlooked was the fact that, hit or not, the film was both stellar in its storytelling and in its cast. It is essentially the story of the roguish, yet charming, Captain Jack Sparrow, for whom the crystalline waters of the Caribbean, and high seas the world over, present a vast playground where adventure and mystery abound. But Jack's idyllic pirate life capsize after his nemesis, the wily Captain Barbossa, steals his ship, the Black Pearl, and later attacks the town of Port Royal, kidnapping the Governor's beautiful daughter, Elizabeth Swann.

Elizabeth's childhood friend, Will Turner joins forces with

Jack to commandeer the fastest ship in the British fleet, the HMS Interceptor, in a gallant attempt to rescue her and recapture the Black Pearl. The duo and their ragtag crew are pursued by Elizabeth's betrothed, the debonair and ambitious Commodore Norrington aboard the HMS Dauntless.

Unbeknownst to Will, a cursed treasure has doomed Barbossa and his crew to live forever as the undead, with only the moonlight eerily transforming them into living skeletons. The curse they carry can only be broken if the plundered treasure is restored in total, and a blood debt repaid.

Against all odds, the Interceptor and Dauntless race toward a thrilling confrontation with Barbossa's pirates on the mysterious Isla de Muerta. At stake is Jack Sparrow's revenge, the Black Pearl, a fortune in forbidden treasure, the lifting of the pirates' curse that has doomed Barbossa and his crew to live forever as skeletons, the fate of the British navy, and the lives of our valiant heroes as they clash their swords in fierce combat against the dreaded Pirates of the Caribbean.

Perhaps that's why Roger Ebert considered it pointless, because, as he put it, although 'the characters keep us interested during entirely pointless swordfights,' he points out that the pirates 'are already dead, they cannot be killed, so doesn't that mean there's no point in fighting them?' But surely this misses the whole point of pirate movies – fighting. Although he may not agree with that summation, he does concede that Johnny's performance was pretty much faultless. 'He seems to be channelling a drunken drag queen, with his eyeliner and the way he minces ashore and slurs his dialogue ever so insouciantly. It can be said that his performance is original in its every atom. There has never been a pirate, or for that matter a human being, like this in any other movie. There's some talk about how he got too much sun while he was stranded on that island, but his behaviour shows a lifetime of rehearsal. He is a peacock in full display.' Even when he arrives on shore in a dilapidated boat, he's told, 'You are without a doubt the worst pirate I have ever heard of.' Yes, he replies, 'but you have heard of me.'

Consider how boring it would have been, Ebert continues, 'if Depp had played the role straight, as an Errol Flynn or Douglas Fairbanks Snr or Jnr might have. To take this material seriously would make it unbearable. Captain Sparrow's behaviour is so rococo that other members of the cast actually comment on it. And yet because it is consistent and because you never catch Depp making fun of the character, it rises to a kind of cockamamie sincerity.' But wasn't that why Johnny was up for an Oscar? Simply because his portrayal was so damn good.

It was probably something director Gore Verbinski had thought about, long before he went after Johnny for the role. 'He's an artist who is known to take on quirky projects. He's a brilliant actor. He's not out to create a fan base for himself, or to simply select work based on salary. It's clear he needs to find a role that gives back to him artistically. I think he also wanted to do something specifically for his kids.'

But, almost ironically, Johnny's character isn't the kind of guy you would want your kids to emulate. Jack Sparrow, says Verbinski, 'is basically a con man. He's a great pirate, he's lazy and he is not going to fight if he doesn't have to. He's always going to take a shortcut. And the big thing for him the myth that he is part of. He's his own biggest agent, and he markets himself very well.'

Verbinksi wasn't the only one to think this. Jerry Bruckheimer was determined that when Johnny created his character, he would have as much free reign as possible. Bruckheimer describes how Johnny took full advantage of his freedom: 'He had a definite vision for Jack Sparrow, which is completely unique. We just let him go and he came up with this off-centre, yet very shrewd pirate. He can't quite hold his balance, his speech is a bit slurred, so you assume he's either drunk, seasick or he's been on a ship too long. But it's all an act perpetrated for effect. As strange as it seems, it's also part of Captain Jack's charm.'

For Johnny, it wasn't only the chance to create something from scratch, but the chance to take on a kind of role that, perhaps, no one would have previously considered him for, 'It was a great opportunity to invent this pirate from the ground up, to create a different kind of pirate than you have seen before.' He also appreciated the mischievous nature and never-say-die attitude of his character, 'In Jack, I saw a guy who was able to run between the raindrops. He can walk across the DMZ, entertain a troop and then sashay back to the other side and tell the enemy another story. He tries to stay on everyone's good side because he's wise enough to know he might need them in the future.'

And no matter how bad things got for Captain Jack, continues Johnny, 'there was always this sort of bizarre optimism about him. I also thought there was something beautiful and poignant about the idea of his objective. All he wants is to get his ship back, which represents nothing more than pure freedom to him. Of course, he'll thieve and do whatever it takes, especially when the opportunity arises, but his main focus is just to get the Black Pearl back at whatever cost.'

Yes, echoes Verbinksi, 'but again it's about the simplicity of the character; his great love and his great freedom are his ship. He's not a villain and he's not the love interest, although he does think he's got a chance with Elizabeth. In the end, Jack Sparrow is a bit of an oddball.' From Verbinski's point of view, Johnny's characterisation is not too unlike Lee Marvin's drunken gunfighter, Kid Shellen, in *Cat Ballou*, Elliott Silverstein's equally hilarious 1965 take on the wild west. As Marvin did, Johnny as Sparrow, 'really just floats through the story affecting all around him while pursuing his goal.'

According to Johnny, his inspiration for Jack Sparrow didn't come from Marvin, but largely from Rolling Stones guitarist, Keith Richards. If pirates were, as he put it, 'the rock and roll stars of the eighteenth century', then who, he wondered, was the coolest in the history of rock and roll today? 'To me it's Keith Richards, hands down. Over the years, I've been lucky enough to get to know him, so I tried not an imitation, but I drew on my memories of Keith – a certain grace, an elegance and a wit that I thought would be useful.' Not that this came across in the script. Nor did Johnny's character description mention anything about the bits of cartoon character Pepé Le Pew, and modern-day Rastafarian characteristics that he also tossed in. 'Jack's got little trinkets hanging in his hair, so that was another inspiration,' Johnny explains. 'I liked the idea that each one of these little pieces is a very vivid and extremely important memory for Jack.'

Another inspired touch was the silver and gold caps he put on his front teeth, in three different carats, to make each one reflect light differently. Although the makeup people found they needed to do very little to keep him as the rugged pretty boy, apart from darken his eyes, glue braids into his own goatee and have a wig made, the studio weren't so happy about the caps, and in the end, Johnny did concede to have them moved to his side teeth.

There were, of course, critical questions voiced about why Johnny had agreed to star in a Jerry Bruckheimer summer blockbuster, particularly one based on a Disneyland ride, especially in view of Johnny's defiantly subversive career choices up until then. Even if Bruckheimer himself didn't share those doubts, he did openly admit that he wasn't thrilled with the first screenplay draft that crossed his desk. In fact, it was only when *Shrek* writers Ted Elliott and Terry Rossio pitched him the idea of a movie with cursed pirates and skeletons in the moonlight that he got excited. The supernatural in a pirate movie wasn't something that anyone else had done before.

Armed with a new script, Bruckheimer flew out to France to try something few have ever done: to get Johnny Deep involved in a potential franchise action movie. A fool's errand, some may have said, but the way Bruckheimer saw it was that, 'Johnny's got kids now, and your point of view changes when you have kids.' His children, Johnny agreed, 'would definitely be one of the reasons. I wanted to make a more accessible movie. I mean, *Fear and Loathing In Las Vegas*, they may want to wait fifteen or twenty years to watch that one.'

Of course, once Johnny was firmly committed to the

movie, there was an immediate rush of both young and established actors anxious to try out for the other parts that were up for grabs. Geoffrey Rush literally jumped at the chance to play Captain Barbossa, Jack Sparrow's cursed nemesis and the thief of his ship, the Black Pearl. An Australian whose past credits include such disparate films as *Shakespeare In Love*, *Quills* and *Ned Kelly*, he proved to be the perfect choice for Barbossa.

It is uncertain whether Johnny screen-tested alongside Rush or not but, once filming began, the pair hit it off immediately. They shared a mutual admiration for each other and were excited to be working side by side. A similar sense of excitement prevailed as the remainder of the cast was assembled. Orlando Bloom, best known for his role as Legolas in the *Lord of the Rings* trilogy, was recruited to play the romantic lead, blacksmith Will Turner; Keira Knightley, the much talked-about star of *Bend It Like Beckham*, and the forthcoming *King Arthur*, was cast as Elizabeth Swann, Will's abducted true love; film and stage veteran Jonathan Pryce would be playing her father, Governor Weatherby Swann; and Jack Davenport, from *This Life*, the British hit television series, accepted the role of Commodore Norrington, the newly appointed commander of the British Naval Fleet in Port Royal, to whom Elizabeth's father hopes his unconventional, bold and sometimes downright audacious daughter will marry.

The attention to detail given to the casting was carried over to the filming itself. Under the watchful eye of production designer Brian Morris, one example of the film's extravagance was the pirate cave where Barbossa stashes the many riches that have been plundered by his crew. It was the centrepiece of the many sets constructed at Walt Disney Studios in Burbank – the largest stage on the Disney lot. It was recently enlarged, and was the prefect location to build a lavishly adorned cavern, complete with winding waterways, a moat, little grottos and treacherous rocky terrain. Interestingly enough, it took 100 craftsmen five months to build the cave set, which was filled with 300,000 gallons of water, and then set dressed over a period of three weeks.

Every object on the set was researched and selected for its authenticity, recalls set decorator Larry Dias. 'It was a big job just trying to stay true to the period and to the style of the movie. We had to make the sets look authentic because the film has a dramatic flair, but it's also comedic, so we tried to set a mood so that the atmosphere would be realistic yet theatrical at the same time.'

No less daunting was the task of the ships. Trouble was that there are very few ships in existence that could pass for a vessel dating back to the eighteenth century. The studio and the producers initially assumed they would have to build every ship featured in the story, never imagining they would stumble across a virtual treasure trove of information and contacts, who knew where to find viable stand-ins. They found such a character when they hired Marine co-ordinator, Matt O'Connor. A boating enthusiast and marine specialist who had been working in the film industry for over fifteen years, he contacted an associate in Seattle and persuaded him to convince his board of directors to allow the production company to use their prized tall ship, along with a fully staffed crew, for an unprecedented amount of time, in a location halfway around the world, but substantial structural modifications to the vessel were necessary.

The offer was too exciting to pass up, and the owners of the ship embraced the challenge, undeterred by the obstacles presented in such an undertaking. So, the Lady Washington was modified and became a valued member of the cast, 'starring' as the Interceptor.

No pirate movie is complete without action sequences, and *Pirates of the Caribbean* was no exception. The incredible sword fights took four hours each day to get right, as the cast practised moves that had been choreographed by the eighty-year-old legendary film swordsman and one-time Errol Flynn double, Bob Anderson. Another unforgettable part for Johnny and Keira Knightley, is the 'walk the plank' scene, as they call it. They spent almost three shooting days standing at the end of a long two by four plank that protruded from the side of the Black Pearl's deck, fifteen feet over the rolling ocean waves. No stunt person, no body double, no look-alike or dead ringer needed to apply – it was Johnny and Keira balanced at the end of that plank.

'I'd been standing on that plank for two days, with nothing but air around me and water below, I was absolutely petrified,' recalls Knightley. 'The plank is quite narrow like a diving board, so it bounces up and down when you move and even when you just stand there. When it came time to jump off the board, Gore told me I didn't have to do it, that he'd have my stunt double, Sonia, do it. I said, "I've been standing up here for two days! Do you really think I'm not going to jump off this thing?" So I jumped in that long dress. I was terrified. I asked Gore if he wanted me to scream and he just said, "whatever comes out". I screamed my head off. The only interesting bit was when I hit the water and the dress went over my head, so I showed off my knickers. I was so girly, but I was proud of myself. I don't know what I must have looked like,' she laughs. Despite her fear, Knightley came up smiling, unscathed by the experience.

Overall, it was an intense movie with an equally intense shooting schedule. But screenwriters Ted Elliott and Terry Rossio had set out with the idea that, if parents feel their children are old enough to go on the *Pirates of the Caribbean* ride, then they would be old enough to see the movie. Elliott himself recalls going on the ride when he was just six years old, and feeling a mix of absolute exhilaration and a little bit of terror. 'Exuberant delight, I guess, you'd call it. And that's what we wanted for everyone who sees the movie. To experience the feeling they had the first time they went on the ride.'

And that excitement was present for those who attended the world première at Disneyland on Saturday 28 June 2003. It was the first time that Disneyland had played host to a movie première, with cast, crew and special guests arriving from 6.30pm to take over the whole place for a special, advanced screening, before the film was released just over a week later.

According to a report that appeared on the Internet soon after, 'the event was crazy, to say the least. Disneyland opened at six in the morning just to give 'normal' people enough hours in the park. Twelve hours later, it was closed and everyone was booted out to make way for the Hollywood folk. The entire west side of the park was swarming with pirates, whores, bands, and security. A smattering of rides were opened for the enjoyment of invited guests, and for the first time, without queues. A whole load of fancy bleachers were set up all around the Rivers of America and a gigantic screen was built on Tom Sawyer Island. The sailing ship Columbia was parked in front of everyone with a band on it, there were speakers everywhere. All at full blast. After the movie there were fireworks that went in perfect timing with the film score. Overall it was an amazing night.' Equally amazing were the giveaways, which included dinner, hats, posters, tattoos, swords, blankets, piggy banks, pictures and games.

Perhaps equally crazy, as far as Johnny is concerned, was the surprise of the countless accolades that he has received for his performance. He never expected such attention. 'I'm very thankful. And I'm very grateful for this past year, and certainly the things that have happened. I had no expectations at all. Certainly not nominations of any sort. So I'm very touched, very moved.'

At the same time, though, he knew he was going through what he called a 'decompression period' since he had completed filming. 'If you're really connected with a character, you always do to some degree. You miss the guy. You miss being that person. The only thing that was in the back of my mind was the hope that there would be a sequel some day, so that I could meet him again.'

CHAPTER 2

*'IN MY HIGH SCHOOL, THERE WERE DIFFERENT
CLASSES OF PEOPLE: THE JOCKS, THE SMART KIDS,
AND THE REDNECKS. THEN THERE WERE THE BURNOUTS.
NONE OF THE GIRLS WANTED TO HANG OUT WITH ME.
I WAS JUST, YOU KNOW, A KIND OF WEEDHEAD –
A WEIRD KID.'*

REBEL WITH A CAUSE

John Depp and his wife Betty Sue were living in Owensboro during the summer of 1963. The city is the third largest in Kentucky, first settled in 1780 by explorers Joseph Blackford and William Smeathers. It was not until 1817, however, and in honour of Colonel Abraham Owens, a local dignitary, that it became established as it is today. And still best known for playing host to the world famous International Bar-B-Q Festival.

Although the Depps already had three children by this time, two of them from Betty Sue's first marriage, daughters, Debbie and Christi, and a son, Dan or "DP" for short, Betty Sue was now heavily pregnant with John's baby, their second together, and if everything went according to plan, John Christopher Depp II, Johnny Depp, would be born on June 9. And according to the local newspaper, where his birth was dutifully announced, he was.

John Snr and Betty Sue could never have been described as anything other than typically conventional parents, and the world in which they circulated was equally typical. John was a public servant, working as a city engineer. Betty Sue worked as a waitress in a local coffee house. According to Johnny, years later, she 'cursed like a sailor, played cards and smoked cigarettes. And sometimes she would come home after working ten hours with $30 in tips. So in turn, when I was growing up, I just got in the habit of tipping.'

All the same, the Depps were, to all intents and purposes, a working-class American family, benefiting from the explosion of cheap tract housing first developed in the Fifties. They lived in a suburban town, had suburban lives and dreamed suburban dreams. It was, after all, the 1960s – the decade in which the post-war promises came of age, and the American dream was possible. If you worked nine to five, then why not? You could have the house, the car and the family, just like on the postcards and in the magazines. Heart and soul, John and Betty Sue were products of the Sixties.

But eight years after Johnny's birth, the war in Vietnam was still grinding on, and Nixon was still in the White House. And just three months after Johnny's eighth birthday, an American court martial finished trying the 25 officers and men charged with involvement in the 1968 civilian massacre at My Lai. Twenty-four of them were released unpunished. Three months later, the American airforce would commence its most intensive bombing campaign yet.

Insurrection at home was crushed no less ruthlessly. The

horror of Kent State, where the National Guard fired upon unarmed student protesters, was still fresh in the mind when Attica State Prison in upstate New York erupted into open rebellion in September 1971. There, too, the solution was unbridled violence, as the prisoners' demands were answered by a thousand shock troops. And the first cogs in the machine that would eventually spit out the national humiliation of Watergate quietly began to turn. A dream, as the Depps had seen it, was ending.

Despite their convictions, Johnny wasn't about to be drawn into what he considered their suburban way of life. Neither did he want to emerge affected by the liberal principles to which he was now exposed, as his almost solitary life with his grandfather would prove.

As a child, Johnny would spend as much time as he could with him. 'I remember picking tobacco back in Kentucky,' he explained. 'We were inseparable, me and Pawpaw. He died when I was seven and that was a real big thing for me. But somehow I believe that he's around. I believe in ghosts. I hope I'm a ghost someday. I think I'd have more energy. But I'm sure my Pawpaw is around – guiding, watching. I have close calls sometimes. I think, Jesus Christ! How did I get out of that? I've just got a feeling that it's Pawpaw.'

Johnny's grandfather was a full-blooded Cherokee Indian who had the same haunting good looks, sharp cheekbones, and sculpted visage that Johnny himself would, in the coming years, lend to magazine covers the world over and cause much of American girlhood to fall for him.

The Depp family, although a fusion of German and Irish ancestry, were Cherokee by heritage. Even Johnny's version of his Cowboys and Indians playtime remained loyal to those same Indian nation bloodlines. Never once did he allow his Indian to be shot, wounded, die or even fall to the ground, no matter how many times his childhood friend, Sal Jenco, aimed and fired off his cap gun pistol.

It was that fiercely independent spirit that was already firing the determination that would dictate his future. Johnny would simply not be assigned rules and regulations. He needed first to want it and feel it. It should come as no surprise that Johnny's first source of conflict with authority was his suspension from school for exposing his buttocks to a teacher. The command to carry out an everyday, mundane task was, in Johnny's eyes, simply the last straw.

But then again, 'I was a weird kid,' Johnny freely admits today. 'A kind of weed-head. I wanted to be Bruce Lee,' he remembers. 'I wanted to be on a SWAT team. And when I was five, I think, I wanted to be Daniel Boone.' But not everyone fitted into his personal iconography of heroes. John Wayne, for instance, was certainly a no-no. 'I know this sounds kind of anti-American, but I never could stand him. He seemed like such a right-wing, radical sort of guy.'

Maybe that was true. Maybe, too, his dislike of the celebrated screen cowboy had something to do with Johnny's own Cherokee heritage. After all, wasn't it Wayne who always made a habit of slaughtering hundreds of Indians in his movies? It is events like that which appal Johnny today. He still reels at the knowledge of how many distant relatives must have been lost in what he calls the genocidal murder of millions of American Indians.

In fact, it was the death of his grandfather, when Johnny was seven, that convinced the Depp family that the time was ripe to move, this time south to Miramar, just down the coast from Miami.

Even more importantly, moving to the working coastal town was a step in the right direction for Johnny's father, who found work there as a public works official. And not unlike Johnny's own future of living in a succession of hotel rooms and rented apartments, his parents would check into one of the town motels, and would not move again for another twelve months.

In the end, though, Johnny recalls, 'We must have moved about 30 times. We'd go from neighbourhood to neighbourhood, sometimes from one house to the house next door. I don't know why. My mom would get ants somehow. But there's a huge history of my family out there. Furniture, my toys, schoolwork, everything, everything, everything was abandoned, left in attics or garages. All gone. We were gypsies, we lived all over the place, always transient. After a while, I thought, I'm not even going to introduce myself to the other kids.'

Those other kids, or schoolmates, Johnny found, shared very little common ground with him. But he didn't care. Why should he? After all, what on earth could a bunch of conforming school kids offer Johnny that rivalled the thrill of what he had in mind for his life in the small communal town?

It was, Johnny continues, like Endora, the dead-end town in the movie *What's Eating Gilbert Grape?* 'Where nothing much happens and nothing much ever will.' Not surprising really when you consider there wasn't much there other than the two grocery stores directly across the street from each other.

'There's a Winn-Dixie here, with a drugstore next door and, next to that, a card and gift store. Across the street was Publix, with its drugstore and card and gift store. The same thing, only different names. Either way, you were just there.'

And there was where he didn't want to be. It was probably what further complicated Johnny's childhood – the difficulty he encountered fitting in at school, for instance. 'I was not the most popular kid,' he mutters. 'I always felt like a total freak. That feeling of wanting to be accepted but not knowing how to be accepted as you are – honestly.' He talked on another occasion of 'wanting to hold a girl, but thinking I'll screw it up'.

In the years to come, of course, he would exact perfect revenge upon them all, by winning the affections of precisely the same sort of people in the movie *Edward Scissorhands*.

Right now, though, all he could do was hope it wouldn't be for ever. By his own admission and by his own lack of interest in his schooling, he arranged to sign up with the town's football team mainly because he thought it would please his father. But that didn't work out either. After a month he quit, and then wondered why he joined up and quit twice more.

But he also learned very quickly to pick up on other interests. Throughout his childhood, he documents, music was a constant passion, and one of his first real love affairs was with the band Kiss, whose performances were as outrageous as their music. He had even tried to emulate their vocalist Gene Simmons. He, too, would eat fire. But the day Johnny tried it for himself, his face went up in flames.

'I was, maybe, 12,' Johnny recalls, 'and we put a T-shirt on the end of a broom handle, soaked it in gasoline and lit it. Then I put gasoline in my mouth and breathed fire like Simmons. Only it set my face on fire; I was running down the street with my face alight. Unfortunately, my mom obviously was going to see that my face was all burned up, so I lied completely. I said we were shooting fireworks off and one went off in my face. And she fell for it. She certainly didn't expect me to say, "Well, I put gasoline in my mouth and blew it into a huge stick of fire, Mom." The fireworks story was easier for her and me; and she bought it, bless her heart. It was one of the dumbest things I've ever done – not the dumbest, but right up there – and I have done lots of stupid things.'

In addition to his musical tastes, Johnny continued to share in the world's admiration of stunt motorcyclist, Evel Knievel, who in the late Seventies was wowing audiences with his death-defying leaps over rows and rows of double-height vehicles on his specially designed star-spangled Chopper bike. But as Johnny watched and played on, he also immersed himself in Vincent Van Gogh, as much for the artist's life and struggle as for his works of art.

Another obsession was the Second World War. As time passed, however, it must have seemed strange to his parents that he couldn't stop reading about Nazi Germany. Nor could he get enough of recreating imaginary episodes of *Hogan's Heroes*. In the back yard, he would dig a tunnel, clamber underground, and sit there waiting for the whole thing to collapse around him. It must have seemed even stranger when John and Betty Sue compared him to his friends. Even when he wasn't digging tunnels, he would be dreaming of becoming the first white member of the Harlem Globetrotters.

Equally influential in Johnny's upbringing, albeit for different reasons, was his uncle. He was, Johnny explained 'a preacher who had this gospel group. He did the whole bit, where he stood up at the podium and held his arms out crying, and said, "Come on, run up, and be saved." And people would come up to his feet. It was that whole weird idol thing.'

Johnny, as much as anyone else in the congregation, couldn't believe how enthralling the art of performance was close up. He was even treated to a masterclass in capturing and holding the attention of an audience. And he witnessed the tricks and techniques his uncle used to convince his congregation of the truth of what he said, of the importance of what he revealed, and of the power of the artifice he employed.

His uncle often encouraged Johnny to express himself in the same way, whether musically or otherwise. Indeed, the influence of his uncle's approach to performance had already hit home. In fact, he couldn't wait to climb up on stage and try it out for himself. In such an environment, the idea of becoming a rock 'n' roll star became second nature to Johnny. Well, it sure beat the gas station attendant job that he feared would await him at the end of his schooling.

'My cousin had a gospel group and they came down and played gospel songs, and that was the first time I ever saw an electric guitar,' observed Johnny. 'I got obsessed with the electric guitar, so my mom bought me one for $25. I was about 12 years old. Then I locked myself in a room for a year and taught myself how to play chords, picking things off records. That's how I got through puberty, just sitting in my room playing guitar, slobbering. Rarely do I remember seeing my family. And then I started playing in little garage bands. The first group I ever played in was called Flame.'

He even introduced a distinctive image for the band. 'At first we would wear T-shirts that said "Flame" on them. Next, at 13, I was wearing plain shirts. Then, I used to steal my mom's clothing. She had all these crushed velvet shirts with French-cut sleeves. And like seersucker bell bottoms; I dreamed of having platforms, but couldn't find any.'

Forever understanding, John and Betty Sue were still concerned about Johnny's schooling. It wasn't really going according to plan. 'I'd been in high school three years, and I may have just walked in yesterday. I had like eight credits, and I was in my third year of high school and I didn't want to be there. I was bored out of my mind, and I hated it.'

It was then, Johnny said, 'I hung around with bad crowds. We used to break and enter places. We'd break into the school and destroy a room or something. I used to steal things from stores.'

Even years later, when Johnny was asked for an autograph by one of his former teachers, he was outraged. 'I mean, what was I supposed to say? He'd failed me. I remember one time this teacher yelled at me so heavily in front of the entire class. He didn't have any time for me then, and now, all of a sudden, he wants my autograph?

They all thought I was going to end up a drug addict, and in jail.'

And maybe they were right, Johnny concedes. It really didn't make any sense for them to keep him in the classroom when he wasn't exactly an exemplary pupil. 'I started smoking at 12, lost my virginity at 13 and did every kind of drug there was by 14. Pretty much any drug you can name, I've done it. I wouldn't say I was bad or malicious, I was just curious,' he admits. 'I certainly had my little experiences with drugs. Eventually, you see where that's headed and you get out.'

That proved to be the least of Johnny's difficulties. In 1978, when Johnny was 15, John and Betty Sue got divorced. It was the second time Betty Sue had suffered a failed marriage and things seemed to deteriorate very quickly from then on. Untreated, and certainly unrested from the emotional turmoil, Betty Sue was a broken-heart victim just waiting to happen. But the whole family, Johnny recalls, pulled together and did the best they could.

'Family is the most important thing in the world,' he says. 'Without that, you have nothing. It's the tightest bond you'll ever have. When you're in your teens, family's family. You think it's always gonna be there. You think, "I want friends and I want cars and I wanna do things different." But there's a certain age you hit when you realise, "What am I doing? This is my family." When my parents split up was when I think I realised these are the most important people in my life and, you know, I'd die for these people. I was 16, and it just sort of happened. You just deal with it, but there's no escaping the hurt. I mean, it definitely hurts.'

Johnny continues, 'I can remember my parents fighting and us kids wondering who was going to go with whom if they got divorced. When they did,' he continues, 'my father left and my mother was deeply hurt and sick physically and emotionally.'

Johnny elected to go with his mother, sister Christie, who is now firmly installed as his manager and adviser, and brother Dan, also now installed as the other half of his production company. Johnny's other sister Debbie went with her father to Hallendale where he still lives and works.

As for Betty Sue, Johnny, taking one step at a time, turned his attention to finding her a place of her own. He began looking around and found one north of Los Angeles. It is where she still lives today with her third husband, Robert Palmer. 'I don't sleep or eat much as a rule,' Johnny proclaimed. 'But at her house, I'm so relaxed, I immediately become starving. Then fall into this deep sleep.

'She's the greatest lady in the world,' he continues. 'Best friend, coolest thing. Just unbelievable. Her whole life she's been a waitress, but I won't let her wait tables any more.' And nowhere is that tribute better expressed than the day he headed for a local tattoo parlour and asked to have her name imprinted into his flesh inside a bright red heart.

He even made a note of when he had it done so he could tell his grandchildren. 'When I'm 90, and I'm sitting around and they go, "Gramps, when did you get that?" I want to be able to say 31 May 1988.'

And the Betty Sue tattoo would be discussed in much the same way as the Indian Chief's head he had engraved some years earlier, this time on his right side, in commemoration of his Cherokee heritage. If Johnny hadn't exactly told anyone about his intense curiosity in tattoos and self-scarring, he certainly sensed that people would soon ask. 'I remember carving my initials on my arm,' he once said. 'And I've scarred myself from time to time since then. In a way your body is a journal and the scars are sort of entries in it.'

He even developed elaborate plans with his friend Sal Jenco to retreat from the turmoil of it all. The two were already seasoned veterans of everything imaginable. Now the two of them planned to live in the back of an old 1967 Impala, simply because Jenco had nowhere else to call home. It had, Johnny recalls, back seats filled with beer cans but little else. A far cry from the civilising essentials such as electricity, running water and all those other modern luxuries Johnny would now live without.

But in contrast to many of the journalists who have examined his early life in Miramar, Johnny balks at calling his upbringing wild and reckless. It was only after he became famous, he asserts, that he was tagged with those labels. Besides, 'the only reason that any of my past came out is because I brought it out. And the reason is that, hopefully, people can learn from it. Kids can say "Jesus, he went through the same thing I'm going through now. Maybe I'm not a bad kid, like everyone says."'

Everyone, he says, has conveniently labelled him 'a bad boy, or a delinquent or a rebel or one of those horrible things. To me, it was much more curiosity. It wasn't like I was some malicious kid who wanted to kick some old lady in the shin and run, you know. I just wanted to find what was out there.'

Nevertheless, he says, he had a fairly normal childhood. 'When you're 13, 14, and you hang out with a bunch of guys and the junior high prom just doesn't do it for you, you go out and do something. Experiment. You live in Miami as a kid, and drugs are everywhere. You try it for the usual reasons. Peer pressure, curiosity, boredom.'

CHAPTER 3

*'I'D SAY I FELT WEIRD FROM THE TIME
I WAS 12 TO THE TIME I WAS 17, BUT THEN
AGAIN, DURING YOUR TEENAGE YEARS, THERE'S
THAT FEELING OF SAFETY, LIKE NOTHING
CAN GO WRONG. BUT THAT KIND OF FEELING
GETS LOST LATER.'*

A ROCK STAR IS ALMOST BORN

'In 1979, when Johnny was 16, he still wasn't going to go back to school. He'd had enough with his fight for academic achievement. And he was tired of being the one who dreaded arriving at school every morning and finding that he had precious little in common with his schoolmates. When the rest of the class talked about *Star Wars*, Johnny would rave about whichever latest stunt Evel Knievel had pulled off, and when they laughed about last night's TV sitcom, Johnny would quote from *Hogan's Heroes*, the mouldy oldie that so enthralled him.

Johnny's musical tastes, too, were also unpopular at school. In the late Seventies punk rock was not exactly embraced by the musical mainstream. It was wild, weird, anti-social, and the people who liked it weren't much better. Indeed, when his schoolmates found out that Johnny liked the New Wave bands he was immediately regarded as an outcast. When they discovered that he was determined to pursue a career playing the same music, his ostracism was confirmed.

Johnny's band, The Kids, started out performing cover versions and warming up audiences for big name bands like the B52s and Talking Heads. And although they concentrated briefly on writing their own material (that Johnny would best describe as 'U2 mixed with the Sex Pistols'), they did little else.

'I'm sure my brain stopped at 17,' Johnny remembers. 'I was really happy then. I was playing in a band, reading books because I hadn't read in school, and there were girls around. In a way, I'm sort of stuck here.'

Forever persevering, the Kids next played some rock 'n' roll clubs in Florida. The only trouble, Johnny concedes, was that 'I was under age. But they would let me come in the back door to play, and then I'd have to leave right after the first set. That's how I made a living on about $25 a night.' There were, however, other times, when they ended up playing gigs for much more, sometimes for over $2,000. 'We used to make that for the entire group and road crew,' which, as Johnny would point out, was a huge sum at that time.

Around two years later, when Johnny was 18, 'we did two shows with Iggy Pop, and after, I got really, really drunk.' He was at the bar after the club had closed, getting ready, as Johnny puts it, 'to puke or something. And I saw Iggy in skimpy little pants wandering around the club with a dog. And for some reason, I started screaming and yelling at him, "Fuck you!" I don't know why, because I always idolised him. And he walked over, and just looked at me. I thought he was gonna hit me. And I said, "You little turd." And then he walked away.'

In the coming years, of course, the two would be reunited when they came together on the set of John Waters' *Cry Baby*. Discussing the incident then, Iggy Pop sighed philosophically. 'I was probably in the same condition as you, maybe worse,' Iggy said.

That was six years after Johnny had already become a musical hero himself around the usual Florida hangouts. It also proved to be the place where he met and eventually married Lori Ann Allison, a make-up artist five years older than Johnny, and whose favourite local band at that time was The Kids. She, too, had been trying her luck in music, as a recording engineer. But it was her sister Suzanne, now dating Bruce Witkin, another of The Kids, who apparently brought them together. If there were two people who could pull off a record deal for the band, it was Johnny and Lori. But their failure to do so, it was said in some quarters, contributed to the ending of their relationship two years later.

Others in the band were well aware of what they were going through, and Johnny remembers how he himself was feeling. 'I was married when I was 20. It was a strong bond with someone, but I can't necessarily say it was love. That's something that comes around once, maybe twice, if you're lucky. And I don't know if I experienced that, let's say, before I turned 30.'

But according to childhood friend Yves Bouhadana, 'I remember him being very excited about getting married to Lori [on 20 December 1983]. In fact, I remember hers as being the first serious relationship that he had, so he was madly in love with her, and ready to be married to her'.

Either way, it was also a sign of how quickly things could change. 'I remember being in seventh grade and having the most intense crush on this very popular girl,' Johnny admitted. 'I pined for this girl, like beyond *Romeo and Juliet*. Shocking. I just chewed my tongue up for her. Eighth grade comes along, we hang out a little at those parties where you end up making out. So we did that, and I just couldn't have been happier. Then she goes for the football guy, and leaves me just dangling in the breeze.'

Years later, Johnny continues, 'after I dropped out of high school, I'm playing a club. I'm on stage and I look out and I'm like "Fuck, it's her!" So I finished the set and I go directly to the bar where she's sitting and I walk up to her and it's that face, man – incredible. And I went, "It's so nice to see you!" And I look at her, and she's 250 pounds! She is mammoth, but her face is still the same. Again I went, "Oh my, nice to see you – how many kids do you have?" And she had four kids – what fitting payback for fucking breaking my heart when I was a little kid.'

All the same, Johnny simply put his time with Lori down to the process of growing up. Not even moving to Hollywood seemed to help.

'I guess I have very traditional kinds of sensibilities about that kind of stuff,' Johnny admitted later. 'You know, a man and a woman sharing their life together and having a baby, whatever. I think for a while I was trying to right the wrong of my parents because they split up when I was a kid, so I thought I could do it differently, make things work. I had the right intentions, but the wrong timing, and the wrong person. But I don't regret it. I had fun and I learned a lot from it.' More importantly, Johnny said, 'It wasn't working out, so we took care of it.'

Before the couple finally called it quits, Johnny, Lori and

the rest of the band made what would best be described as an all-out last-ditch plea for rock 'n' roll stardom. 'Don Ray, a guy who booked all the bands at the Palace in Hollywood thought we should come out,' Johnny remembers. 'He wanted to manage us, so he pitched me some money and we saved up some money, and drove out there.'

But there was, of course, another set-back. The one that probably hadn't even crossed their minds. Getting the band working in Hollywood wasn't as easy as they had first thought. 'It was horrible,' Johnny admits. 'There were so many bands it was impossible to make any money. So we all got side jobs. We used to sell ads over the telephone – telemarketing. We got $100 a week for ripping people off. We'd tell them they'd been chosen by so-and-so in their area to receive a grandfather clock. They would order $500 worth of these fucking things and we would send them a cheap grandfather clock. It was horrible.'

Almost as horrible, Johnny confessed, as the little money he made selling personalised pens to companies over the phone. 'My first acting job,' he would smile later. 'I was working this day job selling ink pens over the phone and getting maybe $10 a week, and I thought, "What have I got to lose?" The last couple of times I did it, I just said, "Listen, you don't want this stuff, man."'

But for most of it, 'I attribute that job as my first training as an actor,' Johnny repeated. 'You would start playing different characters on the telephone because you got bored. And you would come up with different names and different voices and stuff like that. It actually turned out to be kind of fun.'

All the same, The Kids, Johnny says, 'did some good shows in LA. We played with the Bus Boys and Billy Idol.' But that's all there was more or less. Doing the same as they had done in Florida. If there was a career to be made out of playing in a band, hell, it sure didn't come their way.

Johnny and Lori took the disappointment stoically. But still their failing hurt. They both decided to sit back and take stock of their lives. They needed to start putting things back in their rightful place. What they really wanted to do was sort out their increasingly ambivalent feelings for each other. As it turned out, one of those decisions was to dissolve their partnership in The Kids through divorce. They did that as well, almost two years to the day after they met. Johnny was 22, Lori 27.

Even worse, of course, was the pain that was part and parcel of the divorce. The same pain that Johnny and his parents had themselves lived through seven years earlier.

The only bright spot on the horizon was Lori's old friend Nicholas Cage. He was then the newly-emergent star of 1983's *Rumble Fish* and nephew of its director Francis Ford Coppola, best known at the time for his *Godfather* epics. He suggested that Johnny try acting. And with the help of his agent, he landed Johnny an audition call for a movie about to go into production with Wes Craven.

The director of such horror flicks as *The Last House on the Left* and *The Hills Have Eyes*, Craven's latest project was *A Nightmare on Elm Street*, a gruesomely bleak – and frequently unpleasant – slasher story. The screenplay, Craven's own labour of love, did not shy away from the explicit, to put it mildly.

Indeed, Craven had always been fascinated by dreams and the subconscious long before he learned he might be able to bring it to life on celluloid. During his first years of success, the fascination continued to gnaw at the director's mind. Then, some years before *A Nightmare on Elm Street* went into production, he came across a batch of newspaper reports about Laotian refugees so afflicted with horrifying nightmares that they became terrified of falling asleep.

It was this theme that he weaved into his movie, lending it a new character that would redefine horror as much as *The Exorcist* had done for the 1970s. *A Nightmare on Elm Street* defined slasher movies for the next decade and for most of the one that followed with such outings as *Scream, I Know What You Did Last Summer* and, of course, another four *Nightmare* sequels.

Not that Craven would have anything to do with them. When filming of *A Nightmare on Elm Street* commenced in July 1984 for release in October one year later, Craven had no intention of making any others. 'Why do a sequel?' he asked, when this one would be adequate enough on its own. Hell, how many times could the story be told before it would outrun its course?

Producer Robert Shaye, however, had different ideas. He and production company New Line Cinema had seen the potential for making further instalments and even asked Craven to shoot another ending for the continuity aspect of the saga. He refused, and remained in conflict with them over the next ten years throughout the following sequels, right up to his own, *Wes Craven's New Nightmare* in 1994.

It was the story of an outrageous new bogey-man, the hamburger-faced, razor-taloned Freddy Krueger, a child murderer who was burned to death after escaping conviction and who has now returned to his old stomping ground on Elm Street to haunt the inhabitants – mostly teenagers.

There, they share common nightmares as Freddy, played by Robert Englund of television series *V*, stalks them in their dreams, using his claws to carve his way into their homes and their minds. Like some ghastly combination of Peter Pan and the Pied Piper, Freddy makes sure they never grow up.

Well, not exactly everyone. There was one who would survive the film's climax. Nancy Thompson, played by Heather Langenkamp, was the heroine of the piece. But it was the part of her boyfriend, Glen Lantz, who is violently sucked into a bed and churned out in a surge of blood and gore that Craven was now trying to fill.

Johnny, however, had second thoughts about pursuing the role. Even as he arrived to attend the reading he wasn't convinced. After all, he wasn't even remotely like the character he would be playing.

'I was just totally not what Wes had written for the story,' Johnny explained later. 'He had written the part of a big, blond, beach jock, football player guy. And I was sort of emaciated, with old hairspray and spiky hair, earrings, a little fucking catacomb dweller.'

The director had already sat through several other readings with aspiring young actors, but as soon as Johnny walked in, he knew his search had ended. There and then, he says, 'Johnny had a quiet charisma that none of the other actors had. He really had that sort of James Dean attraction. Just had a very powerful, yet very subtle personality.' Even Craven's daughter and her friends raved over him. 'They absolutely flipped,' Craven said at the time. 'He just had real sex appeal for women.' And he was perfect. Five hours later, Johnny's agent called to offer him the part. Now he was an actor.

And now he was about to taste the financial rewards that

his new career in cinema could offer. 'It was amazing to me that someone wanted to pay me that much money. Never had I seen anything like that.' Neither had he imagined the sudden thrust towards movie stardom, even though he really enjoyed playing the part of Glen Lantz, the dispensable kid who, as Johnny points out, 'got sucked into a bed. What kind of reviews can you get opposite Freddy Krueger for that? Johnny Depp was good as the boy who died?'

Indeed, he did. *Newhouse Newspapers* raved, '*A Nightmare on Elm Street* is the real thing. An outstanding example of a genre that would seem to have breathed its last breath.' *The Baltimore Sun* was equally effusive in its praise of the film: '*Nightmare* is so imaginative, so skilfully carried out and so effectively creepy that it has audiences and critics excited about the possibilities of the horror film once again.'

As the *New York Times* critic put it, '*Nightmare* puts the emphasis on bizarre special effects which aren't at all bad.' Britain's *Monthly Film Bulletin* agreed. '*Nightmare* is a superior example of an overworked genre, thanks to Craven's skill at organising individual shock scenes and getting neat performances out of his mostly young cast.'

Although Johnny himself would most probably judge that, in *A Nightmare on Elm Street*, he was some way from a career in movies, the film at least established him as a promising newcomer. 'I just kept working and I did a few more things here and there.'

One of those things was taking acting classes at Loft Studio, the Los Angeles-based drama school for what Johnny considered to be much-needed drama coaching. Not that his acting ability was likely to be drawn out of him in a conventional manner. And when he wasn't doing that, he filled his time with a few minor roles, including one in an episode of *Hotel* and another in *Lady Blue*. Before that, he had played Sherilyn Fenn's boyfriend in *Dummies*. A ten minute student film made for the American Film Institute. It was made as part of the AFI education process, which demanded, during the first year, AFI Fellow students and their teams would make three short "Cycle Project" films, essentially as learning exercises, but not for release or distribution. There would be no release date and no box office receipts. The crew would consist of mainly AFI Fellows and volunteers. For the cycle project in the year that *Dummies* was made, the requirement would have been as it is today, for the actors to be part of the Screen Actors Guild Conservatory, which is a program run for actors just starting out. Both Johnny and Fenn would have fitted into that category.

Perhaps not so certain was how they would become romantically involved with each other during the making of it. Laurie Frank who directed the three-day shoot, confirms, 'their eyes locked and that was it, but the minute we finished shooting, she had this red corvette and they would get into the corvette, and the windows would steam up and we would see this corvette rocking away and then they wouldn't come out again until it was time to do the next shot. They really fell madly in love.'

Although he found little else, there was something. The lead role in another film called *Private Resort*, a movie about teen sexploitation. The ad slogan invited you to 'spend a riotous weekend at the hottest spot in Miami'. And another invited you to 'come to the wildest party of your life'. Either way, Johnny hated it. And so did the critics.

It was, according to the cover blurb on the home video, the story of two free-spirited teenagers, Ben (Rob Morrow) and Jack (Johnny) who check into the luxury hotel to pursue their favourite pastime – women! The object of Jack's lust is the rich, beautiful Dana, and he'll do anything – even pose as a surgeon – to manoeuvre her into operating position. Meanwhile, Ben's pursuit of a gorgeous waitress called Patti may be foiled by a house rule forbidding amorous activities bewteen guests. The boys' escapades are further threatened by a snoopy house detective called Reeves, and a manic thief nicknamed The Maestro, who are out to snatch a priceless diamond.

The climax – no better, Johnny complained, than the rest of the film – begins with the principal players running hell for leather after Jack and Ben. Even the occasional attempts to copy routines lifted unapologetically from countless Marx Brothers movies didn't help either. On reflection, it seemed there was very little on which to recommend *Private Resort*. Not even Johnny's nude scene 15 minutes into the film could soften the first reviews that rolled in following its release. Well aware of the movie's faults, Johnny most probably consoled himself in the belief that no one would ever see it. He certainly wouldn't. 'It was a stupid film.'

Another was the adaptation of Arthur Lions' acclaimed novel *Castles Burning*, a thriller in the Hitchcock genre that was made for cable television.

It was just a matter of knowing that 'I made some shitty movies when I was first starting out,' Johnny concedes. 'But I wasn't embarrassed by them, especially as I didn't think I was going to be an actor. I was just trying to make some money. I was still a musician. When I first started out I was just given the opportunity, and there was no other way to make that kind of money, apart from crime. I couldn't believe how much they were paying me.'

With his hair cut unfashionably spiky, only marginally distinguishable from his roles in *A Nightmare on Elm Street* and *Private Resort*, Johnny's character was neither well-defined or particularly challenging.

Donnie (Johnny) is the smart-arse son of millionaire Simon Fleischer, played by Dan Hedaya (who interestingly enough would eventually reunite with Johnny for *Benny and Joon* seven years later). Jacob Asch (played by Eric Roberts) was the gadget-ridden private eye, formerly a journalist who is hired by artist Gerald McMurty (Raymond J Barry) to track down his ex-wife (Beverly D'Angelo) now married to Fleischer, Donnie's father.

Asch's investigations, of course, uncover the usual cobweb of deceit that is part and parcel of such television movies, as well as Donnie's kidnapping and eventual, gruesome dismemberment. The geometrical convolutions are completed and, of course, further complicated by Donnie's conspiring girlfriend Emily (played by Pam Draper, Johnny's old ally from *Private Resort*).

And that was *Slow Burn*, a TV movie that, as one critic put it, was a limited exercise in recreating a lost genre of film. Johnny's rebuttal would have probably been equally critical. It would also have been understandable.

CHAPTER 4

'I KNOW IT SOUNDS STRANGE, BUT I'VE
NEVER HAD MUCH AMBITION. I NEVER REALLY
WANTED TO BE AN ACTOR OR A DIRECTOR. I WAS
A MUSICIAN AND STILL AM. THE OTHER
STUFF JUST HAPPENED.'

SOLDIER BOY AND A
HIGH SCHOOL COP

With The Kids now disbanded and his well-received performance in *A Nightmare on Elm Street* behind him, Johnny, although still some way from being a great actor, hoped that *Private Resort* and *Slow Burn* might at least nudge him on his way. 'Well, I have no band,' he said at the time, 'and I've had some pretty good luck with this, so why don't I see what this acting stuff is about and just give it a shot?'

He did. The trouble was, he remembers, 'People weren't exactly banging my door down with scripts.' At that point he was about to give up on the idea of a career in movies, when out of the blue, the postman delivered a script accompanied by a letter suggesting he apply for the part of Lerner, the hapless translator in Oliver Stone's upcoming *Platoon*.

Hollywood at the dawn of the 1980s recognised Stone as

one of its most influential directors. Not only for his uncompromising approach to social and political issues, but also for his controversial treatment of them. Francis Ford Coppola and Martin Scorsese were probably his only other serious rivals at the time.

Stone first erupted on to the scene through his scriptural début, Alan Parker's unexpected hit, *Midnight Express*. That was eight years before he met Johnny, but since that time he had scripted another three films before turning his attention to directing after he was given the chance to take on the coruscating *Salvador*. The same year he would make his mark with *Platoon*, his startling Vietnam odyssey based on his own experiences of the no-hope war that the United States could not be deterred from waging despite widespread condemnation from the watching world.

Stone was similarly determined to get the movie made in the first place. Even though almost every studio and independent producer in America were less than enthusiastic about bankrolling the project, Stone simply defected across water to British producers and European funding to end up with a movie that would astound and overwhelm the year's Academy Awards ceremony at which *Platoon* was nominated in four categories: Best Picture, Best Director, Best Sound and Best Editing. It walked away with all of them.

Johnny remembers, 'I went to read for Oliver Stone and he scared the shit out of me! Then he said, "OK. I need you for ten weeks in the jungle." It was a great experience,' he says, even though at the time he was unaware of the misery that was about to envelop him.

That misery, he recalls, was 13 days of hell. Not only for

Johnny, but also for the 30 other actors already recruited from a newly-emergent cast that included Tom Berenger, Willem Dafoe and Charlie Sheen.

In fact, none of them could believe the hard, relentless field training they were about to be put through in the run up to the six weeks principal photography on location in the Philippines. Neither were they prepared for the news that Stone had recruited a real-life Vietnam veteran to knock them into shape.

The training programme, recalled by Dale Dye, was intended to be difficult and physically demanding. 'I believe that the only way a man can portray the rigours of jungle combat is to get a taste of it.' That first taste, as Dye put it, was the 60-mile cross-country trek from Manila into the heart of the jungle that kicked off the first crucial round of punishing routines.

Armed with baggy fatigues, jungle boots, dog tags, rifles, bayonets, ponchos, flashlights, water canteens and other infantry paraphernalia, the cast promptly set about digging their two-man fox holes that they were required to live in during the gruelling manoeuvres. Even worse were the nights and days that ran into each other, the soaring temperatures, the onslaught of red ants, and the rations of 'plastic' meat, cold hot dogs and tubs of what Johnny called 'bean something or other'. Not even the pre-cooked hamburgers helped ease the torment.

No less demanding, of course, was the attention to detail. Everything from instruction of M16 rifle handling to squad radio procedures, interspersed with Stone's own classes on scene study and character analysis. If war was hell, then this, Johnny said, was a close second. He hadn't expected filming to be so arduous. Nor had he expected to have much of his performance end up on the cutting-room floor.

Equally as tough were the 12, even 14-hour work days that Stone incorporated into the shooting schedule for it to be possible to wrap in 54 days. As Stone would later note, 'During the shoot, four or five production people were fired, and there were the usual fights, raging line-producer battles, several broken limbs, one near-fatal viper bite, hordes of insects, early monsoon rains, and too many scary moments in helicopters.'

Indeed, Stone went on to recall that the filming itself placed a lot of pressure on the cast and crew – everyone, in fact. Not insignificant was the unidentified fever bug that struck everybody just 12 days before shooting was meant to be completed. Most of them had suffered illnesses before, but they'd never experienced anything like this. An infection so debilitating that they had no choice but to succumb. That proved to be the primary concern out of all Stone's difficulties. All the same, he did eventually overcome it, even if it meant compromising on some of the shots he wanted to film, and he still made the schedule with hours to spare. Four or five, at least.

Not that anyone would have known. With an $8 million gross at less than 600 cinemas in its first weekend, Oliver Stone's *Platoon* enjoyed the biggest opening of the month during its February 1987 release. And the critics confirmed the public's approval by showering the film with plaudits.

Writing in the *New York Times*, critic Vincent Canby offered one of the most concise summaries in his praise for the cast. 'The members of the supporting cast are no less fine than the principal players, and no less effective, often, for being anonymous.' *Variety* agreed that 'each member of the young cast have their moments to shine'.

And New York's David Denby said much the same. 'Oliver Stone's impassioned, mournful *Platoon* is the kind of Vietnam film many of us have longed for... easily the most powerful film of the year. There are many casting victories in this brilliantly acted film. You can feel the excitement of hungry actors seizing a moment.' Indeed, it was high praise. Not least for Johnny. In fact, he brought such a natural air to his performance that before the cinema-going public even got a chance to see him in the film, the critics were already on his side. And for adherents of Sherilyn Fenn, she too had Johnny to thank for painting her name on the helmet that he wore in the film.

With his work on *Platoon*, and his divorce from Lori Ann Allison finalised just before filming got underway, Johnny looked forward to starting work on *Wonderland Avenue*, another Oliver Stone movie based on the autobiographical reminiscences of an adolescent throwaway who ran with Jim Morrison of *The Doors*. 'It's going to be an interesting, really dark movie,' Johnny said at the time. But only months later he had dropped out of the project saying 'it was taking too long to work out.'

Far more appealing was a friend's nothing-to-lose suggestion that he join up with Rock City Angels. He did. But two months after Johnny started filming *21 Jump Street*, the band, much to Johnny's amazement, signed with David Geffen's record label for what was reportedly the biggest deal since Madonna. Well, according to *Movieline*, it was, even though there was no second album. Johnny was less than ecstatic. 'All I wanted since I was twelve years old was to go on the road.'

Basking in the glow of playing with his new band, Johnny slipped almost unnoticed into his relationship with Sherilyn Fenn, his co-star from *Dummies*, and to whom, only months after meeting on the set of the student film, he was reportedly engaged, and was now living with.

Johnny Depp and Sherilyn Fenn – it could have been a relationship made in tabloid heaven but 'we weren't famous then', recalls Johnny. Fenn, best known at the time for her erotic performance in 1988's *Two Moon Junction*, was still some years away from her role as Audrey Horne in David Lynch's bizarre soap series *Twin Peaks*, and even further from replacing Kim Basinger when she dropped out of 1993's *Boxing Helena*.

Since *Slow Burn*, and far more importantly, *Platoon*, Johnny had been determined he would not return to the small screen, not even when he heard that Fox were trying to fill the part of Tom Hanson, an undercover high school cop for *Jump Street Chapel*, a new series pilot they were producing for network broadcasting. Neither did he want to read the script. It never even crossed his mind. The idea of a long-running television series just didn't figure in Johnny's professional priorities.

'It wasn't that I was snubbing television or anything,' he insisted, 'I just wasn't ready for that kind of commitment.' But that didn't stop the series creator Patrick Hasburgh wanting to cast Johnny Depp, the promising young newcomer from *Platoon*.

But Johnny, Hasburgh had heard through the grapevine, wasn't at all interested. So the studio, already committed to filming the pilot, did exactly that, with Jeff Yagher of television series *V* in the Hanson role. But after three weeks of shooting, that idea fell through as well when Yagher was dropped from the production. The problem now was that Fox were so delighted with the shot footage that they promptly demanded more episodes, and even changed its original title to the newer, snappier, *21 Jump Street*. The only other stumbling block, of course, was they had nobody to play Hanson. Well, not exactly – there was still Johnny Depp.

'I got a call from my agents who said these people want you to come and read for this TV thing,' Johnny explained. 'But I said no, no, no. I didn't want to sign to some big contract that would bind me for years. So they hired somebody else to do it, and they fired him after a month, and then they called me again and said, would you please come in and do it? My agent said, the average span of a TV series is 13 episodes, if that. One season. So I said OK.'

Even though Johnny was now firmly committed to the idea of filming an entire television series, he still remained unconvinced about the project. His misgivings were principally due to the character he would be playing. 'Hanson is not someone I'd want to have pizza with,' Johnny noted unfavourably. 'I don't believe in having undercover cops in high school. It's spying. The only thing I have in common with Tom Hanson is that we look alike.'

Johnny's uncertainty was understandable. After all, he was a character who seemed to have more hang-ups than most. He was a 20-something second-generation cop who had the youthful appearance of a 15-year-old. The only difficulty is that his precinct colleagues and even the bad guys can't help rubbing him up the wrong way about it. And it's sinking him into a trough of depression, made worse by the fact that he needs to prove he's as great a cop as his father was.

Choosing between desk duty and joining an élite group of undercover cops is all it takes to recover his goals and ambitions. The group's mission, out of their abandoned chapel base, is to look young enough to infiltrate the local high school haunts to flush out the teens selling drugs instead of getting on with their studies.

Hanson, of course, has long wanted to join the squad that now floods the classrooms, which included Dustin Nguyen as H T Ioki, Holly Robinson as Judy Hoffs, Peter DeLuise as Doug Penhall, and, running the show, Frederic Forrest as Captain Richard Jenko, replaced seven episodes later by Stephen Williams.

Interestingly enough, the pilot was based on a controversial real-life operation which ran in Los Angeles in 1974. Indeed, the youth anti-drug programme made headline news the year before *21 Jump Street* aired on national television when one of the undercover agents allegedly developed a romantic relationship with a 17-year-old high school student.

For a time, Johnny moved his base to Vancouver close to the *21 Jump Street* set, and even moved his mother Betty Sue and her new husband Robert Palmer out there to join him. If that reunion wasn't enough to awaken Johnny's memory of his Florida childhood, then Sal Jenco, his friend from that time, certainly would.

He was visiting Johnny on the set when his party piece

of inhaling air and blowing it out like a strange-looking fish gave the *Jump Street* producers an idea. They recruited him to play a character nicknamed Blowfish, one of the regulars to drift in and out of the show during the series. Another friend, Peter DeLuise, was also given a small role, much to Johnny's relief. Both proved to be invaluable allies during and after filming. 'If Peter wasn't on the show I would have gone insane or jumped into the river,' Johnny says with a smile. 'He was my saviour.'

He also enjoyed his time in between takes on location with Sherilyn Fenn, and managed to secure her a small cameo role in the ninth episode. She would appear as the daughter of a police officer whose abusive treatment of her results in her contracting Hanson – now working undercover with Penhall as the drug-dealing McQuaid brothers – to murder him.

With prime-time viewing, *21 Jump Street* could do no wrong, and if it's true that every generation gets the show it deserves, there could be no better successor to *The Mod Squad* than this. Proof came in the form of the staggering 10,000 fan letters a month Johnny received; more than Michael J Fox, more than Charlie Sheen, and more than Rob Lowe, all of whom were newly-emergent stars in Hollywood at the time. But then again, affirmed Fan Handle, the Los Angeles star mail handling service, 'TV guys always get more than film guys.'

In the face of such success, Johnny would most probably agree. But at the same time, he couldn't help but be concerned. 'I've gotten weird letters, suicide letters, girls threatening to jump if I don't get in touch with them. So you think, this is bullshit, but then, what if it's not? Who wants to take that chance. I write them back, tell them to hang in there. If things are that bad they have to get better. But I'm not altogether stable myself, so who am I to give advice?

'Even kids,' he continues, 'write to me and say they are having these problems, or they want to commit suicide or something. It's scary. I have to say, "Listen, I'm just an actor, not a professional psychologist. If you need help, you should go and get it."'

It probably didn't help that he also took up permanent residence on the cover of *Tiger Beat* and numerous other teen magazines. Everything, Johnny adds, from '*Sixteen*! *Teen Beat*! *Teen Dream*! *Teen Poop*! *Teen Piss*! *Teen Shit*!' Even more damaging, he recalls, was the fact that 'I was this product. Teen boy. Poster boy. All that stuff that I wasn't. But they made me that. It was horribly uncomfortable.'

Equally uncomfortable was the image that had caused much of American girlhood to fall for him. The iconography of adolescent fantasy. 'It's terrifying,' he admitted later. 'People come up to you and start crying. Everybody compares everyone to James Dean. If you're lucky they mention Brando or De Niro. They invite you to put on an instant image.'

One of those occasions was when the *21 Jump Street* City Tour reached Chicago in August 1988. With echoes of the fan hysteria that greeted The Beatles' first American tour in the sixties, screaming teenagers, men and women, would fight their way to Johnny for autographs.

Neither did he go unnoticed in the plethora of popularity polls with which the teen magazines at the time abounded. Not for the first time in his career, *Rolling Stone* voted him 'Hot Face of 1988', and *US* magazine tagged him one of the 'Ten Sexiest Bachelors'.

As for the scripts, he would question those, too. 'Sometimes there are things that I personally and morally don't agree with.' In one episode, he remembers, 'My character had to set a cross alight. It was supposedly dealing with racism, but I don't think it worked. I found it pretty repulsive, and although in the end I did it, I didn't think the episode dealt with the issue correctly.'

Another episode awakened a different kind of horror. So much so that he wouldn't even agree to appear in it. It was the story of a high school student deliberately murdered after being wrongly suspected of being an informer. Needless to say, the genuine informer stands by without uttering a word.

Johnny, however, spoke out. He pulled out of the episode after a squabble over moral issues, and even if the studio had begged him to reconsider, he was not about to 'sell out' his beliefs. 'I wanted no part of that one.' Fox simply told Hasburgh to write his character out of that episode's story and have new cast member Richard Greico's Dennis Booker take his place.

And in another story, Johnny again condemned the show's content when its theme centred around a student building an electric chair in shop class. 'I was very concerned from the beginning that *Jump Street* would never be preachy or point the finger. I'm not a good-guy role model. Hanson's pretty gung-ho about his job.'

Like others, Hasburgh could see that 'Johnny's a kid who has often experienced the same problems we're dealing with on the show.' Is it possible that Johnny could be put in the same category? And if he could, why on earth was he asked to film a public service announcement that said: 'Hi, I'm Johnny Depp, and listen; stay in school and graduate, because it means the world to me and you'? When Johnny heard that news, he couldn't believe it either. 'I'd been working for these people for four years. Don't they know I'm a drop out? How can I tell people to stay in school? Then they said, "Oh yes, we forgot."'

In the end, though, Johnny did agree to appear in some of the public service announcements that ran alongside the issue-based episodes. 'The first season we hit a lot of good ones,' Johnny explains. 'The second season, the same. We dealt with AIDS, sexual molestation, child molestation, things like that.' Unfortunately, 'Patrick left the show after the second season, and the direction seemed to change.'

Well aware of the show's faults from that time, Johnny also knew that *21 Jump Street*'s biggest downfall was the audience it was quite deliberately targeted at. But, he continued, 'I don't want to bite the hand that feeds me. The show has done a tremendous amount for me. It put me on the map. But in a lot of instances the people pushing the pens have been very irresponsible. And that's scary.'

The tabloid press, of course, was less cautious. Johnny's apparent on-set tantrums, misbehaviour and egotism quickly became newsworthy, and his alleged arrest for assault and mischief in conjunction with a 'noisy' party he attended in March 1989 simply added fuel to an already smouldering fire. Although Johnny feigned nonchalance at the time, 'I have a couple of ideas where the stories came from. I think that there are a couple of people who don't like the fact that I am outspoken about certain things. As far as temper tantrums and throwing punches at my producers, it's such bull that it's hilarious.' Far more important, he explained, 'I don't think my ideas or my principles have changed. But I've learned a lot about this business, how political it is, and how people manipulate other people. It's scary, man. Power is a scary thing.'

Certainly, that is true. At the same time, though, Johnny also recognised the advantage of taking over the directional seat for two public service announcements. One for a child abuse helpline service on American television, and another for the American Make a Wish Foundation.

'It helps cancer patients or people who aren't going to live a long time,' he explained. 'They write in and say, "It's my dream to meet Johnny Depp," or someone, and we meet up with them. It can be heartbreaking, but you meet a lot of very sweet people. I wouldn't trade that in for the world. Ego, money, career – you can take it all so seriously. But faced with a kid who's dying, it all means nothing.'

He even found time to appear in a 15-minute film short he made from a script he co-wrote 'about the things people can do to screw each other up'. And when he wasn't doing that, he would harbour his dream to star in a movie version of Jack Kerouac's *On The Road*, the same work Francis Ford Coppola, the *Godfather II* director, was interested in. A decade later, both Johnny and Coppola's passion for the project remained unabated. Not only that, but it would also feed Johnny's intense interest in Kerouac and the Beat poetry movement of the 1960s.

Nevertheless, he did have second thoughts. At one time, he even considered calling it a day. Going back to music was one option that appealed. 'I could do a Bruce Willis thing and do a record now, but it would just milk my teen boy, pop idol image. And I'd rather do nothing than do that. Music is still part of my life but I wouldn't want to do it now because of the way the people in charge are. They want to take you and make you into something you're not.'

Even as he turned 25 in June 1988, Johnny was rapidly tiring of playing the popular undercover high school cop, no matter how much popularity he generated. It was when he started another season for *21 Jump Street* that the weariness of it all finally exploded into the open. From now on, he announced that he would start revising the scripts. Lines like 'This is a great place, Doug,' would become 'Nice digs, Doug, you dog, dig 'em.' He also hoped it would lead to him being kicked off the show.

For another episode, he even suggested his character could be obsessed with peanut butter, and could get caught by the other characters smearing it over his naked body. In another tirade, Johnny complained, 'For the last two years I didn't even know what my character's name was.'

All the same, responded one producer, 'I don't always agree with him, but I can see where he's coming from. He fights hard for what he believes in and he has a tendency to fight for other people.'

Johnny, however, was adamant. 'My feeling is that the show needs to go deeper into certain issues, like racism and gang violence. In television there are strict boundaries, so there's only so much you can do, but the only way to change something is to fight it.'

Even when *Interview* magazine caught up with him two years later, he told John Waters much the same. 'I think they should make the character start to lose his mind, because the hazards of being a policeman can make you go crazy. I think he should go completely insane. They should really break the boundaries that there are in television. They should put him in an asylum.'

Interestingly enough, a later episode did, in fact, have Hanson undercover in an asylum for juveniles to investigate alleged abuse by the staff on the residents. Hanson's feigned illness and drug addiction is so convincing to the staff that they lock him away, and refuse to believe his delusions about being an undercover cop.

Perhaps more episodes like that would have encouraged Johnny to have remained with the show longer than he did. 'I learned a lot of lessons from it,' Johnny would explain later. 'But when you're doing a series like that there's really no creative control. The word "creative" doesn't really exist in their vocabulary. So I said to myself that at the first chance I got, I was going to do exactly what I wanted to do and not compromise. And that's what I did. Since then, I've been lucky enough to do films I've wanted to do and to work with directors I've wanted to work with.'

Not only that, but Johnny felt no connection whatsoever to his character, Tom Hanson, not any more. He never did. But according to Hasburgh, Johnny 'was very, very new with enormous talents, and *21 Jump Street* was his garage band. And he really, really had an opportunity to hone his skills and his talents every single day. It was remarkable to watch this young actor get better and better by the minute.'

Denise Di Novi, who later produced two of Johnny's movies, agreed. 'When you work with certain actors you start to have a respect for that magical thing that makes a film star. And people really do either have it or they don't have it. They don't acquire it. They don't learn how to do it. It's usually recognisable on the very first thing that they do. I mean you look at *21 Jump Street*. You know, find an old re-run of that, and see that, and you can say he had it on this stupid, you know, TV series.'

That was certainly true. Also true was the fact that, during this same period, Johnny and Sherilyn Fenn broke up. No explanation was offered, although insiders were quick to offer their own conclusions. Some even suggested that he was jilting Fenn on the grounds of her erotic performance in *Two Moon Junction*. This charge came despite the fact that most simply blamed the career conflicts that kept the couple separated for so much of the time. With all the attendant filming and personal appearance outings that *Jump Street* entailed, it wasn't really surprising. From that point alone, it seemed the relationship didn't really stand much of a chance.

Johnny, however, didn't remain alone for long. Some observers noted that he was now seeing Jennifer Grey, best known for her role opposite Patrick Swayze in 1987's *Dirty Dancing*. It was shortly after she met Johnny that he gave her an engagement ring, but six months after that, they had gone their separate ways. Once again, it seemed that most of the couple's life together was spent apart. Johnny was in Vancouver on the set of *21 Jump Street*, while Grey was away working in Los Angeles.

With Johnny's own spare time at a premium, as with Fenn, the relationship once again didn't really stand much of a chance, and although he reinforced that, he had very little else to say on the subject.

Besides, he didn't want that sort of hell. 'It's like when

you're in high school,' he explained, 'and you're going steady with someone and your friends say, "Hey, man, are you seeing this girl?" and they start razzing you. If you love this girl, you're not going to tell your friends. I think you have to shield things; otherwise we'd all be out there cutting our arms open and showing you. Here's my blood. Have a vein.' Why do you think Elvis cloistered Priscilla at Graceland for what was Hollywood's best-kept secret?

CHAPTER 5

*'PEOPLE DON'T REALISE THIS, BUT WE'VE BEEN
TOGETHER ALMOST A YEAR AND A HALF. OUT OF ANY,
WHATEVER, THING I'VE BEEN THROUGH BEFORE, IT
HASN'T BEEN THIS LONG. IT WASN'T LIKE, "HI, NICE TO
MEET YOU, HERE'S A RING." IT WAS ABOUT FIVE MONTHS
BEFORE WE GOT ENGAGED. THEY THOUGHT WE RAN
AWAY TO LAS VEGAS AND GOT MARRIED.'*

TRUE LOVE

The first time Johnny and Winona Ryder clapped eyes on each other they knew it was love at first sight. He knew he was looking at the girl of his dreams. Her stunning natural beauty just hit him. Everything about her was perfect. He didn't want to be seen staring at her as she got a Coke in the lobby of the Ziegfeld Theater in New York but he simply couldn't help it. Not surprising, really. Squeezing herself into a tight white Giorgio di Sant'Angelo lycra mini-dress with plunging neckline, Winona was in town for the première of her film *Great Balls of Fire* in which she played the child bride of Jerry Lee Lewis.

She had already been wowing the paparrazzi with her arrival, and by the time her elfin frame moved inside, Johnny couldn't help but notice the dark-brown velvet eyes that flickered adorably, or the gorgeous bobbed black hair that was swept away from her forehead to offset the pale porcelain skin that he thought echoed visages of a young Elizabeth Taylor with an equally enviable body. The message was simple. She was young, she was hip, and she was cool. Not only that but the whole world was in love with her, or at least those who had seen her movies were. From that point of view, Johnny was no different. The fact that she could also act the socks off her contemporaries must have helped.

Indeed, Winona had already proved that she could rise above the profit margin of the coins in the box office; she had ever since she débuted in David Seltzer's *Lucas*, the first of her many alienated teenager roles. A starring role followed in Daniel Petrie's *Square Dance* before she landed the part of the sensitive-souled misfit heroine of Tim Burton's *Beetlejuice*, and that of a teenage killer in Michael Lehmann's dark, satirical comedy *Heathers*. Both movies delighted audiences and critics with the appearance of a new fully-formed star as she all but took up permanent residence on the covers of the teen magazines.

'It was a classic glance,' raved Johnny, 'like that zoom lens in *West Side Story* when everything else gets foggy.' It wasn't, Winona said, 'a long moment, but it was suspended'.

Dressed more casually for when she was dragged to meet Johnny in his hotel room at the Château Marmont a couple of months later by Josh Richman, a mutual friend through the small parts he played in *Heathers* and *21 Jump Street*, Winona watched entranced by the charm that had caused much of American girlhood to fall for him, and was even more enamoured of the intelligence that his smart, sensitive *21 Jump Street* role had seemed to imbue him with.

Although at first, 'I thought maybe he would be a jerk. I didn't know,' Winona confessed, 'but he was really, really shy.' Shy or not, it was where Johnny and Winona began their intense and often unstable relationship. It was just six months before they were due to film Tim Burton's *Edward Scissorhands* together, although at the time, of course, they had no idea they would be working alongside each other.

Almost before they knew what was happening, they were arranging to see each other again. Their first date, a few weeks later, was a party at the Hollywood home of counterculture guru Timothy Leary, Winona's godfather. Johnny was simply ecstatic. 'When I met Winona and we fell in love, it was absolutely like nothing before. We hung out the whole day ... and night, and we've been hanging out ever since. I love her more than anything in the whole world.'

Even though she may have had some earlier romances, 'I never really had a boyfriend before,' Winona admitted later. At 17, and after a barely worth mentioning two-week fling with her *Heathers* co-star Christian Slater, she hadn't really contemplated or even thought about a serious relationship yet. Not only that, she says, but 'I was no veteran of relationships. It wasn't like I was after Johnny or anything,' she reasoned.

Nevertheless, it looked like it might be fun to pursue. 'I'd heard horror stories about what happens when you dive in real quick.' And she made it clear she wouldn't be diving in quite yet.

She also underestimated the strength of her own emotions. Five months after they met, Johnny gave Winona an engagement ring, and a month later, the couple were living together, even if it was in a succession of hotels and rented apartments. Although Winona soon had him thinking about 'sniffing out a place to own and live. Maybe somewhere on the east coast.'

Not that John Waters, Johnny's soon-to-be director of *Cry Baby*, was convinced. He calls him a homeless movie star. Even after knowing him for a year and a half, he confessed, 'I have a page of addresses for him. The best way to reach him is to write Johnny Depp, A Bench, Vancouver, British Columbia.' Johnny, of course, explained it away by saying, 'I have beds, tables, chairs, a TV set. And they're mine, And I have Winona. That's all I need.'

Johnny Depp and Winona Ryder – it was a relationship made in tabloid heaven. Winona was young, sweet, charming, a child. Johnny, on the other hand, was a hell-raising party monster. Well, according to the press he was. All the same, the gossip columnists couldn't go wrong. Even Timothy Leary would later describe Johnny as both 'wild and charitable', and although Winona focused on the charitable side, the ubiquitous Hollywood insiders found Johnny's apparent past and presumably future indiscretions of considerably greater interest.

There was, for instance, the row of scars that decorated his arms, each commemorating what Johnny deemed an important moment in his life. There was also his own admission that he started smoking at 12, lost his virginity at 13, and by 14 had tried 'every kind of drug there was'. And if that wasn't enough, there was his past record as, one observer put it, 'the kind of passionate fellow who finds scant middle ground between picking someone up and proposing'.

There was also the fact that he had been married and divorced, engaged twice more, and would even spread his engagement to Winona into a trilogy of break-ups and reconciliations, affirmed by the number of times Winona's engagement ring came off and went back again.

And at other times the Irish ring she sometimes wore. The one that, she said, signifies love, friendship and loyalty. Wearing it with the small crown pointing up meant she was taken. But when *Rolling Stone* caught up with her for a May 1989 feature, one month before she spotted Johnny, she was wearing the crown down. 'The longest relationship she had, six months, had just ended because she was away on movie shoots all the time.'

Indeed, it was Johnny's romantic past and presumably future that was the number-one concern. Manhattan was even struck by a brief craze after the announcement of his betrothal to Winona, in which car bumper stickers appeared demanding, 'HONK IF YOU'VE NEVER BEEN ENGAGED TO JOHNNY DEPP'. Not that it bothered him – or did it? 'I'll just answer that I was engaged to Sherilyn, I was engaged to Winona, and I was engaged to Jennifer Grey. But a lot was written about that shit, and it was taken to another level and it was turned into some kind of horrible joke.'

Joke or not, Johnny, of course, had blazed this trail before, pursuing and getting involved with much younger women. His previous engagements as much as his infidelity might well have been his chosen path, but it didn't seem to worry Winona in the slightest, and if it did, she simply shrugged it off. 'People assume it bothers me that he's been engaged before, but it really doesn't. We have a connection on a deeper level. We have the same colouring, but we're from very different backgrounds, so we're interested in each other the whole time.'

Indeed, Johnny had read the Beat poets Winona grew up with, understood the culture that provided the background to her own childhood, and loved to collect the first editions of their work. It was what nourished their appetite for each other, and fuelled their regular weekend visits to the counterculture book store that Winona's father, Michael Horowitz, ran in Petaluma. They also shared a mutual obsession for *The Mission* soundtrack, Jack Kerouac, and J D Salinger's *Catcher in the Rye* – Winona's all-time favourite novel which she said she had read at least 50 times, and affectionately called her personal bible. From that point of view, they shared much more in common than fame.

Not only that but Johnny had never been as involved with a relationship as much as he had with Winona. He even felt the need to set the record straight on his previous liaisons, so widely reported as engagements. 'That's not quite true,' he insisted. 'I was sort of engaged. But if you haven't made some mistakes by 28, it's abnormal. People do whatever they do for whatever reasons, and it's not for anyone else to understand. And basically, it's none of their business.'

Besides, he continues, 'I've never been one of those guys who goes out and screws everything that's in front of him. When you're growing up, you go through a series of misjudgements. Not bad choices, but wrong choices. People make mistakes. We all fuck up. I was really young for the longest time. My relationships weren't as heavy as people think they were. I don't know what it is. Possibly I am trying to rectify my family's situation, or I was just madly in love. There's been nothing throughout my 27 years that has been comparable to the feeling I have with Winona. There's something inside me that knows really well, that no one else has ever known, or will ever know. Life is trial and error, but when you find the one who's really it, there's no mistaking it.' That, he explained, was why he was going to get Winona's name tattooed on his arm for $75.

When Winona heard that news, her initial response was excitement and pride. 'I was thrilled when he got the tattoo,' Winona sighed. 'Wouldn't any woman be?' It was only later that her interest turned to apprehension. As she waited at Sunset Strip Tattoo – 'Tattooers of the Stars Since 1971' – while Johnny's 'Winona Forever' double-banner tattoo was engraved into his right bicep to match the tribute to his mother on his left, those feelings grew stronger.

At the same time, 'I was sort of in shock,' Winona freely admits. Besides, 'I'd never seen anyone get a tattoo before so I was pretty squeamish, I guess.' Even as she repeatedly removed the bandage to stare at the engraving that Mike Messina had so perfectly etched, 'I kept thinking it was going to wash off or something. I couldn't believe it was real. I mean it's a big thing because it's so permanent.'

Johnny himself had no doubts. 'I love Winona. I'm going to love her for ever. Putting her on my arm solidified it. The truth is very powerful, believe me this is not something I took lightly.' But according to Messina, 'It was no big deal for him, mainly because he's had tattoos done before.' Even if the process did hurt. But that was all part of the allure. 'Yeah!' Johnny yelped. 'I liked the pain. It was electric, kind of nice.'

Although Winona had already given him a platinum ring, Johnny insisted that rings could be lost. 'Tattoos are extremely permanent.' But would that permanence turn out to be a burden? In expressing his love for her so strongly, Johnny had effectively caged her. Maybe it was then that she realised that on the rare occasion when she did talk about him to the press, the future, their future, never received a mention. Instead, she would talk purely of the present.

The first few months of the couple's life together, however, was spent apart. Johnny was in Vancouver on the set of *21 Jump Street*, while Winona was in Ohio shooting her next role in Jim Abraham's *Welcome Home Roxy Carmichael*. Although work for both would prove to be an aching separation that only long-distance phonecalls and red-eye flights could bridge, it would also provide a welcome rest from the daily harassment of the gutter press. That, of course, didn't stop Johnny's romantic beckoning. One night, he remembers sending Winona 200 helium balloons – 'she could barely walk to the phone to say thank you,' he recalls fondly. They simply 'took up too much room'.

That same summer of 1989, John Waters was looking for an actor to play the part of a delinquent biker in his next project. If there was one thing Johnny had impressed upon his agent, it was how he hated the whole teen idol thing that *21 Jump Street* had imposed upon him. And the best way to get rid of an image, any image, according to Waters, was to make fun of it.

Indeed, *Cry Baby*, or as Waters called it, Elvis Presley's '*King Creole* on acid' was intended as an antidote to all of that. It was a love story about juvenile delinquents set in the mid-Fifties, just before the onslaught of sex, drugs and rock 'n' roll hit the end of that decade.

In fact, the press release described the film as one that lovingly depicts the happiness of teen rebellion and the tragic pitfalls of early conformity in Baltimore of 1954. 'Our Romeo and Juliet heroes are Wade "Cry Baby" Walker (Johnny), a tough, handsome teenage "hep-cat" from the wrong side of the tracks who falls in love with Allison Vernon Williams (Amy Locane), a beautiful rich "square" girl whose raging hormones combined with the evil influence of rockabilly music drive her into the nightmare world of gang mentality and hoodlum passion.'

According to the publicity blurb, the movie, 'with a background of fast cars, gang wars and sexual frustration, would be filled with both original songs and great unheralded music from this forgotten time. John Waters has satirised one of the only movie genres that hasn't been updated in 30 years. Fresh territory for an "historical" black comedy that rips the lid off the throbbing, searing world of yesterday's juvenile delinquents.'

Long before Waters met Johnny, he had already established himself as one of the few independent film-makers with a reputation for what his nickname suggested, the 'Pope of Trash'.

It probably didn't help that in 1972 he had launched Harris Glenn Milstead, an overweight, 300lb transvestite, best known as Divine, for his performance in Waters' own *Pink Flamingos*. The scene where he literally, but unapologetically, chews on fresh dog excrement had the critics virtually stampeding for the exits.

It was, *Variety* noted, 'the most disgusting caper in film history. Surely one of the most vile, stupid and repulsive films ever made.' Nonetheless, it did nothing to tarnish Waters' reputation, nor Milstead's for that matter.

Well, not according to Waters, it didn't. 'He didn't think it was going to hurt his career because at that point he didn't think he was even going to have a career. When he did it, he did it like a professional. He spat it out, brushed his teeth and then got on with his life.' Although 'it was a pretty crazy thing for us to do, it wasn't that crazy,' freely admits Waters today. Mind you, 'I didn't think we'd still be talking about it 25 years later.'

Maybe, too, they would be talking about his next movie 25 years after its release. Perhaps that's why it should be no surprise that Waters would take on a Fifties teen satire. Even if it did end up as a rock 'n' roll musical, *Cry Baby* would still allow the director to shoot what Waters himself would point out was a spoof.

It was, he said, 'a kind of joke on the really wild, untamed youth movies from the early Fifties, except it's the reverse of those movies because the bad guys are who you root for, and the good guys are the villains.'

But with the death of Glen 'Divine' Milstead in 1988, two weeks after the première of *Hairspray*, John Waters had lost his leading lady. 'When he died, there was just no question about having a man dress up as a woman in my films again. There was just no point. Divine was the best.'

Neither could he tell you who he had in mind for the title character of his latest vehicle. Certainly, when he started to think of the who's who among the cream of young Hollywood hopefuls, he simply had no idea. Not to be discouraged, he remembers, 'I went out and bought about 20 teen magazines, which was really mortifying. I found myself hiding them under my jacket. When I got home and started looking through them, Johnny Depp was on the cover of almost every one of them.'

Johnny, Waters was pleased to learn, had the essential attitude about himself, and about his image, to make *Cry Baby* work. 'I think he was very brave to take this part on because, first off, he told me that it was the most peculiar script he had ever seen, and by portraying *Cry Baby*, he would be right out there, making fun of himself.'

As far as Johnny was concerned, though, the whole thing blew him away. '*Cry Baby* came along at a good time for me,' he recalls. 'I had been looking at film ideas for a while and was getting very disillusioned. Most of what I read was flat, just schlock. I was being sent scripts which just echoed what I was doing on *Jump Street*, and I wanted something that would be totally different.'

John, he continues, 'first sent me a letter, and then we talked, and met, and then he gave me a script. I was so excited because not only was it really funny, but it made fun of those clichés and sensitive heroes I had been reading for so long.'

Universal and Imagine Films, the production companies bankrolling the project, were equally delighted. Up to that point, they had only seen one other John Waters movie, and that was *Hairspray*. They were as enthusiastic about that as they were about the script for *Cry Baby*. In their eyes, it was a slick nineties *West Side Story*.

And they were right, Waters concedes. Even if they were shocked at the sight of Johnny looking the absolute antithesis of the star of the picture. 'He came into this lovely Hollywood office in complete rags,' Waters remembers. And then, 'in the middle of the meeting, he looked at me and gave me a sneer. At that moment, I realised he would do just fine. He understood the whole plot of the film.'

Equally shocked was Waters himself. Not at Johnny, but at the budget for the movie. 'They gave me $8 million to make it,' something the director just wasn't used to. Now for the first time scenes could be laboriously set up over hours of preparation. They wouldn't have to be cut short or abandoned altogether. And the plot, continuous on paper, could be shot at any point of the compass, so to speak, and reassembled later in the edit suite. It was a director's dream.

Johnny agreed. 'For someone who writes and directs, someone who is basically the entire creative force, the real surprise is basically how open John is to ideas and suggestions. He was real accessible, not distant or brooding. He listens to ideas about adding or taking out lines. If I was having a problem with something, he would rehearse me. I mean, he would actually get out there with me. No other director I've worked with has stood there, and danced for me, to help me understand a step.'

At the same time, though, Johnny also recognised another bonus. 'One of the main reasons for doing the movie with John was because it would be contradictory to what everyone sees me as or what I've been labelled as, by some fuckhead with a tie.'

Although Los Angeles singer and songwriter James Intveld was recruited to vocalise the eleven musical numbers, Johnny, contributing his own footnote to the film's musical score, would consult with the crew on the tiniest of details. Every object on the set from vintage guitars to amplifiers were carefully researched and selected for their authenticity. It was something Johnny was more than qualified to be consulted upon.

But the biggest high for *Cry Baby*, Waters continued, 'was that it was an official selection for the Cannes Film Festival. The midnight screening was completely sold out. Standing ovation. They loved it. Standing at the top of that red carpet and turning around to eight million paparazzi with Ricki Lake and Rachael Talalay, my producer, was a huge high for me. That was a fantasy I wanted since I was 14.'

So, *Cry Baby*, he continues, 'was a good experience for me in the long run. Out of all the movies, it was probably the happiest on the set. There were some problems, but I think people had a lot of fun working on it.'

Johnny certainly did. Especially when Winona visited the set. He particularly enjoyed introducing her to everyone, and even more the considerable presence they had at the première in New York the following April. It was there that Johnny dressed in yellow, and Winona in black, with Johnny's Valentine's gift, an antique gold cross set with rubies on an onyx chain – would be wowing the paparazzi once again. It was also where they would be called the 'bumble bee couple' by much of the tabloid press. Not that it mattered. The reviews for the film were excellent.

Peter Travers writing in *Rolling Stone* said, 'Waters' bad taste is unassailable. The subversive comic thrust of *Cry Baby* shows he simply had to find new ways to channel his baser instincts. The wizard of odd still runs amok.'

Variety, too, supported the film, claiming Waters'

'mischievous satire of the teen exploitation genre is entertaining as a rude joyride through another era, full of great clothes and hairdos. Johnny is great as the delinquent jive, delivering the melodramatic lines with straight-faced conviction and putting some Elvis-like snap and wiggle into his moves.'

Britain's *Sight and Sound* was equally complimentary. 'Johnny Depp is a *bona fide* teen idol.' And London's *Evening Standard* film critic Alexander Walker agreed: 'Genuine heart-throb Johnny Depp is everything a boy should be: young, good looking and mean.'

CHAPTER 6

'JOHNNY'S TASTE AND LOOKS SEEM IN COMPLETE
CONTRADICTION TO WINONA'S. EVERYTHING ABOUT
THIS COUPLE SEEMS VERY ENGLISH: DEBUTANTE GIRL
MEETS ECCENTRIC BOHEMIAN BOY. THEIR HOME,
THEIR CLOTHES AND THE WAY THEY ARE TOGETHER
ARE VERY ROMANTIC. WHOEVER WOULD HAVE THOUGHT
THAT IN 1991, IT WOULD BE HIP TO BE ROMANTIC,
BUT THESE TWO ARE DEFINITELY BOTH.'
VOGUE

KING AND QUEEN OF
YOUNG HOLLYWOOD

December 1989 was the coldest ever recorded in Boston, where Winona Ryder was shooting her subsequent movie role in *Mermaids*. It was also the destination for Johnny's regular cross-country treks throughout *21 Jump Street*'s fourth season, his last, as he travelled back and forth to see her, catching the last flight out of Vancouver every Friday and the last one back every Sunday. 'It was worth it, but man, I was a world-weary traveller.'

That alone was enough to suggest this was a different kind of relationship for Johnny. In fact, it was the closest he would come to actually getting married. Although he openly admitted to relishing the idea, he remained uncertain as to whether or not he believed in the concept. Sure, he liked the image, but still questioned whether one person could be with another until 'death them do part'. He simply couldn't tell if that was humanly possible. All the same, he was prepared to give it a try, and who better to try with, than Winona? 'We'll do it when we have a chunk of time and we can do it quietly with a three-month honeymoon. I've heard about places in Australia, islands where you can be dropped off, and there's nothing there at all. I guess you just run around eating coconuts, foliage and bugs.'

Winona would probably have agreed. 'I've got the feeling that this is right. But I don't want to do it just so I can say I did it. I want to have, like, a honeymoon and the whole shebang. We're going to get married as soon as we have time and we're not working.' In another period, she repeated much the same sentiment. 'Johnny and I have both been working really hard on *Edward Scissorhands*, so we haven't had much time to talk about when the marriage will be. But it will be!'

Even Winona's father was enthusiastic. He himself entertained no doubts whatsoever. If anything, his instincts screamed approval. 'He thinks "Marry him!"' said Winona, taking her evidence from the weekends she and Johnny spent at Winona's family home. Once there, she remembers, they were completely pampered. 'They really love him a lot and even bring me and Johnny breakfast in bed. They're so cool.' Yet it could have turned out so differently. 'It would have been easy not to like me,' Johnny added, 'older people might have just seen tattoos.'

Far less cautious, in fact, was Cher, Winona's co-star from *Mermaids*. She did her best to warn Winona. 'Neither one of them knows what they are doing, but they might as well go through it together. At least she's going through it with a person who cares a lot about her.' Not that Winona disguised her determination. As far as she was concerned nobody was going to preach to her about Johnny. 'She really likes Johnny, so I think she's pretty happy for me,' Winona said of her co-star. 'And although she gives me advice, she doesn't expect me to take it. I'm going to do what I'm going to do anyway.'

The tabloid press, of course, was a different matter entirely. 'We don't feel like royalty,' complained Winona, recalling the time that *People* magazine named them the King and Queen of Young Hollywood. 'We read in the papers when they make that comparison and it makes us giggle. It makes us self-conscious in a way that neither of us enjoys. It's uncomfortable to be watched all the time or to have people eavesdropping on your conversations in a restaurant. They make things up about you which is even worse.'

But according to Daniel Waters, the scriptwriter from Winona's movie *Heathers*, she enjoys it more than she's prepared to admit. 'There's a part of her that likes it even though she denies it. Right now, she's got a Natalie Wood obsession.' Not surprising when you consider that Winona would become the first American actress since Wood successfully to transcend a career from adolescence to adulthood in the full glare of the Hollywood spotlight.

Certainly, she and Johnny would have considerable presence at the ShoWest movie event in Las Vegas where the National Association of Theater Owners saluted them both as the Young Stars of Tomorrow. It was where, with matching rings, they publicly announced their engagement, and according to *US* magazine, acted 'like a couple of teenagers, groping each other and falling to the floor'. But did they really? Even if they did, it was no more than what any other young couple in love and just engaged would do. Still, the press couldn't stop talking about it.

Neither could the Hollywood grapevine. 'When I was young, I was the sweetheart of the press,' acknowledged Winona. 'They loved me, but they were kind of waiting for me to mess up. I had no skeletons in my closet, no major past to talk about. I wasn't with anyone. Then I became engaged to Johnny.'

She had just turned 18 and was still getting acquainted with the tabloids. 'Suddenly people are curious about things you wouldn't even tell your friends.' It was Cher, Winona credits, with helping her through much of that. 'She's been through that her whole life – she taught me what I should take seriously and what I should let go.'

Indeed, it was during this time that Johnny developed his hatred for the press, and Winona carefully began to keep her media exposure in check. Most actors have a love-hate relationship with journalists. Although most are willing to be accommodating with film publicity, when their private lives are under the microscope, most celebrities object to the intrusion. Even when things are stable, being asked the same question 10,000 times is understandably irritating.

It was this aspect that annoyed Johnny more than any other. He particularly remembers one occasion when he was 'in the john of some bar and some stranger came up to me, and said, "So, are you and Winona still together?" At the urinal, for Christ's sake!' Another, *Shout* magazine, went even further, when they pleaded with

Johnny to spill the beans on whether he was still, as they put it, 'snogging Winona'!

Neither could he forget just how pernicious the influence of the tabloid press could be. One incident, in particular, had drawn unwanted attention to them both. Winona was due to star in Francis Ford Coppola's *The Godfather Part III* as Mary, the daughter of the Corleone family reprised by Al Pacino and Diane Keaton in the roles they made famous, or had been made famous by, almost two decades before.

It was, recalls Patrick Palmer, Winona's producer from *Mermaids*, an opportunity for her to star in a true American classic that would establish Winona as a genuine adult star, if for nothing other than the love scenes with Andy Garcia. It was something she hadn't really touched upon in her earlier roles, not that she would be participating in any nude, or even semi-nude, scenes for the voyeuristic benefit of the cameras.

Less than a day after Winona finished *Mermaids*, she and Johnny boarded a plane for Rome. Although she was still exhausted from the upper-respiratory problem that had hit her during filming, she was not concerned. Not even as she sniffed and coughed her way across the Atlantic. But almost as soon as they stepped off the plane, they both knew she was in bad shape. She was literally burning up with a 104-degree fever. Not only that, but her lungs were killing her, and the pressurised cabin had made her ears extremely painful. Days later, her condition was exactly the same, but right on schedule, she presented herself for work. Then she collapsed in her hotel room.

Johnny immediately summoned the production team

doctor, who promptly announced Winona too sick to work, and too sick even to fly home for a few days. 'I literally couldn't move. It wasn't my choice. It was out of my hands.' Even when she and Johnny did eventually fly back to Petaluma, all she could do was lie in bed. 'I had nothing left in my system. I was a wreck in every sense of the word and I just needed to rest and do nothing.' But as a result, 'I was getting threats that my career would be over and that I was going to get sued,' she recalls. Even her agent warned that if she walked out of the movie she might as well give up acting there and then. Winona left the agency some time later. But what good did that really do? Everywhere she turned, it seemed, the advice was the same.

The press, of course, was another matter entirely. Winona recalls, 'I was sick physically, and exhausted. That's what happened.' But immediately on her return home, and for months to come, Winona became equally sick of having to defend herself. The standard catalogue of absurd and untruthful rumours circulated around Hollywood about why she had left the movie; she was pregnant, she had overdosed, she was having a nervous breakdown, it was drugs, it was an eating disorder, it was Johnny having an affair, it was an assortment of other disasters.

Some even suggested it had been engineered so that she and Johnny could make *Edward Scissorhands* together. What seemed to escape their attention, though, was the fact that Winona had already agreed to appear in the film long before Johnny was cast alongside her. Later, she would concede that the two movies' schedules did conflict, but that was a bridge she intended to cross when she came to it. Finally losing patience, Winona snapped,

'It's amazing how people want things to be as nasty and complicated as possible.'

The truth, she continued, was simple. 'I was told by my doctor that I couldn't work. I don't know why nobody believed it. Maybe people thought Johnny was influencing me, but he wasn't. He was just taking care of me, ordering room service, sticking his fingers down my throat, helping me to throw up.' Today, Winona credits Johnny alone with helping her through the ensuing storm. But how many times would she have to defend her decision to walk out on *The Godfather*? How many times would she have to explain?

'Sure, it's disappointing, devastating in fact. I wish it didn't happen, but it did. Obviously I would have loved to have worked with those wonderful actors and a great director. But it wasn't a choice. It wasn't like, "Well, I'm not feeling well today. Maybe I won't do this movie." The doctor was there and he said, "You have an upper-respiratory infection. You can't do it." My leaving the movie was a disappointment to everyone. Especially me.'

For the time being though, all Winona could do was lie in bed, and recuperate throughout the period she should have been filming in Rome. She also focused on making sure her relationship with Johnny worked out. But it wouldn't be the only time. 'He is an amazing person whom I have an enormous amount of respect for and very deep feelings for. It's not a possessive, weird little Hollywood promenade.' When she did finally return to work, it would be alongside Johnny on Tim Burton's warm Florida set of *Edward Scissorhands*.

Even in a profession where unconventionality is often a

by-word for success, Tim Burton was never cut out to be a 'typical' Hollywood director. At 29, this native Californian who grew up within earshot of Warner Brothers' massive Burbank lot had erupted on to the scene with his directorial début, Paul Reubens' unexpected hit, *Pee Wee's Big Adventure*. That was five years before he met Johnny, but since that time he had by-passed movies completely only to end up having Hollywood at his feet.

The success of Winona's *Beetlejuice*, with its $73 million dollar gross, and the first *Batman* movie had firmly established him among the upper echelons of Hollywood directors. Although his visions seemed to defy logic, they nevertheless continued to strike a profitable chord with audiences. *Edward Scissorhands*, Burton's peculiar tale of a man-made man with scissors for hands, would prove to be no different. In fact, he ended up with a movie that would eventually gross a respectable $54 million dollars at the box office.

The idea for *Edward Scissorhands* had haunted Burton ever since he was a child, the image living in his mind long before he learned he might be able to bring it to life on celluloid. Through his first years of success, Edward continued to play on the director's mind, until finally, during pre-production on *Beetlejuice*, he commissioned Caroline Thompson to write a screenplay. 'I had read her book, *First Born*, which was about an abortion that came back to life. It was good ... close to the feeling I wanted for *Edward Scissorhands*.'

Nevertheless, it was, according to Thompson, an unusual scripting assignment. 'Tim had the image of this character,' she recalls. 'He said he didn't know what to do with it, but the minute he described it and said the name Edward Scissorhands, I knew what to do. It was Tim who came up with the image of the guy with the hedge-clipper hands and I came up with everything that had to do with them. It was the perfect joining of our talents.'

Originally, the idea was to produce *Edward Scissorhands* as a musical comedy. Thompson even wrote a song, 'I Can't Handle It', but the idea was scrapped in a subsequent revision. Although most of the script remained remarkably similar to the early drafts, it was still a variation of Burton's obsession with the Frankenstein theme.

All the same, he could not explain his fascination with Edward. It was simply 'an image I liked. It came subconsciously and was linked to a character who wants to touch but can't, who was both creative and destructive.' He acknowledged, as Thompson did, that it could have been almost autobiographical, something that 'probably came to the surface when I was a teenager, because it is a very teenage thing. It had to do with relationships. I just felt I couldn't communicate.'

He would work with that same sense of alienation in mind as he set about selecting his cast. Although he agreed to the studio's suggestion that he consider Tom Cruise for the title role, Burton already knew that the *Top Gun* superstar was one of the last people who could capture the bizarre sense of the out-of-the-ordinary that Edward Scissorhands demanded. There were others, of course, equally anxious to try out for the part: William Hurt, Tom Hanks and Robert Downey Jnr. Even Michael Jackson. Not that it mattered. Burton wanted Johnny Depp.

Johnny remembers his first meeting with Tim Burton

very well, mainly because he thought the young, rumpled figure sitting opposite him in the coffee shop of the Bel Age Hotel in Los Angeles looked as if he was in need of sleep. He was, recalls Johnny, 'a pale, frail-looking, sad-eyed man with hair that expressed much more than last night's pillow struggle'.

Johnny, on the other hand, was exactly what Burton had expected. At the time, expounded Burton, 'Johnny was very much known as a teen idol and perceived as dark and difficult and weird and was judged by his looks, but he's almost completely the opposite of this perception. So the themes of Edward, of image and perception, of somebody being perceived to be the opposite of what he is, was a theme he could relate to.'

All the same, Johnny remained uncertain about entering into Burton's world of visionary imagination. In his eyes, he thought, 'I was a TV boy. No director in his right mind would hire me to play this character. I had done nothing workwise to show that I could handle this kind of role. How could I convince the director that I was Edward, that I knew him inside out?'

But did he know him well enough to play the part? It turned out that he did. 'I connected with it really well, I sort of already knew the character and what he represented. Edward seemed more of a feeling than a person. The metaphor of the scissors is about wanting to touch, but if you touch you destroy. Nothing you do seems right. It's the feeling you get when you're growing up, very adolescent. I felt that way. I think everyone did.'

Even after the meeting with Burton, Johnny was not entirely convinced that he would be offered the part. 'My chances were slim at best. Better-known people than me were not only being considered for the role, but were battling, fighting, screaming for it. I waited for weeks, not hearing a thing in my favour. All the while I was researching the part. It was now not something I merely wanted to do, but something I had to do. Not for any ambitious, greedy, actory box-office draw reason, but because this story had now taken residence in the middle of my heart and refused to be evicted.'

When Johnny finally got the call, and the part, he was ecstatic. 'I couldn't fucking believe it.' Burton, he said, 'was willing to risk everything on me in the role. Headbutting the studio's wishes, hopes and dreams for a big star with established box-office draw, he chose me. I became instantly religious, positive that divine intervention had taken place. This role for me was not a career move. This role was freedom. Freedom to create, experiment, learn and exorcise something in me.'

That something was, as Johnny explains, like being 'rescued from the world of mass-product, bang-'em-out TV death by this odd, brilliant guy who had spent his youth drawing pictures'.

The decision to cast Winona was equally instinctive. 'She's the best,' Burton raved. 'She has something you can't even talk about. She's a throwback to movie stars throughout film history. There's something about her skin and her eyes and her ability and her gravity that you can't verbalise. Magical.' For Winona, it wasn't only the chance to work with Burton again, but also with Denise Di Novi, her producer from *Heathers*, and now president of Tim Burton Productions. Later, of course, she learned Johnny was also being approached, but as far as she was concerned that was simply a bonus even if it was a nerve-wracking one.'

'Working with Johnny turned out to be really great, but I was scared and nervous about it. I mean, if there's one person that I want to impress with my acting, it's him. So there was a lot of insecurity during the first couple of days, but it turned out to be a really motivating situation. I think we have pretty good chemistry.'

Johnny agreed. 'The fact that we're together and we're in love certainly won't hurt the movie. But I was nervous. It's like another level of exposing yourself to someone. You know, you can be together, but then to act together, be different people, especially someone like Edward. It was scary at first. She was nervous, too. But it was great. Besides the fact that I love her and everything, she has a lot of talent, she's a great actress, very giving and considerate. It was really easy working with her because stuff automatically happens. You don't have to try. Stuff comes out. I'm sure we're going to do more things together. People have had great success at that, like John Cassavetes and Gena Rowlands. In a perfect world, I'd just do movies with Winona, John Waters and Tim Burton, and live happily ever after.'

Neither did it worry Burton in the slightest that his two stars were in a relationship. He knew Winona too well, and his instincts screamed approval of Johnny. They were, he laughed approvingly, 'kind of an evil version of Tracy and Hepburn'. Indeed, once the filming was over, he confirmed, 'I don't think their relationship affected the movie in a negative way. Perhaps it might have if it had been a different kind of movie, something that was tapping more into some positive or negative side of their relationship. But this was such a fantasy. They were very professional and didn't bring any weird stuff to the set.'

Indeed, to depict a love between such dramatically opposed characters of Edward and Kim was a bold move on Burton's part but a necessary one. He was aiming to disrupt and to upset the viewers preconceptions without alienating them. Just as his stars adapted to roles that were completely contrary to any they had previously played, he hoped his audience would adapt by accepting the unexpected strangeness of Edward and Kim's relationship. Similarly, the film's setting – a slice of Florida suburbia strikingly repainted in bright pastels by production designer Bo Welsch – was selected to convey a sense of startling peculiarity depicted nonetheless as warmly familiar.

Edward Scissorhands wastes no time introducing the world which Edward is about to be thrown into. From the winding suburban development that ends at the foot of a hill dominated by a large, derelict Gothic mansion, Avon Lady Peg Boggs (Dianne Wiest) makes an out of the way call to discover the greatest of secrets: Edward, a boy living alone whose hands are an array of lethal blades. So she does what any normal Avon Lady would do. She takes him home with her to live with her family and, as if to ignite the comedy of errors and misunderstandings that follow, she even boards him in a bedroom with a waterbed.

Although Edward is quickly welcomed into the neighbourhood as a sort of sideshow attraction as he creates a gallery of living sculptures, clipped hedges, spruced lawns, coiffed poodles and even crafted hairstyles for his benefactress and others, his popularity, just as quickly, breeds resentment.

A main reason for this is his obvious affection for Kim (Winona), his hostess's cheerleading daughter, whose increasing awareness of Edward's feelings provokes her jock boyfriend (Anthony Michael Hall) into a succession of bullying outrages. Even the middle-aged seductress (Kathy Bates) whose advances are spurned by Edward soon joins the fray, and as misunderstandings mount, so does the climax of the movie. It begins with a hunt scene lifted, almost unapologetically, from countless Frankenstein pictures. The only real difference is that this time the monster survives, but the affinity, of course, is deliberate.

Equally deliberate was Burton's casting of his greatest cinematic idol, the veteran American actor Vincent Price as Edward's inventor, who doubles up as his father in echoes of Disney's *Pinocchio*, and whose presence in so many gothic horror movies were made so memorable. The two men would subsequently become close friends. In fact, Burton's next project, *Conversations with Vincent*, was a documentary of Price's life, who himself would make no further movies before his death in 1993. While the film remains unfinished and unreleased, *Edward Scissorhands* stands as a fitting tribute to Price's genius.

As much as Burton, Johnny, too, remained close friends with Price up until his death. In fact, he was thoroughly enamoured with him. One of those times, Johnny recalls was when he was sitting with him in his trailer, during a break in filming, and 'I was showing him the first edition book I have of the complete works of Edgar Allan Poe with really amazing illustrations. Vincent was going nuts over the drawings, and he started talking bout *The Tomb of Ligeia*.

Then he closed the book and began to recite it to me in this beautiful voice, filling the room with huge sounds. I looked in the book later, and it was verbatim. Word perfect.' For Johnny it was something he said he would never forget.

Neither would he forget the time when Price encouraged him to make sure he avoided the vestiges that typecasting hell could bring - something that had dogged his own career through a string of movies that Johnny considered never less than brilliant.

But above all else, Price's suggestion to buy art was 'a piece of advice I'll treasure forever,' says Johnny. But where would he keep such treasures? As Johnny confessed at the time, 'I haven't bought a home yet.' Neither did it look as if he was about to.

Even at the height of his fame, he wasn't sure 'if, when I do, it's going to be in the States. It may be in France somewhere. But I have bought a lot of paintings and drawings and some photographs. It's good to have things around that feed you.' One of those things were the original *Edward Scissorhands* scissor hands resting peacefully on a wooden chest at the top of the stairs of Winona's new Los Angeles home she would be sharing with Johnny by late spring 1991.

It was also where, among the mementos and messages stuck to the refrigerator door, there was a photo of Johnny with his *Cry Baby* director and the couple's close friend, John Waters, and a piece of yellow note paper bearing Jason Robard's phone number. He'd been Winona's co-star from *Square Dance*, her first starring movie role. It was Robards, Winona credits to this day, who 'taught me how to be natural in front of the camera'.

Down the line, of course, Burton's creation exorcised demons – both his own and those of his cast. Discussing Johnny's portrayal of Edward, the director remarked, 'I think a lot of the character is him. He has this kind of naïve quality which as you get older gets tested and has holes poked into it. I would imagine Johnny is somebody who would want to protect that to some degree.'

Certainly, a sizeable portion of the movie was devoted to that theme, first in the eyes of the audience when Kim's boyfriend leads Edward directly into trouble with the law, and much more literally, when the boyfriend is killed by the cornered Edward. 'That was probably some sort of junior high or high school revenge fantasy,' Burton confessed. 'Perhaps I was just letting off steam.'

Edward Scissorhands also fascinated the media not only as a movie, but also because of the real life relationship between its stars. Certainly the tenderness between Edward and Kim was derived at least in part from Johnny and Winona's real-life feelings, and several reviewers picked up on that chemistry following the movie's Christmas 1990 release in America, and the following summer in Britain.

Even more intriguing were the hundreds of scripts that Johnny and Winona were sent subsequently. 'They're so obvious,' Johnny noted. 'They offered us a gangster movie. I'm a mobster and Winona's my moll.' There was, however, one idea that Johnny simply adored. *Movieline* had suggested that he try and talk John Waters, his director from *Cry Baby*, into directing him and Winona in a 'whacked-out remake of *Viva Las Vegas* with Johnny taking over from Elvis Presley's hip-swivelling grease monkey, and Winona from the frenzied, lip-smacking

Ann Margret'. 'That would be beautiful,' conceded Johnny. 'I would love to do something like that, especially with the Dead Kennedys' version of the theme song.'

All the same, the public perception of Johnny and Winona's relationship was already so troubled that when Johnny and Winona attended a Tim Burton tribute at the Montreaux Film Festival, their presence was described as a notable reconciliation simply because the couple hadn't been seen out for a few weeks. Not together, anyway.

Even Burton was stunned by the posse of paparazzi that were at Los Angeles Airport when he, Johnny and Winona flew back from Florida after completing *Edward Scissorhands*. 'It was one of the most horrible things I've ever seen in my life,' he recalled with contempt. 'I'm sort of a believer that if you're in the public eye you've got to accept a certain amount of that. But I've never seen anything so hostile.'

Winona agreed. 'We got off the plane, and about 50 paparazzi jumped out and started taking our pictures. We couldn't, like, see where we were going because the bulbs were popping. One guy stuck out his foot and tried to trip me! They were yelling at us, trying to get an "interesting picture". Finally, Johnny got so mad that he turned around and flipped them off. Now you'll see his picture in a magazine and he's going to look like some asshole.' Besides, Winona continues, 'aren't we allowed to be in a bad mood sometimes? Everybody else is.'

Indeed, one of those pictures, still unpublished, did exactly what Winona predicted. Even the press copy that went with it did much the same: 'Hollywood has a new Bad Boy. It was shades of Sean Penn [known for his violent temper] as actor Johnny Depp and his fiancée, actress Winona Ryder, arrived at Los Angeles International Airport on a flight from Tampa, Florida. Depp, of Fox TV's *21 Jump Street*, was snapped as he spat at clicking photographers, flung his lit cigarettes in their faces, telling them to 'FUCK OFF!' Clearly embarrassed, Ryder shielded her face with a small piece of luggage, ducked her head and kept walking.'

But that wasn't the only occasion. The papers, cursed Winona, 'were always trying to put me with other people. I mean I work with actors and I know them, and sometimes I might have lunch with them, but that's the end of it. And Johnny does the same thing with actresses. I guess part of it is that they want to get a reaction, and they also want to start a scandal, an affair, or whatever.'

She was right. It was even confirmed when she was allegedly reported to have had a 'very cosy dinner with Christian Slater at the Hard Rock Café in Los Angeles holding hands when they weren't chowing down on their cheeseburgers and fries,' two years after she had ended her two-week fling with the actor. But, Winona snarled, none of that is true.

Neither was the story, on another occasion, when *People* magazine asked HOW DEPP IS HER DEVOTION? after she had been spotted at a Hollywood party with *Dracula* co-star Gary Oldman. According to sources, wrote Mitchell Fink, the pair were 'looking a lot closer than two actors who happen to be making a movie together'.

But Fink continued, 'A source close to Ryder, while acknowledging that Winona is "an affectionate kitten", says Ryder doesn't even like Oldman. "He may have hit on her at one time," says the source, but her relationship with

Johnny Depp is "stronger than ever". They have gone through some difficult times, but they are still engaged.'

Although Winona admitted the gossip hurt, 'I don't really read those papers,' she vowed at the time. But she also acknowledged there was no way to avoid finding out what they alleged. 'You hear about it, but you can't pay too much attention because it's too tiresome.' Again, she was right.

Long before all of that nonsense, of course, Johnny had asked John Waters, now a mail-order minister, to marry him and Winona in Las Vegas. It was the one claim to fame that Johnny was most proud of. 'I'm responsible for having John Waters ordained. I sent off to the Universal Life Church and had him ordained by mail. He's now Reverend John Waters and we want him to perform the ceremony. Who better?'

Who better indeed, but Waters, although enthusiastic, was initially reluctant. 'I told them I wouldn't do it without their parents' blessing. I've met her parents. They've eaten dinner here and I'm not gonna just horrify them.' There were other times when Waters, as he put it, would counsel the couple. 'Too young! I tell them to wait, wait, wait. But, yes, I'd be thrilled to perform the ceremony. I'd feel like the Pope!' There was also another stumbling block. Winona herself. Although Johnny said she loved the idea, when she became the party-pooper and refused to go along with the scheme, it did nothing more than prompt a fresh deluge of stories, this time about jilted grooms and unrepentant brides.

It was if no one could believe Winona might have tamed the wild Johnny Depp. Although he made no secret of his past liaisons, there never seemed to be a lack of 'close friends' willing to testify that they weren't all in the past. And it only made matters worse when the couple did answer questions about their private life. Did they throw wild parties? Did Winona really snap polaroids of Johnny in uncompromising positions and then take them to the local pharmacy for developing? Did they go out to the New York nightclubs? Not according to Johnny, who claimed he didn't even know where they were. 'We walk, wander, folic, and then we rent movies and go home.' Just like any other couple. By making stardom sound so mundane, they also moved reporters to dig deeper.

Even when Winona was once asked about her desires for stage work it was no different. If she believed she would be bored with doing the same thing over and over every night, why then did she get engaged at 18? Wasn't that the same thing every night? No, it wasn't. 'And anyway,' she hinted shyly, 'it's definitely not the same thing every night.'

Besides, she continued, 'We're both young, and I think we should be making the most of our relationship at this stage.' But, according to the press, there had to be something else going on, hadn't there? 'I don't know what the obsession is,' condemned Johnny. 'It's so crazy that newspapers make up all these stories about me that never really happened. Part of it is my fault because I spoke fairly openly about my relationship with Nonie.'

Neither was he convinced that his romance with Winona was, as some observers put it, 'treated with kid gloves by casting them as romantic innocents amid all the usual gossip about Bruce Willis and Demi Moore, or Julia Roberts and Kiefer Sutherland'. True, Hollywood had always thrived on celebrity romance, but for Johnny to see his love life diagnosed like a cultural symptom, or publicly consummated and consumed, did nothing more than irritate. But neither could he condemn the fact that, to all intents and purposes, Johnny and Winona were also being packaged as the fairytale couple, a symbol of 'Hollywood Romance'. Even the occasional fashion shoots they did together – embracing and kissing – insisted they were.

Although they weren't short of money, they never blew it on wild excesses. Instead, explained Johnny, 'I like to shop for weird things if I'm with Winona. We found a genie inside an old lamp, and clown posters. Clowns have always scared me, so I think if I surround myself with them, it'll ward off evil.' He even let it slip in one interview that he had a nine-foot cock which raised a few eyebrows. 'I always thought it was good to say that I had the biggest cock in Los Angeles. I am not saying there are no grounds for that without him, but when you have a nine-foot rooster you can say that to anyone.' He had bought that as well, a fibre-glass rooster that he found outside a shop in Hollywood. 'I had to have it. It used to protect me from the clowns.'

As a child, Johnny was horribly aware of his phobia. 'I don't remember one particular incident, I've just always hated them.' His fears were most probably magnified the day he bought a painting of a clown by convicted murderer John Wayne Gacy. 'Before he was caught, Gacy used to go around as Pogo the Clown. Now on death row, he paints clowns, and if you send him a photo, he'll paint you.' It was, as far as Johnny was concerned, 'really sick'.

Less fatefully, of course, were the little gifts and presents

Johnny and Winona used to buy each other. For Winona: roses, clothes, and jewellery, including her first pearl necklace. And for Johnny: antique locks for his Houdini hobby, first editions of their favourite authors, and bugs for his collection, mounted traditionally with pins in glass boxes. Even though he used to catch chameleons when he was seven years old and train them, spiders were a definite no-no. And he makes no bones about the impact they had on his life. Not even when a friend went out and bought him a tarantula for his birthday did it help. 'I thought, well, this is great. Now maybe I won't be scared of them any more. So I'd try to touch him and when I did, I'd scream, so I had to get rid of him.'

There was also the galactic star located in the Northern sky in the constellation Cepheus, not visible to the naked eye, that Winona bought and named 'Jun' after him. Much the same way as you can buy acres of rain forest. Some, however, had seen that as an attempt at a reconciliation. According to Mitchell Fink writing in *People Weekly*, 'A woman in the throes of splitting up does not pay to name a star for her man.' Nor does she pay an extra $44 to get him a framed certificate. Indeed, insisted Johnny, they were simply a young couple still very much in love.

If that was true, then work would again provide an aching separation for both. While Winona contended with her own set of demons on Francis Ford Coppola's *Dracula* shoot, her first role as an adult, Johnny himself was thrown into an equal nightmare on *Arizona Dream*, a movie with a temperamental cast and an even more temperamental director.

Emir Kusturica first came to the Yugoslavian public's

attention with 1984's *When Father Was Away on Business*, a documentary study of the national betrayals of Yugoslavia in the fifties seen through the eyes of a young boy. Five years later Kusturica made his mark at Cannes with his Best Director prize for *The Time of the Gypsies*, and was now firmly committed to the idea of filming the mythical American dream filtered through European eyes.

Indeed, the brainchild of *Arizona Dream* came from David Atkin, a student of Kusturica's film classes at Columbia University. It was, he explained, 'a little piece about a young boy who didn't know what to do with his life. Somehow, I was interested in exploring the declining empire of the car industry in the States, because America is always the country of cars and movies. I saw something similar to what I wanted to do.'

It was the story of Axel Blackmar, a 20-year-old, orphaned after his parents' death in an unfortunate car accident six years earlier in which his uncle Leo was driving and who still hasn't forgiven himself for the fatal crash. Axel, however, has since found contentment living in Manhattan 'where you can see everybody and nobody can see you', and counting fish for New York's Department of Fish and Game. His simple contentment, however, is swiftly interrupted when he is summoned back to his Arizona hometown for Leo's wedding to his 'little posh cupcake', half his age and half his size. It is where Leo begs Axel to be his best man, and where, afterwards, he should remain to learn about being a Cadillac salesman at his uncle's showrooms.

Already in this setting is Paul, Leo's other salesman, who's on hand to show Axel the ropes. But he has other things on his mind – dreams of becoming an actor. He can already recite the dialogue from *Raging Bull*, and even comes up with one of the finest moments in the movie, his confounding impression of Cary Grant running from the crop-duster in Hitchcock's *North By Northwest* without saying a word.

Equally confounding is the manic depressive Elaine Stalker and her oppressed stepdaughter Grace, with whom Axel swiftly becomes entangled. Although Elaine fatally shot her husband (the circumstances aren't too clear), she and Grace blame each other whenever it's convenient.

Grace has also already inherited the state's third-largest copper mine and the two women, bonded more by love and loneliness than hatred, live in a vast Victorian ranch house just outside town. Axel initially is more taken in with the glamorous and sexy Elaine and her dream of building a flying machine than he is with Grace, who never stops talking of suicide and her hopes for reincarnation as a turtle.

The *Los Angeles Times* critic Kevin Thomas would describe the film as 'a dazzling, daring slice of cockamamie, tragi-comic Americana envisioned with magic realism by a major distinctive film-maker'.

With $17 million dollars of French money and two French producers, Claude Ossard and Yves Marmon, Kusturica developed a script for a movie that underwent three title changes from *Arrowtooth Waltz* to *American Dream* to *Arizona Dream*. 'The American dream is the dream of everyone in Western civilisation,' Kusturica insisted. 'To have a car, a little money and a house. But when I was living in America for two years, I found that

America itself was very different. People were unhappy and much poorer than I expected. There was a problem then, because in destroying the illusion of the American dream you are also destroying part of your youth, a childhood spent watching movies.'

Johnny agreed. 'I was thrilled to work with Kusturica because I saw *Time of the Gypsies* and it was one of the greatest things I've ever seen.' Not only that, but Johnny applauded the idea of working with yet another director not yet established in the upper echelons of Hollywood, and one, he thought, who would be more open to exploring and experimenting with his material.

He also saw something in the script of which even Kusturica was not probably aware. The role, Johnny notes enthusiastically, was another offbeat oddball taking a unique path in life. Something Johnny himself could relate to, in retrospect, at least. From that point of view, Johnny's fascination with Axel Blackmar should not have been surprising. It has since proven characteristic of his favourite kind of role.

'There's a part of me that always wanted to change. For example, ever since I was a kid, I was fascinated by the idea of time travel, of being someone else in another time. I think that's probably a normal thing. Well, let's hope it is. What interests me is that so-called "normal" society considers them outcasts or on the fringe or oddballs. With any part you play, there is a certain amount of yourself in it.'

There has to be, he reasoned, 'otherwise, it's just not acting. It's lying. That's not to say that I feel different than others. Maybe they have a more difficult time saying "I don't feel accepted" or "I feel insecure". These characters are passive; I see them as receivers. I've identified with them since I was very young.'

Certainly, that was the opinion of the star names rushing to try out for the other parts. Jerry Lewis, a veteran of 17 Dean Martin movies was cast as Uncle Leo; Faye Dunaway and Lili Taylor were recruited to play the mother and daughter team, Elaine and Grace Stalker; and Vincent Gallo, the seventies underground musician and accomplished painter from New York accepted the part of Paul Blackmar.

All the same, filming itself, on location in Alaska, New York and Arizona, placed a lot of pressure on Kusturica's shoulders. As he himself would later point out, he suffered what he called a nervous breakdown.

Not surprising really. After weeks of exhausting night shoots, escalating budgets, an increasingly erratic cast and looming money-men, he upped sticks and returned to New York, refusing to shoot any more footage of the uncompleted film until his backers would give him more time, more space and more money to realise his vision.

Such antics are generally known as the amorphous creative differences which scupper so many other Hollywood projects. Most films would have seen the director replaced and the movie completed, but the producers swiftly discovered that Kusturica had the cast, including Johnny, right behind him. Indeed, the entire cast and crew refused to consider continuing with anyone other than Kusturica.

'I'm a European director,' he snapped, 'not an American and I just wasn't ready for what they throw at you. They don't want imagination. They want a beginning, a middle and an end, with the end nice and convenient and happy.'

Although Kusturica freely acknowledged that his bizarre all-or-nothing approach led to most of the problems, he was not prepared to acknowledge defeat. 'I don't know what's the matter with me. Perhaps I'm just crazy, but I have this vision and I just have to complete it, no matter what the cost. I'd hate to be my producer.' With *Arizona Dream*, he said, 'I thought I was going to die at least twice. It's too much of a strain.'

Even Vincent Gallo observed the scenes of the dramas that were going on behind the cameras. But he also noted a change in Johnny, too. He had apparently re-invented himself since the two first met on the set of *21 Jump Street*. He was, Gallo recalls, dating Winona, and they were wearing thrift shop clothes for the first time. 'He was tattooed and earringed and on a TV show. I just hated them.'

There were even rumours of a conflict between the two. Their friendship, it seemed, was under strain during the making of the movie. Johnny, he explained, had found a soulmate in Emir Kusturica and constantly demanded his attention. 'And he was not completely nice to me to get it,' Gallo recalls. 'He had this need to be heavily involved with Kusturica. It was almost like a love affair. Emir and Johnny carried around Dostoevsky and Kerouac books and wore black. They had never worn black in their lives.' Not only that, continues Gallo, but 'they kept everybody in the cast and crew awake all night, because they were blasting music and getting drunk.'

The tragedy of Johnny Depp, Gallo continues, 'is that the exterior, the TV pop star turned bad boy, waif lover, hipster friend of Jim Jarmusch, is totally uninteresting. It's tragic that he has this poser part of himself, that he has to invent himself like that. If only he would allow himself to be who he really is, somebody who's traumatised and trapped by his childhood and emotional life, then he would be interesting, a great person, a great talent. He is one of the most funny, talented, likeable, sweet, authentic people I've ever met.'

All the same, Gallo felt no reservations about Johnny's on-screen ability. If you want to see Johnny's greatest moments on film, he insisted, 'look at the scenes where he has no dialogue. He is the most brilliant listener in a movie. There's a scene where we're at a movie theatre and they're showing *Raging Bull*. All he's doing is watching me hustle these girls. I'm telling her we can make love but do not touch my face or my hair, and I start rambling on. "Do you think anybody touches Brando's face? Touch Pacino's face? Does anybody touch De Niro's face? Does anybody touch fucking Johnny Depp's face?" I said, "Do you think fucking Johnny Depp lets anybody touch his face?" I just said it.

'I was goofing because I thought we were just shooting a rehearsal. Johnny is flawless in the scene. He's just brilliant in the scene, he doesn't flinch. I say his name in the scene and he doesn't flinch. He blows me off the screen, and it's my most animated scene in the film.'

There were, of course, other demons Kusturica needed to contend with as the *Arizona Dream* shoot rolled on. Tantamount among these was his relationship with Faye Dunaway. What had started out as a genuine respect for each other became more difficult. It probably didn't help that Kusturica didn't seem to be as attentive towards Dunaway as he was Johnny.

Whatever the reason, it appears the tension between the two was enough to ignite the difficulties, 'But,' Kusturica said, 'we overcame that problem together. I said to her that this is a movie where all the people must act together with each other all the time. If you have any problems, just let me know.' She did that as well. But, admitted Kusturica later, 'she will be very good in the movie.'

In Elaine, agreed The Detroit News, 'Dunaway in particular has found one of her most challenging roles as an extremely mercurial, outrageous woman with an image of a crazed nymphomaniac whose vulnerability and longing actually express an acute perception.' Much the same as they said about Jerry Lewis. 'He also gives a serious, endearing performance of one of the most normal men he has ever played.'

And that is what Kusturica had expected from him. Aside from his acclaimed performance in Martin Scorsese's The King of Comedy, Lewis hadn't worked that much in movies of late. 'I had heard a lot of bad things about Jerry,' Kusturica smiled. 'But they must have been lies. For me, Jerry was crazy, and extremely pleased because I was laughing at what he did, but at the same time, I had to control him, because in this movie he is dying and had many serious scenes. He is a very good actor. The reason that the cast is electric somehow relates to the States and even to the movies, to things like Jerry's comedies.'

It was something Kusturica learned when he and Johnny left for Cannes to promote the then unfinished movie. All the same, it was a trip that Vincent Gallo believes was as much for Johnny's ego than the purpose of selling the film to distributors. 'Johnny had this need to go to Cannes, and stay at the Hotel du Cap, and then refuse to do interviews – perhaps he had read in an article that Brando refused to do interviews.'

Even when the film did finally make it out to the screens, the expected wide release was as disappointing as the bemused critical reaction following its international début. It won the competition prize at the Berlin Film Festival in 1993, and two years later it received a limited British release in art houses.

Still, Kusturica was not concerned. If anything, it only cemented his determination to work with Johnny again. Unconfirmed rumours began to circulate linking the two together for a modern version of *Crime and Punishment*, set this time in modern-day Brooklyn, but the project apparently fell through when Kusturica's potential Italian backers Penta shut down their failed American operation.

CHAPTER 7

*'IT WAS A REALLY GOOD THING THAT IT ENDED,
I THINK, FOR BOTH OF US. I DON'T KNOW HOW
MUCH THE MEDIA HAD TO DO WITH IT, BECAUSE WE
REALLY HAD DRIFTED APART A LONG TIME BEFORE THE
PRESS FOUND OUT THAT IT HAD ENDED. SO IT WAS OLD.
I THINK HE'S GREAT, AND I HAVE NOTHING BUT KIND
THINGS TO SAY ABOUT HIM, BUT IT WAS JUST OVER.'*
WINONA RYDER

DEATH OF A FAIRYTALE

By April 1993, it seemed that Johnny's life with Winona was ending. It had been for over a year. They rarely saw one another any more, and although they kept up appearances when they went out, they didn't go out that much. It was apparent that they had begun to drift apart. They may have shared the same home, but they didn't share the same life. It was just the beginning of what would be a painful end to Hollywood's fairytale romance.

Making matters worse was the difficulty they found in maintaining a relationship amidst successful careers and punishing work schedules that kept them separated much of the time. Constant rumours that they had both been stepping out with other young stars continued to add fuel to the fire. And although they ignored the gossip, refusing to even dignify the tales with a response, the stories still persisted, sometimes even touching on accusations of sleeping with their co-stars, rowing furiously, and not even being together any more.

One of those occasions was while Winona was filming *The Age of Innocence*, Martin Scorsese's adaptation of the Edith Wharton novel, in New York, and Johnny was at home writing a movie with his brother, Dan.

According to insiders, Winona and Daniel Day-Lewis had apparently struck up a close friendship. 'She and Dan Day-Lewis were mad for each other all through the production. It was like a freeing of the soul.' But then again, 'Winona was in love with just being there. She had such a good time. She had so much energy.'

It probably didn't help matters when Day-Lewis revealed how they would sing together. Winona's most impressive number he told the *New York Post* was 'I'm Just a Girl Who Can't Say No'.

Inevitably, headlines soon suggested as much when the film was finally released. Several reviewers picked up on the chemistry between the co-stars, suggesting that their relationship was not just confined to the screen following the movie's release five months after Winona and Johnny had split.

Even if the speculation had been true, and according to Winona's publicist it wasn't, what most failed to acknowledge was the fact that Winona and Johnny were no longer a couple. They hadn't been for at least a year, long before filming started.

On the other hand, Johnny himself apparently wasn't quite so blameless. According to Tally Chanel, a B-movie actress who had met Johnny at the Hollywood première of Bruce Willis' *Die Hard 2* in July 1990, she said she almost got the opportunity to marry him.

Not only that, but according to some, they dated for a

year by spending quiet nights at Johnny's Hollywood Hills home ordering in food from a Chinese restuarant. If that was true, and it probably wasn't, the fact that he was engaged to Winona at the same time didn't seem to matter. Neither, apparently, did his confession that 'he sort of had a crush' on Patty Hearst when they came together on the set of John Waters' *Cry Baby*.

Not that Waters would agree. 'Johnny's a serial monogamist if anything. He's been with very few women since I've known him and for long periods. And he's been very faithful to his women so he's hardly a womaniser.'

Whatever the reasons, Winona was clear about where she laid most of the blame for the eventual collapse of her romance with Johnny. 'I remember us desperately hating being hounded. It was horrible and it definitely took its toll on our relationship. Every day we heard that we were either cheating on each other or were broken up when we weren't. It was like this constant mosquito buzzing around us.'

The end of their romance, of course, was dutifully reported in the press. 'Stick a fork into the relationship of Winona Ryder and Johnny Depp, and you will discover it's done,' wrote *People Weekly*. 'Ryder's representative confirms, after months of press speculation, that Ryder and Depp are a couple no more. The two young movie stars have called off their engagement and gone their separate ways.'

Even Winona's diary entry at the time revealed that she was feeling 'fragile, a little confused, heartachy and a little tired'. As for Johnny, 'He's a special guy. I was just really young. I don't know what his excuse is, but that's mine.' But whatever she said in public, she still looked for ways to relieve her private agony of the break-up.

'I attempted being an alcoholic for two weeks,' she would smile later, remembering all the nights 'in my hotel room, drinking screwdrivers from the mini-bar and smoking cigarettes' while the doleful sounds of Tom Waits' *Nighthawks at the Diner* album played over and over on the stereo.

For a time the drinking may have helped, but the night she passed out with a lit cigarette still burning between her fingers, she awoke quickly, before any harm was done, but the thought of what could have happened had simply terrified her. But according to Britain's *Evening Standard*, the drinking and smoking binge did in fact end up with her almost burning herself to death, wrote Liz Hodgson. 'Winona said she woke up to find her hotel room in flames." Although at the time, Winona added she hadn't visited that dark side ever since, or the mini-bar, recent claims that she has a whooper of an addiction to painkiller medication during her notorious arrest for shoplifting in 2001, suggests that she has. But for now, she knew that the dizzy oblivion of alcohol was no solution for confronting the painful feelings she felt over the ending of her relationship with Johnny.

All the same, she would soon after, check herself into a psychiatric clinic, some say because of the break-up. Just twenty years old at the time, she was also having trouble dealing, not only with the ending of her relationship with Johnny, but also with the stresses arising from too much work, too little sleep and too little emotional grounding. 'I was actually in the clinic for five days,' she confessed. 'The public thinks actors aren't allowed to be depressed,' she accuses. 'We're sickening well paid, get amazing perks, and live charmed lives. What the public doesn't see is the ugly side of our lives, and that's the stuff that breaks us down. I had broken up with my first real love and there were huge pressures from my career. I needed desperately to take stock of my life and for that I needed sleep.'

Johnny, however, believed his relationship with Winona slowly unravelled over time, the pressure of their film careers, and being constantly hounded by the press taking its final toll. In June 1993, he announced publicly, 'We split up a month ago. When you're with someone and you love them, it's never easy to cut the string, to sever the connection. But, with us, it just came to seem the natural thing to do – a natural progression, just something that had to happen. I wouldn't say that our splitting was exactly a devastating experience for either of us really. We're still friends. We still talk. And everything's fine, very amicable, very nice.' But was it?

As much as Winona was devastated, Johnny was inconsolable. A friend confided anonymously to *People* magazine that 'he was so desperately in love with Winona, that when they broke up, he wouldn't admit that it was over for the longest time.'

Johnny and Winona had started out their life together by being open with the press in the hope that it would satisfy their demand for celebrity news and gossip and finally leave the couple alone, but that did not happen. 'It's very hard to have a personal life in Hollywood,' revealed Johnny at the time, explaining that the decision to be as open as they were was, in fact, a mistake.

'I thought it would destroy the curiosity monster. Instead it fed it. I had nothing but bad luck after talking about this stuff. It became such a public thing. Everyone felt like they were part of it, or owned part of it, or that they'd somehow got the right to ask me about her. I hated it.'

Although Winona filed away her engagement ring along with her other memories, for Johnny the visible tokens of his love for Winona were going to prove far more difficult and far more painful to dispose of. Having seen his 'Winona Forever' tattoo become the object of many an interviewer's questions, and the butt end of as many comedians' jokes over the next year, he began to have second thoughts about removing it.

'I think of my tattoos like a journal and to have it removed, or erase it, is to try and say it never happened. We were together for three years and at the time, I really did think it would be forever. If I alter it in some way, make it funny, put her next boyfriend's name on top of it – that would be honest.' Over the next year, however, Johnny acknowledged that he was, in fact, going to have it removed.

Even if taking it off would hurt more than putting it on? Johnny agreed. 'Especially if they don't give you the anaesthetic. But it's worth it, the pain going on and off. They're both worth it.' One journalist caught it shortly after the treatment began. 'At the moment, it reads "Wino Forever"'. And still does to this day.

When asked, Winona felt there was little to be done about the tattoo. 'What do you want me to say? It's like, "It's there, oh well". If I hated him, I'd probably say something poignant. He's a great guy, but I don't really think about it.' Johnny, of course, was less reticent on the subject of the ending of the relationship. Where had all the rebel love gone? He had no idea.

'It's one of the mysteries of everybody's life. It's not like you suddenly go, "You know what? I just don't love you."

She's a sweet kid, man, and it's always a little weird. We used to do this and that, and we used to have fun and hang out together. But at least we were able to feel that for each other. I feel real lucky that we got that.'

All the same, GQ magazine wondered if they were simply too young and gorgeous to be left alone by the tabloids. 'They kept doing their ridiculously romantic things. She bought him a star. He tattooed her name on his body. It was more than romantic. It was reckless.'

And maybe they were right. Nonetheless, Johnny didn't relish the thought of being alone again after such a long relationship. Being lonely, he confessed, was scary. 'I've been lonely many times.'

People Weekly, meanwhile, was quick to notice that Winona did not remain alone for long. 'We hear from other sources that Ryder is now seeing David Pirner, lead singer of the rock group Soul Asylum. Pirner apparently left his girlfriend of 11 years to be with Ryder.'

Although the relationship threatened to be as well documented as her previous one with Johnny, and although Winona was not screaming her business from the top of the Hollywood Hills, it was immediately apparent that she felt much more comfortable talking about her relationship with Pirner than she ever did discussing Johnny. 'Our relationship is different from any I've ever had,' she explained. 'It's more casual, it's more of a friendship, really. What I'm basically saying is that it's not full of drama.'

From the pain and turmoil of his relationship ending with Winona, Johnny moved into shooting *Benny and Joon*, a movie based on a screenplay by Barry Berman and Leslie McNeil. The two men had first discussed the project in the early 1980s when both were up-and-coming scriptwriters. A decade later, their passion for the story remained unabated.

Berman, of course, was suitably qualified to pen the story in the first place. He had, after all, been a graduate of Ringling Brothers and Barnum & Bailey's highly competitive Clown College in Florida, earned his apprenticeship in the world-renowned circus, and had loved watching reels of Buster Keaton and Charlie Chaplin's silent comedy classics in between performances under the big top. More importantly, it was what influenced him to create the character of Sam for *Benny and Joon*.

In fact, Berman's screenplay had come to the attention of Susan Arnold and Donna Roth in late 1989. 'Someone told us about this screenplay by Barry Berman, a young, relatively unknown screenwriter,' recalls Arnold. 'The first time Donna and I read the script we could both see that it was filled with jewels. It was simultaneously funny, romantic and poignant. Both of us felt passionate enough about this project to get it made.'

Not only that, but Arnold could also identify with the character of Joon. The producer had previously worked with Imagination Workshop, a California-based arts programme that worked with underprivileged and disenfranchised people as well as with psychiatric patients. 'My experience with the workshop certainly peaked my desire to make a movie about someone who had a little harder time in life than most of us.'

It was the theme that lies at the heart of the movie. The story centred on Juniper Pearl, Joon for short, a smart and talented, but emotionally unbalanced, young girl, who was cared for by her irrepressible, seemingly unselfish, car-

Winona Ryder, shown here with Johnny at the *Edward Scissorhands* première in December 1990, was his highest profile girlfriend before Kate Moss. They were introduced by a mutual friend in 1989.

After his relationship with Winona failed, Johnny began dating
Kate Moss. They are shown here in London.

Johnny with Hunter S Thompson at their reading from *Fear and Loathing in Las Vegas* at the Virgin Megastore in Times Square in New York on 28 May 1998.

Top: On holiday in Mustique with Kate, Noel Gallagher and his wife Meg, Johnny displays his dislike of the ever ravenous paparazzi.

Bottom: The spectacular south of France villa, near St Tropez, that Johnny purchased in 1999. It is pictured surrounded by scorched trees from the July 2003 blaze that swept the area. He and Vanessa Paradis and their two children spend most of their time there living 'a simple life' whenever Johnny isn't working.

Two years after *Sleepy Hollow*, Johnny won his second Saturn Award nomination, again for Best Actor, for his portrayal of the real-life Inspector Fred Abberline in *From Hell*.

Johnny must surely have relished the prospect of starring in the frenetic drug-crazed road movie *Fear and Loathing in Las Vegas*. He is shown here at the première.

Top: For co-star Keira Knightley, making *Pirates of the Caribbean* with Johnny, shown here during the filming of one of their favourite scenes together, was a thrill. 'I can't say enough good things about him, it was a dream, it was a pleasure. He was wicked. Really cool.'

Bottom: Although he ultimately lost out at the Oscars to Sean Penn, Johnny was thrilled that his work in *Pirates of the Caribbean* had earned him so many accolades, including his first Academy Award nomination, for Best Actor. He is shown here, with his mother and Vanessa, arriving at the ceremony in February 2004.

Top: Johnny, shown here at the Disneyland premiere of *Pirates of the Caribbean*, with co-stars Orlando Bloom and Keira Knightley, is to this day completely shocked that he was in a film that ended up as the summer blockbuster of 2003, 'made a whole lot of money' and placed him as the number one box-office star in Hollywood.

Bottom: After completing his work on Tim Burton's *Sleepy Hollow*, Johnny was awarded a star on the Hollywood Walk of Fame in November 1999. It is situated at 7020 Hollywood Boulevard, just two places up from Winona Ryder's.

(Photo: Nigel Goodall)

Top left: *Sweeney Todd* saw Johnny collaborate with Tim Burton once more – here, he is pictured at the 2008 Paris première of the musical film.

Top right: Johnny has found long-term happiness at last with singer and actress Vanessa Paradis. The couple have two children and divide their time between LA, their villa in the south of France and the island they own in the Bahamas.

Bottom left: In January 2009, Johnny appeared on *The Late Show with David Letterman*, one of America's top rated TV talk shows.

Bottom right: 2009's *Public Enemies* paired Johnny with Marion Cotillard and Christian Bale to tell the story of bank robber John Dillinger, America's first Public Enemy Number One.

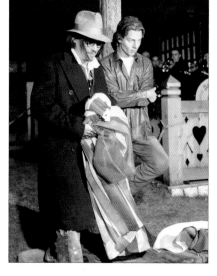

Top: Johnny still draws crowds of hundreds of adoring fans wherever he goes.

Bottom left: Johnny pictured with *Public Enemies* co-star Marion Cotillard and director Michael Mann.

Bottom right: Perhaps one of Johnny's more bizarre engagements – unveiling a statue of himself during the International Kustendorf Film Festival in Serbia. Johnny was guest of honour at the event organised by award-winning Serbian director Emir Kusturica.

Top left: 2010 was the year of the huge hit *Alice in Wonderland* for Johnny – here, he is pictured at the press conference held in California to launch the film.

Top right: Johnny with acclaimed director Wes Anderson and Monty Python star Terry Gilliam (*left*), who directed *The Imaginarium of Doctor Parnassus*. Johnny was one of the actors drafted in when Heath Ledger died during filming – he played a 'physically transformed version' of Ledger's character alongside Jude Law and Colin Farrell.

Bottom: The London première of *Alice in Wonderland*. Johnny met Prince Charles and the Duchess of Cornwall at the glittering event.

Top: Johnny on the set of The Tourist in early 2010 – the film is set for release in 2011 and also stars Angelina Jolie.

Bottom: Johnny with director and friend Tim Burton on *Friday Night with Jonathan Ross*. The pair talked about *Alice in Wonderland* and their other film collaborations, which include *Sweeney Todd* and *Charlie and the Chocolate Factory*.

repairing brother, Benjamin, or Benny, ever since their parents had died in a fatal car accident.

Joon paints and reads, has a passion for fire and nudging her housekeepers into retirement as Benny works his car clinic, plays poker, and gives up any hope of a serious relationship because he has no idea of how Joon is going to fit in.

The natural order and occasionally clichéd creakiness of this life is suddenly shattered, however, when, at a poker game, Joon loses her hand and wins her opponent's cousin Sam, a beguiling and whimsical misfit, who at 26 can't even read, spends all day polishing plastic forks, stays up all night watching old movies on TV, and when he does sleep, it's under the sink.

He, of course, charms his way into Joon's heart with his silent comedy capers, does the housework and listens to the rock music blasting from the radio even when it incurs Joon's wrath.

That is enough for Joon to throw him out, as she puts it, 'for cleaning the house'. He, of course, returns with Benny's blessing and Sam's promise to look out for his sister. Not so blessed, as far as Benny is concerned, is the gentle romance that begins for Sam and Joon. Although they are seen simply as two outcasts enjoying each other's company, they are also deadly serious. Serious enough to tell Benny at least. After all, for Joon, Sam offers the only stable love and sweetness she has seen in her troubled world. Their confession, of course, hits Benny like a ton of bricks, who in turn swiftly condemns the affair and in a moment of rage throws Sam out. This time for good.

Complicating matters even further is Benny's admission

that he has been considering a placement in a psychiatric home for Joon. Joon leaves after a fight with her brother, joins up with Sam and catches a bus out of town, and out of Benny's life. But Joon can't really cope with the outside world, least of all the claustrophobic confinement of the bus and, as a result, she hurls herself into a state of emotional turmoil.

She is rushed into a psychiatric unit from which, it appears, she may never be released. Benny, however, is so overcome with despair that he even dismisses Sam's offer of help. Matters worsen, however, when the hospital confirms its refusal to release Joon, or even to allow Benny to visit with her. Distraught and helpless, Benny turns once again to Sam for help. After another round of Keaton-style capers to extricate her, Joon returns to live again with Benny as he begins to understand her needs as much as he does his own.

Strangely enough, Johnny was not the first choice for the role of Sam even though he had, for some time, thought it was perfect for him. Unfortunately, a lot of critics completely disagreed. They thought he was in danger of pushing himself into a corner with his odd choice of roles, and any calculated attempts to shake off his oddball typecasting was, as far as they were concerned, less than satisfactory.

Johnny, too, asked much the same. 'Do I search out the weirdest thing I can find and then do it just because it is the weirdest thing I can find?' No, he didn't. 'I just do the things that I like. I have to admit, however, that what I like does tend to be left-field.'

Besides, he continued, 'I feel somehow much more comfortable playing it. I relate more easily than I do when I run across straight roles. I hate the obvious stuff, I just don't respond to it.'

Although Johnny did not share his critics' doubts, they still questioned whether it was a movie for him. The character he would be playing could easily have been taken out of any Buster Keaton silent comedy. Perhaps it's not surprising that he had been flirting with the idea of playing Charlie Chaplin in Richard Attenborough's biopic, the one that had linked Winona Ryder to the project in the role of Chaplin's third wife Paulette Goddard. And that could possibly have been why he turned down the role. After all, it would have turned out to be a very different experience from the one when the couple worked together on *Edward Scissorhands*. As Winona herself would point out, 'I'd work with Johnny again, but right now it might be awkward.'

All the same, continues Johnny, 'I wasn't really a contender for Chaplin. I met with Richard Attenborough, knowing I was totally wrong for the part. I just wanted to meet him. I knew right from the start that I was not right for the role, not physically right, I mean. Robert (Downey Jnr) was the perfect choice. He kind of looks like Chaplin and he's built more like him.'

Certainly that was true, but in any event Johnny saw no cause to regret his decision to accept the role of Sam. It was a perfect alternative to the Chaplin part. More importantly, it offered him the opportunity to work with Jeremiah Chechik, a Canadian-born director not yet established in the Hollywood A-list, and one who probably wouldn't enforce the restrictions that an established director might. It was something that had haunted Johnny ever since working with Oliver Stone on *Platoon*. And one that had caused him to question his own performance as a result.

Chechik also loved the script and, more importantly, the

characters. He understood that the moment he read it. 'In the most simple way, it's a romance between two oddities who meet and fall in love.' The story, he observed, 'is universal because every human heart contains the potential for both pain and pleasure. It has a fable quality to it, but it's also very believable.'

He also knew that Johnny would be equally believable. How could he not be? When the two first met, he understood that even more. But he also 'began to understand how much he had brought to the role of *Edward Scissorhands*. He is so emotionally expressive, doing what seems to be so little. It was clear that he would bring a thoroughly original and exciting energy to the role of Sam.'

Johnny, though, wasn't the only cast member to end up as second, or even third choice. For a while, Chechik sought Tom Hanks for Johnny's role of Sam, and Julia Roberts for Joon. Not surprising, really, since they were two of the hottest names in Hollywood at the time. But when the idea of Hanks and Roberts fell through, the studio, MGM, simply told Chechik to look to casting real-life Hollywood couple Tim Robbins and Susan Sarandon who had already starred together with great success in Kevin Costner's 1988 baseball comedy *Bull Durham*. But that didn't work out either. Eventually, they settled on Johnny for Sam; Laura Dern for Joon; and the still relatively new, affable bartender from *Cheers*, Woody Harrelson, as Benny.

Shooting was already scheduled to get under way in June 1993 when two of the trio quit the production. Dern, who had by now secured an Oscar nomination for her role in 1991's *Rambling Rose* was not prepared to accept third billing below the two male leads, and Harrelson was already in negotiation with director Adrian Lyne to secure the hotly-contested role of Demi Moore's husband in Robert Redford's starring vehicle, *Indecent Proposal*.

As far as MGM were concerned, Harrelson was in breach of his contract and was seriously delaying the production of a major motion picture, and the studio intended to make him aware of that. The actor was promptly sued for $5 million dollars and threatened with an injunction if he were to play any other roles throughout the period he should have been filming *Benny and Joon*. To complicate matters further, Harrelson countered with a claim that he couldn't work with Chechik.

MGM, however, were not convinced and their lawsuit contained what they believed to be the true circumstances behind Harrelson's departure. 'Sudden success has caused Harrelson to attempt to take advantage of his new popularity by disregarding his existing obligation in favour of another motion picture project he now considers more favourable.' Eventually, though, Harrelson's gamble paid off, and he did play the role of Moore's architect husband David Murphy in Lyne's blockbuster movie.

Aidan Quinn, still a couple of years away from Brad Pitt's *Legends of the Fall*, and Mary Stuart Masterson, of *Fried Green Tomatoes* fame, were quickly recruited to fill their places as the remainder of the cast was also assembled. Julianne Moore accepted the part of waitress Ruthie, Benny's would-be love interest. Other roles were filled by CCH Pounder as Joon's counsellor Dr Garvey; and Oliver Platt, Dan Hedaya and William Burch as Benny's pals.

Chechik's final choice of casting Quinn as the protective, straight-laced brother may have been an unconventional one but also proved to be the right one. 'Benny's got the weight of the world on him,' explained Quinn. 'He's the mud of reality, while the others are the sprites of magic. My character is very much a straight man.'

Masterson, on the other hand, would admit that her role was one of the most intriguing she had ever taken on. Not only that but the first day on the set, 'my husband and I had just split up, and I was in the hysterical funk you get in when you're trying to be pulled together. But when Johnny walked in, the energy in the room changed. There's something really amazing about him, his generosity of spirit.'

All the same it was, she confirmed later, 'really revealing to play a character whose confidence is shaken by the confusion she lives with everyday. My own insecurities came right to the surface as a result. But this story is basically about love. There are circumstances that are universal in this story, such as learning how much you can love someone and still allow them to be free.' It was that theme, she said, that lies at the heart of the movie.

Nonetheless, it was not an easy role to prepare for, as much for Johnny as Masterson. As with *Edward Scissorhands*, the role of Sam demanded that Johnny interact not only emotionally but also physically with his character. An on-set mime artist, magician and silent film buff, Dan Kamin, was recruited to coach and choreograph the comedy routines of the screen legends that were all part and parcel of Sam's character. Johnny was thankful for his help as he consulted with Kamin on the tiniest of details. 'He gave me some pointers on movement,' Johnny explained. 'I enjoyed the slapstick part of the movie, although I sustained some injuries.'

Johnny's research was augmented by watching the silent movies of the period – especially the Keaton and Chaplin stuff. 'Since Sam's brand of comedy is physical rather than verbal, in much the same way as silent film heroes, we concentrated on a style of movement,' Kamin explained. 'We started with magic tricks, using sleight of hand and worked our way up to recreating Keaton's patented falls. The subtle movements are the hardest to capture, but Johnny did a marvellous job. He was really courageous and worked hard, even at the small things.'

In one memorable review, the *Mail on Sunday* critic Tom Hutchinson summed up the general critical opinion when he credited Johnny as 'the clowning minder to a mentally ill girl, Depp tenderly reinforces the role of eccentric outsider which has become his province. Delightfully played, it is a fable with potential to touch the heart.' The *Spectator* agreed, remarking how Johnny was 'curiously serious and not so much simple-minded as innocent in *Edward Scissorhands* and *Cry Baby*, and he is all those things again here, and charming. The charm is not forced.' Certainly that was true. In the end though, *Benny and Joon* was a delightful movie.

Although the London *Evening Standard* had called *Benny and Joon* 'too kooky for words', Johnny was not concerned. 'I don't think I'm limiting myself, because I'm doing things that are true to me. I see these characters as much more normal than what's considered normal. There seems to be this constant theme in the things that I do which deal with people who are considered "freaks" by so-called normal people. I guess I'm attracted to these off-beat roles because my life has been a bit abnormal. The only thing I have a problem with is being labelled.'

And he laughed, because that yearning could also be read as a justification of Johnny's next role, the title character in Lasse Hallstrom's *What Eating Gilbert Grape?*, a movie based on Peter Hedges' 1993 novel.

It was the story of the title character who looks after his mother, brother and two sisters in the home that their father built just before he was 'hung out to dry' 17 years earlier in Endora, 'where nothing ever much happens, and nothing much ever will'.

Mama used to be the 'prettiest gal in these parts' but is now a 600lb mountain of a woman who hasn't stepped outside the front door in at least seven years and whose oversized proportions play havoc with the infrastructure of the house they still live in.

Gilbert's younger brother Arnie is mentally impaired and was never expected to survive much beyond childhood, and may not much longer. In fact, it could be any day now. 'Sometimes you want him to live. And sometimes you don't.' His older sister Amy is a home-maker who yearns for normal domestic bliss while the youngest, Ellen, has just turned 15 and had her braces removed.

Gilbert's troubles, however, stretch far beyond his family, extending to his friends, employers and customers. He works at Lamson Groceries which is battling against the huge Foodmarket where everyone else shops on the outskirts of town; he's having an affair with Mrs Betty Carver; and his best friend, Tucker, is going crazy about the opening of a franchise burger joint, the best employment opportunity, he thinks, to hit Endora since, well, since he can remember.

Into this self-contained world bursts Becky and her grandmother, caravanning tourists who find themselves stranded in the dead-end town for a while with mechanical problems. It is where Becky is forced to involve herself with community life during her brief stay and, of course, Gilbert. At the heart of the movie, though, is Gilbert's indecision – whether to remain loyal to his family responsibilities, or whether to pursue his own freedom for happiness – in the shape of Becky.

Either way, Gilbert is stuck in Endora, explained Hedges of his scripted screenplay. 'He's working in a grocery store and everybody's gnawing at him; his family, his friends, his lover. But into town rolls a girl who collides with everything that has been closed up inside him.'

Indeed, Hedges' novel had only been published for a few days when Swedish director Lasse Hallstrom, best known for 1985's *My Life As a Dog* and more fatefully as the director who had quit Winona's 1990 movie, *Mermaids*, started calling.

That was, Hedges recalled, 'One of my favourite films. I realised that Lasse could bring great humanity to these characters where another director might make fun of them.' Not only that, but when Hallstrom announced who he had in mind for the title role, he was even more excited. 'Gilbert is very much an observer, a reactor in the movie, and Johnny Depp was the perfect actor,' Hallstrom said at the time. 'He has the sensitivity that Gilbert Grape needs.'

Hedges agreed. He had already watched Johnny's performances in *Edward Scissorhands* and *Benny and Joon*, and instantly knew the choice was the correct one. 'He has an almost burning desire to make ugly choices. He comes with a physical beauty that's just astonishing, and at the same time he has no interest in being that. When I met him he had this really long hair and showed up at the meeting, very quiet, really shy, and was teaching us magic tricks. I thought, I suppose he could be Gilbert.'

As Johnny slipped into his character he knew 'Gilbert Grape had to leave his dreams behind because of circumstances. He has a hostility that he can't express because of his duties and responsibilities to his family. To be able to deal with himself everyday, he's had to make himself sort of numb so that he's not affected too much by everything.' Far more important to his portrayal, Johnny concedes, was the fact that 'there were things that have happened in my life that parallel things in Gilbert's life'.

For Johnny, playing the small-town son who takes care of his mother and retarded brother was, in many ways, a throwback to his own childhood; his parents' divorce, looking after his heartbroken mother, and picking up the support cheques from his father. 'It's always taxing to play something that's close to reality, but sometimes you play roles that are close to you. You identify with the guy. Not that you become the person, because I don't buy into that shit at all.'

What he did buy into, however, was the emotional upheaval of not being with Winona any more. Although it does not appear to have affected his performance, he did openly admit that it was one of the most difficult times he ever had on a movie. 'I poisoned myself constantly; drinking, didn't eat right, no sleep, lots of cigarettes. It was really a lonely, really fucking, lonely time.'

All the same, Johnny immersed himself in the role without hesitation. He even had his teeth bonded and chipped. On set, he vowed, he would dye his hair trailer-park red in homage to his friend Bones who had courageously beat out the flames that had set the actor's face alight back in his teens.

In the same way, Johnny elaborates, 'Gilbert would seem like a pretty normal kind of guy, but I was interested in what was going on underneath, in the hostility and the rage that he has and that he's only able to show a couple of times in the film. I understand that feeling of being stuck in a place, whether it is geographical or emotional. I can understand the rage of wanting to completely escape from it and from everybody and everything, you know, and start a new life.'

From that point of view, it is not difficult to appreciate the appeal of the film or the character. It was, Johnny said, 'like Gilbert at some point or another allowed himself to die inside, slowly kind of killing or martyring himself for his family, becoming a surrogate father – even to his mother. That kind of loyalty may start out as pure love, but it can work against you, with love and devotion turning into resentment and guilt and losing yourself, which is the worst thing anyone can do – because then you hate others because of what you have done to yourself.'

Equally instinctive as choosing Johnny for Gilbert was the choice of Leonardo DiCaprio as his mentally handicapped brother Arnie. 'I needed someone who wasn't good looking,' recalls Hallstrom. 'But of all the actors who auditioned for the role, Leonardo was the most observant.'

He had, in fact, been acting since he was 14, ever since he did a fistful of commercials and educational outings before he moved into what Johnny would identify as television hell by playing the homeless Luke in *Growing Pains*. Soon after, he crossed over to movies, and although still some years away from establishing himself in the heart-throb stakes for the 1996 version of William Shakespeare's *Romeo & Juliet*, and two years later in James Cameron's *Titanic*, his performance opposite Robert De Niro in *This Boy's Life*, the same year he made *Gilbert Grape*, established him as the promising youngster he turned out to be.

In fact, DiCaprio was so brilliant in *Gilbert Grape* that he was suddenly in danger of being typecast, not merely as a troubled teenager, but as a *very* troubled teenager. It was even confirmed by the additional acclaim of his peers – a nomination for Best Supporting Actor at the 1994 Academy Awards.

But it didn't happen by accident. As DiCaprio himself explains, 'It was one of the hardest things I've ever done. I had to really research and get into the mind of somebody with a disability like that. I spent a few days at a home for mentally retarded teens. We just talked and I watched their mannerisms. People have these expectations that mentally retarded children are really crazy, but it's not so. It's refreshing to see them, because everything is new to them. They are completely spontaneous and focus on what is directly in their vision, what they experience at the moment. Playing Arnie was fun because everything I did was spontaneous.'

Hallstrom, too, noticed the focus. There was one particular autistic boy, he remembers, who very much became DiCaprio's role model. 'I took a lot of his mannerisms and made them my own,' confirmed the actor. 'I developed the character even more by adding the mannerisms of some of the other people I had met.'

Executive Producer, Alan C Blomquist couldn't agree more. 'Leonardo gives Arnie this child-like quality, playing him as very free and open and honest. He's a great counterpart to Johnny's Gilbert, who is so solemn and serious about life.' Some even thought that DiCaprio stole all Johnny's scenes, and everybody else's.

All the same, Johnny and DiCaprio were a marvellous combination. On location in Austin, Texas, DiCaprio recalls their brotherly relationship on and off camera. It was, he said, important 'to be just buddy-buddy with each other. Brothers don't necessarily have to say anything to each other. They can just sit in a room and be together and just be completely comfortable with each other.'

In many ways, Johnny was extremely like Gilbert, continues DiCaprio. 'But it wasn't something Johnny was trying to do. It naturally came out of him. I never quite understood what he was going through, because it wasn't some big emotional drama that was happening on the set every day, but subtle things I'd see in him. There's an element of Johnny that is extremely nice and extremely cool, but at the same time he's hard to figure out. But that makes him interesting.'

One of those things, elaborates DiCaprio, was when Johnny 'loved to see my facial expressions when I was disgusted by the smell of something gross, like decaying honeycomb, rotten eggs and pickled sausage. He'd give it to me to smell and I would do this gagging thing. In the end I couldn't stand it and charged him for the pleasure. I made about $500 dollars!'

Johnny, though, had once been on the receiving end himself. It happened when he inhaled the scent of a television remote control that had found its way into the anatomy of a girlfriend of Gibby Haynes, his friend and subsequent guitar player for Johnny's band. 'The look on his face was priceless,' Haynes laughs. But then again, Johnny openly admits he was 'an equal opportunities sniffer'.

Slowly, the rest of the cast took shape around the core of Johnny and DiCaprio. Juliette Lewis, best known at the time for her role in Woody Allen's *Husbands and Wives* would portray Johnny's love interest. But unlike Johnny and DiCaprio, she chose to remain aloof during filming. Even when she had the scenes with Johnny, it was no different. 'We never even talked to each other really. I worked with him, but I don't have a clue who he is as a person. When I'm at work, I just sort of go. My purpose is to do the job as well as possible and not go dancing and do all that other bullshit.'

And that, for now, meant concentrating on playing Becky. The caravanning tourist who gets stranded with her grandmother in Endora long enough to fall for Gilbert. 'I wanted to play her real still. Didn't want to fiddle and do a bunch of facial gestures or go crazy with her because she's sort of the same element in the movie. So I made a decision to be still and logical. My mind works like a computer. I can read scenes, and I'll know exactly how to behave. It just happens automatically. I don't have to do a lot of outside stuff to figure it out.'

Neither did Darlene Cates, albeit for different reasons. She actually did weigh 600lb, and came to the part almost by accident. She had been spotted by Hedges on a chat show about obesity and the problems associated with it, and although not a professional actress, she was the perfect choice. Not merely for her size, but also for the understanding she would have for the character.

At that point, conceded Cates, 'I hadn't left my house in five years, so I started taking correspondence courses to get my high school diploma. Then I found I was going to be a grandmother for the first time, and I wanted to be in the delivery room. It just seemed like I needed to do that, and so I went and did the talk show. I thought I was only one of a very small number, but there are many people like me out there.'

The hardest thing for her was the scene where Gilbert's mother leaves the family home for the first time in seven years and is driven by Gilbert to the police headquarters to fetch Arnie from the cell he has now been thrown into. His recent climbing escapades have left both police and emergency services alike in a quandary as to what to do with him for his own safety, so for the time being, they lock him up. Gilbert's mother is outraged, and storms into the police station to demand that her boy is released right there and then. No one, of course, argues. Not even Gerry, the duty sergeant. With Arnie back in the safe hands, the family leave as they arrived – together, amidst a crowd of onlookers who stop dead in their tracks to stare at the spectacle.

That scene, shudders Cates, 'was so real for me. I had to take time out afterwards because I burst into tears. But then so much of the film was real to me. An integral part of the story is letting people see how much bigotry and cruelty big people go through. I hope we set a trend. I hope it helped change people's attitudes and made them more tolerant.'

Certainly, that is what she hoped for. 'I think she shares what many overweight people do – a feeling that we are unacceptable. I'm glad to say that I don't feel that way any more. I found out that I do have something to offer, just like everyone else. The trick, I think, is just being patient until God reveals to you just what that something is.'

As far as the critics were concerned, it was one quirky role too many for Johnny. Richard Corliss writing in *Entertainment Weekly* was far more complimentary than most. 'DiCaprio and Cates bring loopy authenticity to their roles, and Depp is, as always, a most effacing star. Here, as in *Edward Scissorhands* and *Benny and Joon*, he behaves wonderfully on screen.'

But not everyone thought so. Quentin Curtis in his review of the film for the *Independent on Sunday* said it was a 're-run of his wistful comedy *Benny and Joon*, down to the nowheresville setting and the loopy kid he looks after'. The *Sunday Times* critic Anne Bilson went further when she observed that Johnny, 'might have been the next Tom Cruise except that his career choices are so wilfully non-commercial'. *Sky* magazine added: 'Depp's avoided one kind of stereotyping, but he faces the opposite danger; will he still be playing kooks when he's 40?'

But Johnny was not concerned. 'I've been real lucky. People have mentioned that I like doing offbeat roles, but I've been lucky in the sense that I haven't been typecast. It's important to keep changing. There's a lot of stuff that I just don't buy into, like being an actor who takes himself so seriously that he pretends to be this tortured artist. I think that everybody has pain and an actor doesn't necessarily have more of it than others.'

Besides, he didn't need that sort of hell and he was damned if he was going to let it need him. But what he didn't know at the time was that he was about to underestimate the strength of his own emotions. Probably more than he thought possible.

CHAPTER 8

'SINCE I WAS A TEENAGER I'VE BEEN AFRAID OF
BEING A LOSER, A GUY WITH NO TALENT OR AMBITION.
NO MATTER HOW MUCH MONEY I'VE MADE AS AN
ACTOR, I CAN'T SEEM TO GET RID OF THIS IMAGE
OF MYSELF AS A WHITE TRASH LOSER.'

A NIGHTMARE ON SUNSET BOULEVARD

There are times in everybody's life when, suddenly and inexplicably, everything seems to go wrong. As Halloween night 1993 neared, Johnny was closer to that state than he had ever felt before when one of Hollywood's most promising new young stars died of a drug overdose outside his club, The Viper Room.

In little more than 12 years, River Phoenix had established himself among the most significant actors of his generation and the least likely to hit the A-list of premature departures. In fact, his unique childhood raised by unconventional parents did everything to suggest the opposite. Time and again, his often bold decisions to speak out about the dangers of hard drugs and of his attitudes toward them did nothing but affirm his general aversion to recreational drugs of any sort. It was what won him the respect and admiration of fans around the world as he was propelled from teen star to cultural icon.

All the same, he spent as little time as he could in Hollywood. As much as his friends Keanu Reeves and Winona Ryder did their best to retreat from the hype of tinsel town, so did Phoenix. He simply deplored what he called its 'bad influences and superficial values'.

Indeed, both fans and the Hollywood insiders themselves have since struggled to make sense of the actor's death. Even a casual observer of tabloid headlines would not have put Phoenix down as the one likely to run into trouble.

It simply beggared belief that the child of hippie parents – someone with such Utopian ideals, who refused meat, dairy and fish products, campaigned for environmental issues such as saving the rainforests and the humane treatment of animals, refused to wear leather, and characteristically chose to hide away from the celebrity spotlight – could have died of a drug overdose. It just wasn't possible.

Situated on the corner of Larabee Street and Sunset Boulevard, Johnny's club was co-owned with rock star Chuck E Weiss, and had been ever since it opened in late summer 1993. The two had refurbished the little place into what was, for Johnny, a characteristically 1920s speakeasy around which the rest of the décor would subsequently revolve. Even the cigarette girls Johnny hired were throwbacks to the period.

As much, in fact, as the tiny centrepiece dance floor that was surrounded by five equally tiny booths. One was seemingly permanently reserved for Johnny's agent Tracey Jacobs, adorned with a 'Don't Fuck With It' gold plaque.

The corner stage would accommodate Johnny, his friends and musicians for the informal jamming sessions that often took place. Several, Johnny recalls, with Phoenix's band, Aleka's Attic, who were all set to play on the evening Phoenix died from the same lethal drug combination that killed John Belushi 11 years earlier.

For Phoenix, it was an evening that had started out much earlier that Saturday night at his suite in The Nikko Hotel, west of Los Angeles. Even room service noted how chaotic it was – loud music, and a highly intoxicated-looking Phoenix, which could probably be attributed to drugs and alcohol.

But Phoenix wasn't concerned. Nor apparently was his party; Sammantha Mathis, his girlfriend at the time and co-star of his then latest movie *The Thing Called Love*; his brother Leaf, sister Rain and Red Hot Chilli Pepper guitarist Flea. What Phoenix must have wondered, however, was how on earth he was going to make it through the evening, even as he made his way across town slumped in the back of his car.

It hit him almost as soon as he arrived at The Viper Room. Barely able to stand, concedes one waitress, 'he kept leaping up and bumping into things. His words were so slurred you could barely understand him.' But still the drinks kept coming.

Although unclear as to exactly what happened next, some suggested the actor moved into a backroom behind the corner stage to consume what is called a 'speedball', a lethal cocktail of drugs. Then he returned to his table, and without warning, he started vomiting. That was when some of his party took him to the bathroom to clean him up. There they splashed cold water on his face in their attempts to stop the actor trembling. But, sadly, to no avail. By the time they returned to their table it was clear he was well on the way to becoming an overdose victim. 'He just looked completely stoned,' observed one guest that evening. 'It was quite apparent that he was on something. He was table-hopping and bumping into tables.'

Not only that, but he was having seizures, falling down hard on to the table and sliding away beneath it. Even more frightening was the difficulty he had breathing. Even as he passed Johnny playing on stage on his way outside to grab some fresh air with Sammantha, Leaf and Rain, it was no better. In fact, he was now only minutes away from losing his life. He collapsed on to the pavement in a fit of violent twitching and thrashing. According to one photographer outside the club, he looked 'like a fish out of water, flapping around the sidewalk like a guppy'.

The strange thing, he continues, was that 'people walked by, no crowd formed and no one stopped to help'. It was, after all, Hallowe'en when every oddball in the area was on parade either dressed as victims of drive-by killings, or bloody surfers cut in two by their surfboards. The only difference was that the scene on the pavement in front of The Viper Room was real, even if the passers-by did shrug it off as just another part of the freak show.

From that moment, Leaf panicked, rushed into the Viper Room foyer, picked up the phone and dialled 911, begging the emergency services to hurry. The same message was later played repeatedly on radio and television in the aftermath of the tragedy. 'My brother's having seizures,' Leaf sobbed. 'I'm thinking he had Valium or something. You must get here. Please, because he's dying.' But, sadly, it was too late. By the time the medics arrived, just minutes later, River Phoenix was pronounced to be in full fatal cardiac arrest. It was nine minutes before two o'clock on Hallowe'en morning, just three hours after he had arrived at Johnny's club.

'There hasn't been anything this catastrophic and dramatic,' declared *Variety* columnist Amy Archerd, 'since James Dean and Natalie Wood died.' It was endorsed by the tributes that swiftly accumulated outside The Viper Room. 'The Eternal River Flows' read an inscription on a watercolour etching at the pavement altar festooned with incense candles. 'A true individual who will be remembered,' said a note as a teenager stared quietly while others wept. 'It's too sad,' sobbed a man from Glasgow standing next to four girls in baseball caps. 'He was no age at all, was he?'

'He had this ability to observe everything going on around him without really being part of it,' said another. 'He seemed able to separate himself from his surroundings.' But not everyone was sympathetic. Rush Limbaugh, the right-wing television and radio chat show host, certainly wasn't. She even condemned the media's attention to it.

'From the moment his death was discovered, you would have thought the President of the United States had been assassinated here ... that we've lost some great contributor to the social and human condition. This guy, look at his name! River Phoenix! He's the son of a couple of whacked-out hippies.'

Johnny was astounded, and a lot of other people shared his indignation. It was probably one of the reasons he couldn't bring himself to talk about the incident. Well, not immediately anyway. 'The thing is, he came with his guitar to the club. What a beautiful thing that he shows up with his girl on one arm and his guitar on the other. He came to play and he didn't think he was going to die – nobody thinks they're gonna die. He wanted to have a good time. It's dangerous, but that's the thing that breaks my heart – first he died, but also that he showed up with his guitar. That's not an unhappy kid.'

Neither did he see Phoenix's use of drugs as anything more than a dreadful mistake, one he himself could understand. 'He was a great actor and a great young man, a great human being. He had a great family, a very level view of life and a promising future. This is my quarrel with the press – they could have said, "Look, this was a normal guy, who had some things he was confused about, and he made a mistake. Anybody could make that same fatal mistake, and it could be any one of us. Watch yourself!" But nobody said that.'

Even sicker than the media's attempts to snare Johnny, however, were the allegations against him of contributing to Phoenix's death by running a club like the Viper Room in the first place. And, secondly, by allowing back-room drug abuse, which, the papers suggested, Johnny knew all about. Not surprisingly, he was adamant. 'There was a lot of speculation going on,' he retorted.

'A lot of people were playing backyard detective and exploiting the situation to get ratings and to sell newspapers and magazines. The tabloids were complete fiction. It's really tragic and sad. How many times did we need to hear that 911 tape? How many times did they have to print that stuff? For how long does Leaf have to live with the rewinding in his head? We've become a society of ambulance chasers. Everybody focused on the bad, nobody's interested in the good ... I've worked in this business for ten years, and to say I opened a nightclub to allow people to do drugs, even in the bathroom – do people think I'm insane? Do they think I'm going to throw eveything away – even my own children's future, so people could get high in a nightclub? It's ridiculous.'

Once again, Johnny asserted, 'the press was trying to tarnish his memory in the minds of all those people who loved him. What it all boils down to is a very sweet guy who made one big, fatal mistake. It's a mistake we're all capable of. What took place was so heavy that I didn't even retaliate against the accusations towards me. The fact is, I was there that night. It was my club. I said, "I refuse to be a part of this morbid circus that you fucking ambulance chasers have going. Fuck off!"'

Even Sal Jenco, Johnny's childhood friend from Florida, now running the Viper Room for him, had to put up with another scandal when Kylie Minogue's first love, television soap co-star and her former PWL Records label mate Jason Donovan, collapsed, less fatefully, of course, outside the club, ironically echoing of the River Phoenix tragedy. The difference being that Donovan survived.

He would not, however, be so concerned with the tabloid onslaught that followed. Britain's *News of the World*, for instance, went as far to call Johnny's club DEPP'S DEN OF SEX, DRUGS AND DEATH.

In a weekend so dominated by such wild accusations, the stories fell horribly flat. After all, Johnny had never said, 'I run a place that is filled with drugs and people screwing on the tables.' He defended the Viper Room by saying, 'This is a nightclub – it's a decent place. The Mayor of West Hollywood is having her reception here, for Christ's sake, why don't they write about that? Because it doesn't sell magazines unless they get a photograph of the Mayor with a syringe stuck in the back of her neck ...'

Johnny was less reticent, of course, on the Viper Room's notoriety. 'It became a scene instantly when we opened it. I never had any idea that it was going to do that. I really thought it was gonna just be this cool little underground place. You can't even see the place. There's no sign on Sunset. It's just a black building and the only sign is on Larabee, a tiny little sign, real subtle, and I figured it would be low key.

'What soured me was what happened after all that took place on Hallowe'en, the unfortunate passing of River. I closed it down for two weeks out of respect, so the kids could write their messages and leave flowers. I thought that was real sweet of them. I knew for the next month or so it was just gonna be a gawk feast, just filled with gawkers and tourists, Grave-line Tours, all that shit. I just didn't go around for a while. We've weeded out the gawkers, now it's back to being a good place.'

Johnny was also back to being in a good place. Indeed, it was February 1994, four months after River Phoenix's death, when a friend introduced him to Kate Moss, the waif model from Calvin Klein's Obsession fragrance and Yves Saint Laurent ads.

She was visiting New York and had stopped off at Manhattan's Café Tebac. Johnny, too, was in town where he would also have coffee at the same bistro. 'It wasn't all that romantic,' remembers Johnny. 'She was sitting at a table with some friends, and I knew one of them.' He invited them over. 'And that's how we met and we haven't been apart since. We're just having fun. A lot of fun. She's a real down-to-earth English girl who gives me no chance to get big-headed about my life.'

Kate Moss and Johnny Depp – it was another relationship made in tabloid heaven. As much, or perhaps even more, than Johnny and Winona. Even though Kate wasn't an actress and didn't have the whole world in love with her, she had nonetheless firmly established herself among the supermodels of her generation – Claudia Schiffer, Cindy Crawford and Naomi Campbell were the others.

Born in Addiscombe, Surrey, on 16 January 1974, when Johnny was 11, and raised in Croydon, another London suburb, Kate was spotted in between flights at New York's John F Kennedy Airport by Storm Model Agency boss Sara Doukas. She immediately decided that she wanted to represent her. Even if Kate was shocked by this sudden turn of events, she was also excited. 'I'd seen her judging a *Clothes Show* competition so I knew she was for real.' She was just 14 at the time.

Even if Kate's fame was not exactly handed to her on a plate, it was at least delivered to her door. Two years after she met Doukas, the same year Johnny met Winona, the agent came up trumps. That summer, British magazine *The Face* was looking for a girl to define the waif look for the cover of their next issue. If there was one thing Kate definintely was, she was waifish. And waifish still remains the word that best describes her.

In fact, some even suggested, that the picture - shot by Corrine Day - with Kate's skeletal frame went a long way to encouraging *anorexia nervosa* and other eating disorders in young teenage girls who would try to emulate her. In fact, it was now a red-hot favourite for debate. A far cry from Winona Ryder, who although elfin, simply demanded a flock of role model wannabes.

Kate was suddenly everywhere. Magazines, catwalks, billboards. Even aeroplanes. Quite an accomplishment for a model whose CV now includes such culture-defining names as Chanel and Gianni Versace. Kate remembers, 'Corrine phoned me the other day and said "You know, you don't know how famous you are. You're topless on every other bus."' Kate was still down-to-earth enough to be astonished.

Kate, of course, wished the tabloid press had been less attentive to the critical comments that followed. How many times would she have to defend her appearance? How many times would she have to explain that she had an exceptionally fast metabolism? It irritated her even more the day she was tagged 'Superwaif'. Finally, losing patience she snapped, 'All those anorexic things do bother me. I know I'm going to be called a waif for ever. And I hate it.'

Far more damaging, of course, was everything else the gossip columnists blamed her for, everything from elder women's self-hatred, the rise in child abuse, the fall in the exchange rate, global warming, football hooliganism ...

In the years to come, of course, Johnny would also snap at the constant swiping at Kate's ultra-slim appearance. 'She eats like a champ,' he reflected years later. 'She really puts it away. Why punish somebody because they have a good metabolism? Because they digest their food better? It doesn't make any sense.'

Kate agreed. 'I am just on my way out to dinner,' she wrote

years later in the introduction to her book of photographs, 'to eat a massive steak, loads of very fattening potatoes with lots of butter.' Not that it would make much difference as far as the press were concerned. 'You'd like to believe her,' wrote one of those critics, 'but you can't imagine how she'd fit it all in. Even if her legs are hollow, there wouldn't be room for much more than a chip.'

But maybe that was something to do with the pictures that adorned the pages of her lavish coffee table hardback. Everything from Kate lolloping down a Mexican beach to shadow-boxing in New York. Looking very 1970s, looking scary, looking wise, innocent, carefree, hunted, glamorous, gorgeous, asleep. Kate close up, Kate far away. In knickers, in feathers, in need of a wash.

Perhaps it is because her rise to megastardom was so straightforward that Kate has not lost the qualities that so entranced the fashion-spotters who first saw her. 'What Kate Moss has is a brilliant and quite unerring fashion instinct,' wrote the fashion critic in Britain's *Guardian*.

'She's fantastic at interpreting photographers' ideas, an exceptional trendsetter, a great artist-as-model. When you flick through her book, one is struck by her versatility, her never-ending, ever-changing ability to put over clothes. It's an odd talent.'

Two years before that high praise, of course, was the offer that would elevate Kate out of simple modelling assignments to establish her as a genuine supermodel. Calvin Klein wanted her to appear topless alongside Marky Mark in their latest advertising campaign. Kate accepted.

But again, there was a sting in the tail. And this time it wasn't simply the critical objections to her appearance that tormented her. Kate also found herself the victim of the gossip factory. It was what she attributes to the breakdown of her failed relationship with photographer Mario Sorrenti several months before she met Johnny.

Even then, when the couple went public with their relationship, the tabloids hounded them. Johnny, though, was unconcerned. At that point, he said, 'the press said so many shitty things that I couldn't give a fuck any more. As long as they're not hurting my family or someone I love, they can say I have a fetish for midget amputees for all I care.'

Deep inside, however, that was his only defence. 'I don't talk about it and she doesn't talk about it, because it's nobody's business,' he insisted. 'This is a rumour-filled society and if people want to sit around and talk about whom I've dated, then I'd say they have a lot of spare time and should consider other topics. Or masturbation.'

As Johnny had already pointed out, Kate did her best to shrug off the attention. But she also acknowledged there was no way to avoid enthusing about her new found love. Not even to the *Daily Mail*. In echoes of Johnny and Winona, she raved, 'I can't believe it. It's like nothing that has ever happened to me before. I knew straight away, knew that it was different. I just never felt anything like this before. I knew, this was it.' Not only that, she continues, but 'I fancied him before I met him!'

Once again, the gossip columnists couldn't go wrong. And, of course, the age gap between Johnny and Kate was their number one concern, much as it had been over Johnny and Winona. Although this time, the gap was even greater.

Even though the couple initially focused on the juvenile side of their relationship, the ubiquitous Hollywood insiders found their mutual passion for funfair rides a far cry from the fascination for Beat poetry and literature Johnny had shared with Winona. 'We love going to Magic Mountain,' confessed Johnny, 'and doing all the fastest rides, but you have to go first thing in the morning, or you just end up spending all day signing autographs.'

'I knew from the first moment we talked that we were going to be together,' admitted Kate later. The first few months of the couple's life was indeed spent together. Even when she turned 21, Johnny threw a surprise birthday party at The Viper Room, where he covered the club in fresh roses and balloons. Gloria Gaynor sang 'I Will Survive'. An Elvis impersonator joined Thelma Houston in another singalong, and Johnny played on stage with INXS vocalist Michael Hutchence.

Born in Sydney on 20 January 1960, Hutchence was three years older than Johnny. The eldest son of a salesman and an ex-model, he like Johnny, had a nomadic childhood. When he was four, he moved with his family to Hong Kong, not returning to Sydney again until he was twelve. When he was fifteen, his parents split and Michael moved with his mother to Los Angeles for a year. Soon after his return home again, Michael and some friends formed a band that by 1979 was called INXS. Although an accomplished vocalist and musician, he probably became equally famous for his ungallant and oft-reported boast that Kylie Minogue was the best fuck in the world.

The first time out in public for Johnny and Kate was at the Los Angeles night spot Smashbox where Johnny would launch his film short on the dangers of drug addiction during a *Vogue* benefit to aid the Drug Abuse Resistance Education programme before an audience of 800.

Banter followed in the form of the public information promo shorts Johnny had made from his *21 Jump Street* days, and the 15-minute question and answer AIDS documentary he appeared in with Winona being made at the time for her mother's production video company.

Now, he had the opportunity to turn his own personal experiences into a plea for youngsters to avoid drugs at all costs. According to *Esquire*, the film was 'a gruesome but provocative excursion into the world of hard drugs'. It also questioned Johnny's own reported drug use. With the River Phoenix tragedy continuing to prey on his mind, perhaps nobody realised just how much it had affected Johnny until he spoke out.

'It's all in the past,' he swore. 'I've been taunted by the press and put in a position of having to defend myself. I've done nothing wrong. I've even made an anti-drug movie, and I hope kids learn a lot from it, that drugs are no escape. There are other ways of escaping, like books, painting and writing.'

Only a few weeks after the Smashbox gig, Johnny and Kate were spotted again, this time vacationing on St Barts. On another occasion, while Johnny was writing *The Brave*, they were seen in Mustique with Noel Gallagher and his then girlfriend, later wife, Meg Mathews. Long before that, of course, the couple were spotted at Manhattan's Fez Club for a Johnny Cash concert. And less than a day after he finished filming *Don Juan DeMarco*, Johnny caught a flight to Paris and made his way to Kate's catwalk and couture shows where she gave him a ring-shaped platinum rattle filled with black pearls. And for Kate, a strand of diamonds. They couldn't, insisted one observer, keep their hands, lips, mouths and legs off each other.

Maybe that was true. But he also confessed that a persistent favourite was feet. Or at least, that's what he told *FHM* magazine. 'They are very, very important,' he insisted. 'They are way up there on the priority list. About top two. A bad pair of feet, let's see, would be with long toenails. I can remember seeing my great grandmother's toenails. She was a full-blooded Cherokee. Her toenails were really long and curled like cashews. Long toenails are a bad move. Horrible, can't even think about it. Just an awful image. Feet say a lot. If a girl doesn't take care of her feet there may be problems elsewhere.'

Good feet or not, 'she must be great,' said Sarah Jessica Parker, Johnny's co-star from *Ed Wood*, in her praise for Kate. 'I'm going to assume that and endow her with good qualities because I can't imagine Johnny spending time with anyone who wasn't his equal.'

'He is incorruptible,' agreed Faye Dunaway, his leading lady from *Arizona Dream*. 'He always believes in this pure way about love. He's got those kinds of values and it's instinctive with him. This isn't something he's worked out in his head. I love that he believes in love.'

But not everyone agreed. Tally Chanel, the B-movie actress whom Johnny had met in July 1990, was far more negative in her perception of Kate, inviting her not to put up with the actor's temper tantrums. 'Johnny needs an accomplice to end up in trouble, and it's obvious Kate has a lot to do with his recent behaviour.'

One of those occasions came seven months after Johnny and Kate had met, and was at the Mark Hotel in New York City. 'Let's say my stay wasn't particularly comfortable,' was the way Johnny explained it after attending some *Ed Wood* press conferences he was in town for.

The difficulties seemed to start from the moment he checked in. He had already been put out because of not being able to book into his regular haunt The Carlyle. It wasn't the fact that the Mark's Presidential Suite wasn't up to scratch. Far from it. As far as Johnny was concerned, it was the night security guard Jim Keegan who ranked highly among his problems. It was an instinct that would later prove to be the correct one.

'It seemed like the guy couldn't stand Johnny,' recalls Jonathan Shaw, his friend and tattooist. It probably didn't help that 'Johnny was dressed in leather and jeans, not at all fancy like everybody else in the joint.' Johnny couldn't agree more. 'The guy was a little froggy and he decided he was going to "get in the famous guy's face". I don't really take too well to that.'

Kate was also in town and stayed with Johnny in the hotel from that first Monday through to the early hours of Tuesday. In fact, it was early that morning, just before dawn, something happened that would alter the course of Johnny's public profile – and image – for ever.

Occupying the suite next to Johnny and Kate was Roger Daltry, lead singer of the sixties rock group the Who, and in his time was probably as famous for his hotel trashing as for his band's musical focus. But that didn't stop him calling the front desk to complain about a disturbance next door. The only difference, explained Johnny later, is that the Who would have done a better job, 'and then been applauded for it. I was arrested and incarcerated. Age is a wonderful thing, isn't it? Keith Moon would have been very embarrassed for him ... But he was probably used to being embarrassed for him.'

All the same, the complaint was enough to send Keegan rushing to investigate. The security guard was, according to Johnny, fired up from the start of their confrontation. He had, since Johnny's arrival, monitored his every move in and out of the hotel. 'The guy probably had too many cups of coffee that night,' laughs Johnny at the memory. 'He was particularly feisty, and he decided to call the shots in a way that I didn't think was particularly necessary.'

Johnny explains, 'If I walk into an antique shop and I bend down and look at something over here and I accidentally knock a pot off the rack, it's $3,000, of course, I'd pay for it. If I bust a piece of glass, I smash a mirror or whatever, I'll pay for it. I can probably handle the bill. That's it.'

But it wasn't it as far as Keegan was concerned. He took exception to whatever had gone on in the Presidential Suite and instructed him to leave the room – and the hotel – there and then. If not, he would call the police. Johnny apologetically offered to pay for any damage he had caused, but certainly didn't feel it was necessary for him to check out. True to his word, Keegan called the New York Police Department and 30 minutes later, Johnny was escorted by three officers from the 19th Precinct – out of the hotel and in handcuffs.

For the next 48 hours, Johnny was detained in three different cells at Precinct House, at Central Booking, and in the 'tombs' behind New York Central Police Headquarters where he was apparently mobbed by a horde of female police officers. Apart from one. Officer Eileen Perez was seemingly unimpressed by Johnny's presence. 'I don't think she likes me,' he smiled. 'But I bet if she saw me in a mall, she'd ask for my autograph.'

That is probably true. But at the same time, in the official police report, Keegan listed ten damaged items: two damaged seventeenth century picture frames and prints; a china lamp stand; a Chinese pot; a shattered glass tabletop; broken coffee table legs; broken wooden shelves; a shattered vase; cigarette burns on the carpet; and a split red desk chair.

David Breitbart, Johnny's attorney and New York criminal lawyer, attached to the litigation, said, 'That crazy damage figure they asked for was also for what he owed for the room two nights before, three nights after, something like that.' Even Marlon Brando was concerned. According to Breitbart, 'he said he was very concerned about Johnny's well-being and if there was anything he could do to help, he would like to.' Interestingly enough, neither Keegan nor the hotel's general manager Raymond Bickson would discuss the incident. Not with the press anyway.

Although Johnny didn't dispute the incident, he did offer an explanation. 'It wasn't a great night for me. I'm not trying to excuse what I did or anything like that, because it's someone else's property and you got to respect that. But you get into a head space, and you're human.'

The press, of course, was another matter entirely. Pictures of Johnny's arrest that decorated the front pages did nothing more than reinforce his image as a hell-raising party monster. Once again, the gossip columnists couldn't go wrong. 'I was just stressed out,' was how Johnny would explain away his behaviour. 'I'm human and I get angry like everyone else. I get frustrated and I just lashed out. Big deal. We're talking about an actor who might have assaulted a piece of furniture. I found myself on the covers of all the newspapers, as if this incident was of more importance than the invasion of Haiti. Firstly, you should be allowed to be a human being. Secondly, you should be allowed to have emotion, and thirdly, you should be allowed to have a private life.' Apparently, a private life was out of the question.

Even Betty Sue, Johnny's mother, now married to her third husband, Robert Palmer, was in shock. All the same, she got over it, Johnny recalls. 'She didn't like seeing me in handcuffs on TV, but she knows I'm not a bad person.' Neither did she like the way Johnny was kitted out – especially the green knitted hat and the sunglasses. 'She thought she'd taught me how to dress better than that.' Not that John Waters, Johnny's director from *Cry Baby*, would agree.

'He looked good under arrest. I loved the handcuffs – they always work. Criminal movie star is a really good look for Johnny. The success of hotel room trashing should be calculated by the amount of damage, divided by the amount of column inches.' Even more damaging, of course, was the ostracism that his teenage niece and nephew would have to put up with at high school. Friends and pupils alike would tell them, 'Your uncle Johnny is a fucking maniac.'

Even though, as Johnny himself would point out, 'they gotta live with that stuff, too,' there was no let-up in the aftermath of the Mark Hotel débâcle. If anything it got worse. Johnny's alleged past with drugs and alcohol was still news. Now more so than ever since he had joined the litany of celebrity hotel trashers first started when Beethoven slung a chair through the window of a Vienna hotel room.

Even Leonardo DiCaprio's cameo role as a teen idol rowing furiously with his girlfriend and trashing a hotel room in Woody Allen's 1998 ensemble piece *Celebrity* was considered by many a depiction of Johnny's own Mark Hotel incident.

True or not, Johnny said, 'Now they can say they have this little bit of history, this ridiculous morsel of history. They can say "We had Johnny Depp arrested". Hotels are my home. I live in hotels more than I live in my house. If it had been you, nothing would have happened. They would have come to the room and said, "What's going on?" You would have said, "I'll pay for the damages, and I'm terribly sorry."'

Overlooking the negative aspects of the incident, Faye Dunaway agrees with that summation. 'Sometimes you feel like you've just to kick over the traces, and the Mark took advantage of it. A publicity trip; it's outrageous. I would probably have smashed up the lobby after that. I think they should count themselves luckly that he didn't.'

Johnny, on the other hand, would later find the whole thing preposterous. Not surprising really when you consider 'I had to go to jail for assaulting a picture frame and a lamp!' The papers' depiction of him drunk and having a huge fight with Kate, he said, was 'complete bullshit. But, you know, let's say the guy over here in the bar, he's having a hard day, and eventually – one more stabbing in the toe – the guy's got to hit something. So you punch a wall, or do this and that. Fuck it, I'm normal and I want to be normal. But somehow, I'm just not allowed to be. Why can't I be human? I have a lot of love inside me, and a lot of anger inside as well. If I love somebody, then I'm going to love them. If I'm angry and I've got to lash out or hit somebody, I'm going to do it and I don't care what the repercussions are.'

Of course, the Mark Hotel wasn't the only episode in which Johnny had fallen out with the authorities. In fact his past seemed littered with similar bewildering lapses of behaviour. But why, Johnny asked, 'should I be considered any different than Joe the garbageman or the guy selling doughnuts down the street? Why can't I be as human as anybody, as emotional as anybody?'

Because, he concludes, 'we live in such an ambulance-chasing society. Where there's this judgemental mentality of waiting to expose the dirt on everyone. You'll never see one of those tabloids say, "God, what a nice guy Johnny Depp is!" because people just aren't interested.'

Certainly, he has a point. He had, after all, been variously reported to have been caught hanging, in a dangerously drunken stupor, from the top of the five-storey Beverly Center parking garage in Los Angeles with Nicholas Cage; blowing gasoline on to open flames; and he'd even been spotted screaming at Kate in the dining room of New York's Royalton Hotel. And while filming *21 Jump Street* at the show's Vancouver location in 1989, Johnny had allegedly assaulted a security guard, although the charges were later dropped.

And so they should have been, Johnny asserts. He was

visiting with some friends late one evening at a hotel where he had once stayed. Although known to the staff, the security guard was determined to keep him out.

'He had a boner for me,' Johnny recalls. 'He had a wild hair up his ass, and he got real mouthy about with me, saying, "I know who you are, but you can't come up here unless you are a guest." The mistake he eventually made was to put his hands on me. I pushed him back, and then we sort of wrestled around a bit, and I ended up spitting in his face.'

On another occasion in the same period, Johnny and Gibby Haynes spotted some guy's motorcycle in Sherilyn Fenn's driveway, kidnapped the helmet, painted it garish colours, including the visor, and returned it with a love note. Overall, though, it was nothing more than a bit of harmless fun.

It did, though, occasionally get a little out of hand. One night, Johnny remembers, after a drinking competition with Iggy Pop, he was sued for smashing the window of the Lone Star Roadhouse on New York's 52nd Street, that showered glass over the woman who sued him. And if that wasn't enough, he had also been charged that same year with jaywalking in Beverly Hills, and even got into a squabble with the cop writing out the ticket when he was asked to put his cigarette out. Johnny refused, so the cop held his wrist until the cigarette fell from his hand. He lit another. 'Next thing I know, him and his partner handcuffed me and put me in a cell for a few hours. I'm not scared by those people. They just make me angry. You get the feeling there's nothing you can do.' But there is, he believes, 'Don't take shit from them.' But then again, he adds, 'I've known some cops who've seen way too many episodes of *Starksy and Hutch*.'

On another occasion when Johnny was drinking at London's Globe underground club, photographer Jonathan Walpole, a direct descendant of Sir Robert Walpole, told the *Evening Standard* how, when he accidentally picked up Johnny's drink, 'he pulled both my ears very hard. I informed him that this was not the customary way of greeting people in England, then some ape leapt on my back, put his arm around my neck and tried to force my head to the floor.'

But according to *Icon* magazine, some years later, Johnny had pulled Walpole's ears 'for repeatedly asking Kate Moss's friend for a cigarette and then taking a sip of her drink'. Not for the first time, Johnny's actions, it seemed, continued to be misinterpreted. But according to one friend it's just 'Johnny being Johnny'.

All the same, such antics were not altogether to Johnny's benefit, as Nicholas Cage shuddered when another reputed Hollywood bad boy, Mickey Rourke, trashed his New York Plaza suite just two months after the Mark Hotel incident, 'What's he trying to be? Johnny Depp?'

Sarah Jessica Parker, Johnny's co-star from *Ed Wood*, was far more complimentary. 'Johnny has a very wise spirit, and he pays no heed to things that don't matter. He is internal in a way that is reflective but not isolating. He's a gentle, lovely person. And when I think of those things that have been written in the papers about him, it's as if they're talking about a totally different person.'

From the nightmare of the Mark Hotel and the rumours which still haunted Hollywood about the River Phoenix tragedy, Johnny, according to some, was in danger of walking the same path of self-destruction.

Johnny, however, did not agree. 'There have been times when I wasn't in a good place at all, I couldn't get a grip on what was going on around me, and I'd just get tanked. That's all right for a little while, but when it becomes a way of life, it's not good. It's really bad. And you spend all this time trying to recreate that first high you got, like when you're 13 or 14 and you get drunk or smoke a joint, or have sex, and it's the greatest – it never comes back. You're never going to get that feeling again.'

The hardest thing was the years 'I spent getting loaded to escape. But I never escaped, not once. I've got my demons. Alcohol or drugs can unleash those demons, or open up the doors for those demons to fly around.'

For some time, the press would refer to Johnny's Mark Hotel fiasco as nothing more than that. Even when, months later, Johnny would provide journalists with some new variations of what happened inside the Presidential Suite, his own sense of humour and mischievousness came through for most of it.

According to the *Sunday Times*, he said, 'I was sitting on the couch in my hotel room when a really big dachshund jumped out of the closet. I felt it was my duty to retrieve this animal, so I chased it for 20 minutes, but it wouldn't co-operate. Finally, it dived out the window and there I was, stuck with all this evidence.'

In another interview with *Empire* magazine, the sequence of events was even wilder. 'I think it was an armadillo. It felt like it was an armadillo. It may have been an elephant.'

But whatever he said, Johnny received another setback when he recovered his belongings from the Mark Hotel and checked back into his regular haunt The Carlyle, now with vacancies, for the rest of his stay. What he didn't expect to find, however, was the Marlon Brando autobiography that he'd been reading to be defaced – according to Johnny, it was clearly by someone at the Mark Hotel.

'Fuck you Johnny Depp' was the first message he came across as he flicked through the 468-page book. There were, of course, other messages on other pages. 'You're an asshole' read one. 'I hate you' ranted another.

That was the end; the fiasco had gone too far. If Johnny was incensed, then it was understandable. Far more important, he decided, was the basic need to get through it all with a minimum of scars.

He even developed elaborate plans to retreat from the hype of it all to catch up playing with his band Pee, or just simply 'P'. Now the five of them – Shane McGowan, Gibby Haynes, Bill Carter, Sal Jenco and Johnny – planned to sign with EMI's Capitol Records in mid-1995, aiming to produce their first album for release exactly one year later. Even the advance information sounded promising.

'With titles such as 'Michael Stipe', 'White Man Sings the Blues' and Daniel Johnston's 'I Save Cigarette Butts', the record barrels down P's rock 'n' roll highway and the four lanes sound irreverent, brash, raw and tough. Between the tongue-in-cheek cover of Abba's 'Dancing Queen' and the defiant 'Oklahoma', Carter's musical proficiency and Haynes' screwball vision blend with Depp's liquid guitar and Jenco's kinetic drumming in a volatile brew.'

And contributing his own footnote to Britain's musical legacy two years later, his friend Noel Gallagher of Oasis invited him to play on their latest album, *Be Here Now*.

Johnny's 'actually one of the best guitarists I've ever seen,' Gallagher raves to this day. 'That's why we got him to play the slide guitar solo on "Fade In–Out" because I couldn't play it. Afterwards, when we were rehearsing for the tour, it took me about six months to work it out to see what he was actually playing.'

If, above all else, playing with P and Oasis was to reinforce or maybe remind people of his musical inspirations, then his next two movie roles would simultaneously prove to be the most controversial and challenging he had yet accepted.

CHAPTER 9

*'I'VE ALWAYS BEEN ATTRACTED TO LOSERS.
I'VE NEVER PLAYED THE HOLLYWOOD GAME JUST
FOR THE SAKE OF WINNING. I DO WHAT I WANT AND,
IF IT WORKS WITHIN MY CAREER, GREAT. IF NOT,
FUCK IT. I WON'T BE A SLAVE TO SUCCESS.'*

RISKY ROLES

It was no surprise that Johnny agreed to link up with Tim Burton again for his next movie project. Neither was it surprising that Burton was so keen to cast Johnny in the title role. As Burton himself explains, 'I feel close to Johnny because I think somewhere inside we respond to similar things, and this was a chance after working on *Edward Scissorhands* to be more open.'

Ed Wood, Burton's marvellous biopic of Edward D Wood Jr, the ever optimistic Hollywood hack of the title, occasional transvestite, and dubbed the world's worst film director could have been custom-written for Burton's peculiar sensibilities, and the title role seemed to have been created for Johnny himself. Denise Di Novi, Johnny's producer from *Edward Scissorhands*, agreed. 'Ed Wood was extremely handsome and lovable, as is Johnny. More importantly, Johnny is an actor who takes risks and gives unusual characters the special treatment and dignity they deserve.'

Before any work could commence, however, Columbia, who had the picture in development, put the project on ice when Burton insisted on total creative licence for his film – and he wanted to shoot in black and white. That was the last straw as far as the studio was concerned and, one month before shooting was scheduled to start, Warners, Paramount and Fox all clamoured to pick up the option to make the movie. Burton shrugged and simply defected across town to Disney who ended up with a movie made on a respectable budget of $18 million.

It wasn't the first time that Columbia had pulled out of a Burton project. Before *Ed Wood*, Burton was set to direct an adaptation of Valerie Martin's spellbinding novel *Mary Reilly* with his *Beetlejuice* and *Edward Scissorhands* favourite, and now Johnny's ex-fiancée, Winona Ryder in the title role. It was the marvellous retelling of Robert Louis Stevenson's classic *Dr Jekyll and Mr Hyde* told through the eyes of a servant girl in the doctor's household, but Columbia took both Burton and Winona off the project.

'What happened was the studio wanted to push it,' Burton remembered. 'Whereas before, I could take my time to decide about things, in Hollywood you get shoved into this whole commercial thing. They want the movie.' But the last straw came when the studio, exasperated by what they perceived as his lack of urgency, told him they had another five directors who were interested in the project, insinuating that if he didn't get started, one of the others would.

They probably just wanted to hurry him up, but they

chased him off instead. The whole process, Burton growls, turned him off, and he let the studio know it. 'Well, if you've got five other people who want to do it, maybe you should have them do it.'

Looking back, Burton reasons, 'Basically, they speeded me out of the project because they saw it in a certain way,' and he saw it in another. But this wasn't his only reason for dropping the project he had been so keen to complete. 'They also saw it with Julia Roberts replacing Winona, and once Stephen Frears had taken over as director, that is what they got.

Burton and Winona took the disappointment stoically, although Burton did not have long to mourn. *Ed Wood* awaited him just around the corner. In fact, he had quickly become interested in the project when it was brought to his attention by Larry Karaszewski and Scott Alexander, screenwriters of the *Problem Child* movies. They had toyed with the idea of writing a film about Wood ever since they were room-mates at the University of Southern California film school. Irritated at being thought of as solely writers of kids' movies, they wrote a ten-page treatment and pitched the idea to *Heathers* director Michael Lehmann with whom they shared much of their time at the USC. He, in turn, took the project to his *Heathers* producer Denise Di Novi who immediately struck up a deal for Lehmann to direct, and herself to produce alongside Burton.

It was really when *Mary Reilly* fell through that Burton became more interested in directing *Ed Wood* himself, but only on the understanding it could be done quickly. With this in mind, Karaszewski and Alexander set about writing their screenplay, and delivered it to Burton six weeks later.

He read the first draft and deemed it suitable enough to direct as it stood, without any changes or rewrites. That in itself was unusual.

Wood, the director of such cult classics as *Glen or Glenda*, *Bride of the Monster* and, most infamously, *Plan 9 from Outer Space*, died in 1978 aged 54, penniless and forgotten. Sadly, he achieved near legendary status only posthumously, in the early eighties. Just as video recorders began to liberate viewers from the tyranny of television programming schedules, the films of Ed Wood captured cult followings as he all but took up permanent residence in Michael and Harry Medved's book of *The Golden Turkey Awards* in which he was granted the dubious honour of being the 'World's Worst Film Director'.

Born in Poughkeepsie, New York in 1924, Wood lived his entire life on the cusp of Hollywood, aspiring to be the next Orson Welles, but never even coming remotely close. A famed transvestite with a fondness for Angora sweaters and an engaging personality, Wood surrounded himself with a bizarre côterie of admirers and wannabes – his girlfriend Dolores Fuller, television horror hostess, Vampira (the stage name for Maila Nurmi), Swedish wrestler Tor Johnson and camp television psychic Criswell, all of whom believed Ed would one day make them stars.

In 1953, Wood met his idol Bela Lugosi, a Hungarian immigrant and the celebrated star of Universal's 1930 version of *Dracula*, but in the two decades that had passed since the release of the classic horror tale, Lugosi had slipped into virtual obscurity, had became addicted to morphine, and was by the time Wood found him, trying out coffins in a mortuary. Wood, however, was not discouraged, and vowed to revitalise Lugosi's career by casting him in his movies, and subsequently landed him with roles in *Glen or Glenda*, Wood's autobiographical tale of a transvestite, played by Wood himself under the name of Daniel Davis, and *Bride of the Monster*. Even the small amount of footage he shot of Lugosi leaving his home shortly before his death found its way into Wood's worst movie, *Plan 9 from Outer Space*, the one Wood was certain would establish his name. It did, but for all the wrong reasons.

Karaszewski and Alexander's script centred around Wood's life through the three movies, and focused on his relationship with Lugosi. Burton acknowledged that it was not unlike his own friendship with Vincent Price. 'There was an aspect of Wood's relationship with Bela Lugosi that I liked,' he explained. 'He befriended him at the end of his life, and without really knowing what that was like, I connected with it on the level that I did with Vincent Price, in terms of how I felt about him. Meeting Vincent had an incredible impact on me, the same impact Ed must have felt meeting and working with his idol.'

Burton's first choice of actor was, of course, Johnny, whom Burton called the minute he knew the project was on. As soon as he answered the phone, Johnny recalls, 'Tim asked me to meet him right away at the Formosa Café.' Twenty minutes later, they were talking about the project over some beer at the bar. And five minutes after that, Johnny continues, 'I was committed, completely committed. I was already familiar with Wood's films, and I knew that nobody could tell his story better than Tim. Tim's passion became my passion. I've turned parts down and regretted them in the future, and I think I would have been as sick as a dog if I had walked away from this one.'

All the same, it was not an easy role for Johnny to prepare for. In fact, he would most probably say it was one of the most difficult he had taken on. Never before had he played a real-life person, and he knew it would be very different from his past portrayals of fictional characters. 'I think it would be foolish for any film-maker to say they could hit the nail right on the head when trying to capture someone's life,' explained Johnny. Right from the start, 'Tim and the writers wanted to make something that captured a real Hollywood icon, and I think we did that. It isn't really about exploitation. This is a homage. A real, weird homage, but nevertheless, a respectable one.'

Equally difficult was the lack of visual material available for Johnny to tackle. Aside from Wood's own film appearance in *Glen or Glenda*, some rare silent behind-the-scenes footage, and a few black-and-white stills, there was little else. Not for the first time, Johnny would have to rely upon his own instincts, and indeed, his own perceptions of what he considered Wood to be like in reality. But that didn't stop him leaping into the role without hesitation.

'I read whatever I could get my hands on,' Johnny continued to explain. 'It was completely accepted that the details of Wood's life were a little muddled. Tim wanted to capture the spirit of the guy, and I had to exhibit that. I watched the films, and then put different people together in my brain. I wanted to make him extremely optimistic, innocent and a brilliant showman all at the same time. He was a man who loved making films.' It was, Johnny elaborated, 'his whole life and he didn't allow anything to discourage him'. Neither did Johnny. In fact, his performance as Ed Wood is a role which many people still consider Johnny's broadest and most theatrical.

Slowly, the rest of the cast took shape around the core of Johnny. Martin Landau was recruited to play Bela Lugosi; Bill Murray became Wood's transvestite friend Bunny Breckinridge; Jeffrey Jones, from Burton's own *Beetlejuice*, was chosen for the role of Criswell; Lisa Marie, a former model and now Burton's girlfriend, would play Vampira; real-life wrestler George 'The Animal' Steele became his Swedish counterpart Tor Johnson; Sarah Jessica Parker played Wood's girfriend Dolores; and Patricia Arquette was cast as Ed's wife Kathy. Once again, Burton proved his casting choices to be another excellent mix of talent.

That is certainly what he strived for. Aside from Johnny, 'I wanted to go with some knowns and unknowns,' Burton confirmed. 'It was like trying to get a mix of people, just like in Ed Wood's movies. I wanted it to have its own kind of weird energy,' just as *Beetlejuice* and *Edward Scissorhands* before had done. As far as Burton was concerned, weird was good, weird was acceptable, and weird was successful. One of his strongest beliefs – that Hollywood conventions are simply there to be broken and that an audience will happily watch you break them as long as they are entertained – from that point of view, *Ed Wood* would be no different.

Outside his own circle of colleagues, Johnny was considered an odd choice for the part. In fact, rumours circulated around Hollywood that he had already taken his research for the role far beyond what was expected.

But according to Scott Alexander, he was only wearing woman's underwear and Angora sweaters as part of his everyday routine to prepare for the role. He even told Alexander how he would grab the little hairs over his nipples and just try to twist them around, absent-mindedly, while he was pacing around.

If Burton was concerned, it was only the fact that 'Ed would have to be in drag through portions of the film, and people in drag are real easy targets, but Johnny was so credible that he pulls it off without making it laughable. Besides, he really looks great in those clothes.'

There had, of course, been others before him who had appeared in drag. Most notably Robin Williams in *Mrs Doubtfire* and Dustin Hoffman in 1982's *Tootsie*. The only difference was that both were already middle-aged by the time they made those movies, and would most probably be far less concerned about the consequences of dressing up in women's clothing. But Johnny needn't have worried. If anything, his performance, whether in or out of drag, delighted both audiences and critics alike on the film's release.

Not even Landau was concerned. 'When I played a homosexual in Hitchcock's *North by Northwest*, I was asked if I was concerned that people would think I was gay. "Of course not," I said. It's like with Johnny – if you're comfortable with yourself, you're comfortable with yourself. Otherwise, you shouldn't be an actor.'

Not only that, but before filming got under way, Johnny recalls, 'I got a package from Miss Vera's Finishing School in New York City. They teach men to become transvestites, how to behave like women. It was a bunch of stuff, literature and photographs. The letter said, "We heard you were doing this film. We could help you become a woman." I pondered the thought of going there to investigate what they were doing.'

According to costume designer Colleen Atwood, that wasn't really necessary at all. Although it would prove challenging to transform one of Hollywood's hottest young actors into an actress, she knew exactly how to do it. 'When Ed is dressed as a man, he's a basic guy with shirt, dark slacks, tie, vest. That way, when he's in drag, it's a very big shock, and the distinction is clear cut. When he's a woman, we pad out his hips and give him a bust and stuff. Actually Johnny looks great as a woman. The first time we put him in Angora we were saying "God, he looks beautiful".'

Johnny, however, was not convinced, and he commented on how strange it was to play someone who had dressed in women's clothing. 'When I first looked in the mirror,' he confessed, 'I thought I was the ugliest woman I had ever seen. I mean, I looked huge in those clothes. Enormous!' The comfort, however, was unexpected. It even led him to understand the character he was playing. 'It was spookily comfortable. The only time I felt weird was when I had to do a striptease. But I didn't have any fear about what the audience might think. It would have spoiled the effect if I had looked uneasy in any way. However, I am getting better at walking in high heels.

'I've got some nice slips and hosiery and garters, a couple of nice brassières,' he continued. 'And I love Angora sweaters. Oh man, they're unbelievable. They feel really good. This girl I dated when I was a teenager, she had an

Angora sweater. When we broke up, I was upset, but not about her. It was the sweater.'

All the same, he was a natural said Patricia Arquette, who also talked him through some tips on undressing. 'He was amazing, but very strict who he undressed in front of. I think he energised everyone on set. In fact, he was as much a guiding force on the movie as Tim was. We had these very intimate scenes together, and he would get right into the part and stay there for hours. I'm not that disciplined. I still have fits of laughter during a scene, but Johnny could do it straight.'

In the end though, Johnny admitted that 'the idea of being thirty years old and getting dressed up as a woman and walking out onto a movie set, talking to these sort of big apeish, broodish grips, and you see them getting a little uncomfortable, there's a lot of humour in it.'

The attention to detail was just as essential a part of the filming itself. Under the watchful eye of designer Tom Duffield, building identical sets for Wood's ultra low-budget movies was the most challenging. Each one, he remembers, far exceeded the cost that Wood probably spent on all his movies put together. 'The hardest thing was to not make anything look nice. Items we couldn't find we had to build. Ed's sets were made from inexpensive things he threw together, but our sets were hand-crafted, tailor-made, and far from cheap.'

Burton also took pains to highlight the film's auto-biographical nature, pulling in elements of 68 different locations, many of which were, in fact, Wood's own past stomping grounds. 'It was a vibrant shoot,' recalls Johnny. 'I mean, it was really tough because we were filming in some of the most claustrophobic, badly ventilated, most uncomfortable locations in Hollywood. My adrenalin was pumping all the way, but everyone from the ground up was giving the movie 200 per cent.' That is why, he explained, it was the most ensemble picture he had yet made. 'I don't think I've worked on anything where everyone was so close knit.'

Wood's second wife Kathy, too, was equally effusive in her praise of the film and, in particular, of Johnny's performance. They didn't meet until Kathy decided to visit the location filming. Johnny remembers how nervous he was as she watched him playing her husband. 'It was a real eye-opener for the part. She gave me Edward's wallet and his phone book. I was initially a little fazed by it because I really didn't know how to take it. But it really took the sting out of meeting someone who really knew the person you are playing on film. The wallet and the phone book became real important to the way that I finally fleshed out the part.'

With such high praise, it should be no surprise that Johnny was looking forward to watching the finished film. In fact, it was the first time he'd felt comfortable about seeing something he was in. 'I'm really excited as it was such a great experience. The whole time we were doing it, it felt like a really good departure from any of the other shit that I've done.'

More importantly, Johnny admitted later, 'Ed was someone who was not afraid to take chances and did exactly what he wanted to do. He did the best he could do with what was available to him and he was able to put together images that were surreal, with moments of genius, I think. His movies were all his and they were genuine. I hope Ed is remembered as an artist.' Not only that, continued Johnny, 'but I thought it would be nice to make a film that was a real love letter to him, and to try to clean up what filth had been thrown on his name.' That is certainly how he played the part.

In fact, it was strangely ironic that only a few months after the film was released, Johnny joined Disney and the other principals from the movie in a campaign to have a star placed on Hollywood Boulevard. He was 'trying to get Eddie a star on the Walk of Fame, because it's important. Someone said there's a star next to Bela Lugosi that's available.' That, said Johnny, 'would just be perfect',

Ed Wood opened in America in October 1994 to excellent reviews despite its less-than-mediocre box office. Writing in *Entertainment Weekly*, Richard Corliss called Johnny 'an exemplary actor who can't do much more than smile heroically in the face of every humiliation.' *Première* magazine shared those sentiments: 'Depp plays Wood as a wide innocent caught up in the illusions of cinema. He's another *Edward Scissorhands*. He looks petrified with glee throughout the film,' and the *Village Voice* said much the same by adding that the film was 'flawlessly crafted – as fastidious as any previous Burton production.'

In Britain, where the movie was released in the following May, the reception was much the same. *Empire* magazine had no doubts whatsoever about Johnny's portrayal. 'Depp gives a truly mesmerising performance, both in and out of drag, notching up another distinctly oddball role that again reveals the measure of the young actor's talents. A sublime treat.'

Indeed, *Ed Wood* was Johnny's third movie to earn him a

Golden Globe nomination, again for Best Comedic Actor. More importantly, for the film itself, it walked away with two Oscars at the 1995 Academy Awards ceremony. One for Best Make-Up and one for Martin Landau, for Best Actor, for his portrayal of Bela Lugosi.

Interestingly enough, seven months later, Johnny would purchase Lugosi's old home, or The Castle as it is still known, for a reputed $2.3 million. It was situated on a 2.5-acre plot of land near Hollywood's Sunset Strip with walls and gates surrounding its 9,000 sq ft estate. It had been owned since 1980 by celebrated Hollywood divorce lawyer Marvin Mitchelson, who had been forced to sell it following his conviction for tax fraud 13 years later.

'It's great,' Johnny still raves to this day. 'Lugosi lived in it in the forties; they shot part of the *Wizard of Oz* there, and those things are very interesting titbits, nice to know. But I just love the house, it's such a strange design, very unusual architecture. It's like a weird little castle in the middle of Hollywood, but I'm hardly ever there.' But Mr Pink, as Johnny calls him, is always on hand.

'He's a friend of mine who lives in the house and takes care of the property. I don't know why he's called that. For 25 years he has been Mr Pink. He used to work with Pink Floyd and it would make sense if it was because of that. He's a good guy. If I lived there alone, the place would be a wreck. They'd call in the health department. There's no way I could take care of all that stuff myself. Mr Pink is great, sort of a good friend who just takes care of everything.'

But he wasn't the only resident. Years later, Johnny turned his mind towards bizarre garden furniture again. He began looking for something unusual to place in his front yard. By 1997, he came across the ideal piece – an 8ft yellow gorilla. 'He comes from *Fear and Loathing*,' laughed Johnny. 'He's got the words "You Can Run But You Cannot Hide" emblazoned on his stomach. I saw him and fell in love with him, as one does with an 8ft gorilla, and I thought, "Aah, I've got a good idea. I'll rig him up for those bastard neighbours who've been complaining about the construction and fucking leaves in their garden." That was horrible shit.'

As Johnny himself would point out, 'they're real trainspotters, real nit-pickers. I had the construction crew on the film build his hand so he was flicking the bird (giving the finger). He also has a giant erection; we built a pump into him so he's constantly peeing into a bucket. The neighbours haven't commented yet, but they must know he was put there for them. I've had him moved now, but he used to stand facing their little veranda where they sit and have coffee every morning. Now he's right at the end of my driveway, so just as you park your car there's this enormous gorilla with a giant hard-on – welcome to Johnny's.'

Aside from Mr Pink, there was also Moo, Johnny's pitbull terrier, a present from Kate. 'He doesn't bite. That's just the propaganda against pitbulls. It depends what the owner's like. I don't bite too hard either. I miss him when I'm away. I also have two Rottweilers, called Red and Black. So it's Moo, Pink, Red, Black and me. I don't have a colourful name yet. I'm looking forward to one, though.'

From *Ed Wood*, Johnny moved on to shooting *Don Juan DeMarco*, a movie that advance reports insisted would prove as uproarious as its predecessor was outrageous. The idea was the brainchild of Jeremy Levin whose 1990's screenplay was loosely based on Lord Byron's mythical character of the same name. 'I always wanted to do a movie about women, love, romance and sex,' explained Levin. 'And I always wondered whether anyone had done a movie about Don Juan.' They hadn't.

Not only that, continues Levin, but 'Byron's piece is a very long tome that has a tremendous amount of politics, but some absolutely wonderful scenes. I freely appropriated some of these scenes, and then worked them into a screenplay about another issue.' That other issue was his own personal experiences as a psychotherapist and his fascination with Don Juan.

Born and raised in Woodbridge, Connecticut, Levin's career had been pre-ordained since his primary school days; even then, he was dedicated to writing in one form or another. Pursuing his interest, he published two novels: *Creator* and *Satan: His Psychotherapy and Cure, By The Unfortunate Dr Kassler, JSPS*. Later, he founded and directed *The Proposition*, a satirical theatre group which he ran in Cambridge, Massachusetts for ten years and off-Broadway for a further four. Over the following years, he worked as a television director, school teacher, state hospital psychologist, Harvard University faculty member, and a clinical physiologist before moving into writing and directing films in 1980 with the screen adaptation of his own novel, *Creator*, and another, *Playing For Keeps*.

For his *Don Juan DeMarco* screenplay he introduced psychiatrist Jack Mickler (Marlon Brando) as the catalyst for his exploration of the grey area between fantasy and reality. After nearly 30 years of listening, encouraging and

unravelling other people's miseries, he is all but burnt out.
He has little left for either his colleagues or his long-suffering
wife, played by Faye Dunaway. He is simply living out the
emotions of someone awaiting imminent retirement.

That is until Don Juan DeMarco provides him with the
most intriguing and fascinating case of his career. Indeed,
DeMarco's tales of love and passion are exactly what
Mickler needs to restore his professional etiquette and
flagging marriage.

The opening sequence wastes no time introducing the
main character, a young man perched precariously on the
narrow catwalk at the top of an advertising billboard 40 feet
above street level. With his face hidden by a mask, cloaked
in flowing cape, and wielding a raised sabre, the figure
claims to be Don Juan (Johnny), the world's greatest lover,
and the seducer of at least 1,500 women, but he is
distraught. And he has every reason to be.

Although he has loved an almost countless number of
women, the one woman he actually does love has rejected
him. Convincing himself there is nothing, or no one left to
love, suicide seems to be the most promising option.
Promising that is until Dr Mickler bursts into his enclosed
world of angst-ridden self-pity and succeeds where police
officers have failed in talking the cloaked madman down
from his suicidal perch.

Even on the fringe of professional retreat, Mickler swiftly
decides he has nothing to lose by evaluating his now
seemingly disillusioned patient with a ten-day course of
diagnosis and treatment. Mickler is as delusive as his patient
is distraught, and Don Juan takes his new mentor through a
series of stories that are at best nothing more than wild

erotic adventures. Everything from a childhood in a small Mexican town, a journey to Arabia where he is secretly pressed into service in a harem and an eventual shipwreck which washes him up on to a desert island to encounter his one true love, only to be rejected for openly admitting his past promiscuities.

Needless to say, Mickler, drawn into DeMarco's sagas of love, passion, and romance – strikingly photographed in gorgeous, colourful flashback sequences – finds himself restoring his already flagging marriage as a result of his patient's revelations.

Indeed, confirmed Levin, *Don Juan DeMarco* is a light, fantasy confection of a movie. And who better for the title role than Johnny? Although at the time of finishing his screenplay, the director had no preconceived ideas about an actor to play the part. 'I was told Johnny wanted to do it, and Don Juan as Johnny plays him is someone who's just unmitigatedly in love with love. Whether or not he's the real thing is inconsequential. He causes a tremendous transformation in Mickler.'

On a practical level, of course, many considered Johnny's haunting good looks suitably Latin for Don Juan. Mark Salisbury writing in *Empire* magazine couldn't agree more. 'It's a role Depp was born to play; his beauteous looks and doe-eyes are the perfect accompaniments to a lifetime of seduction and loving.'

Although Johnny was now firmly committed to the idea of filming *Don Juan DeMarco*, there was still one more bridge to cross. He would only appear in the film if Marlon Brando agreed to play the psychiatrist. At that point, Levin was worried. 'I thought the project was dead in the water, only to receive a second shock, hearing that Marlon was, in fact, interested.'

But then again, he knew Johnny loved the script. 'It's incredible writing,' Johnny still proclaims. 'My character's dialogue is so poetic and beautiful. The challenge for me was creating a character who was slightly cocky and noble, but likeable. I needed to create someone who has a strong sense of himself, but is still lost.'

The other thing, of course, was the fact that if Johnny was to have a hero or personal god it would be Brando. More importantly, the now ageing star was also Johnny's favourite actor, and to have the opportunity to work alongside him was like a dream come true. That's not to say Johnny's name alone wasn't enough to green-light the movie. Far from it. What was uncertain, however, was whether he had the clout to attract an actor of Brando's reputation to what could be considered a typically stereotyped, Johnny Depp oddball movie. Apparently, he did.

Brando himself, of course, more controversial than not during his 40-year career, had made 35 films, and could be said to have influenced much of the screen charisma Johnny now exuded, in much the same way as James Dean and Elvis Presley. Nominated seven times for Academy Awards as Best Actor, Brando had won twice, once in 1954 for *On the Waterfront*, and again in 1972 for his remarkable performance as Vito Corleone in Francis Ford Coppola's *The Godfather*. In doing so, he created a body of work that stands proud in its integrity, everything from *A Streetcar Named Desire*, *Viva Zapata!* and *Julius Caesar* to *The Wild One*, *Mutiny on the Bounty*, the controversial *Last Tango in*

Paris, and, of course, his 15-minute cameo appearance in Christopher Reeves' *Superman: The Movie*.

Equally inspirational was the casting of Faye Dunaway in the pivotal role of Brando's wife. She, too, was thoroughly enamoured with Brando. 'He's an idol, a dream. He's a myth to every working actor in the world. And Johnny's a close second.'

'It was tremendously exciting working with Marlon and Faye,' Johnny recalls. 'They are actors with incredible careers. I was privileged to work alongside them and learn.' If he was assailed by self-doubt for any reason, within hours the tension, the nervousness, and perhaps the feeling of a star-struck boy from Kentucky soon fell away. 'You just jump in,' he adds, 'I was real nervous on my way over to his house. Then, as soon as I saw him, he just instantly, magically, put me at ease within seconds of saying "Hello". He became this great wonderful guy I was working with. He was a big, big factor in me doing the film.'

It was something producer Patrick Palmer noticed as well. 'Let's face it, we've got the most talented actor over the age of 60, the most talented actor under the age of 30, and one of the most acclaimed actresses in Hollywood.'

And he was right. In fact, the reviews for the film couldn't have been better if Levin had written them himself. 'I wanted *Don Juan* to be about so many things – about what's important in life, and the connection between people. It's a story about life beginning again, about humanity and the way we're all living. Most importantly, it's about staying alive in life.'

The critics agreed. The movie was utterly delightful, the general consensus ran – 'Johnny Depp stands up to Brando as the best young actor in Hollywood. The part seems made for him, and he plays it without narcissism or camp,' wrote Derek Malcolm in *The Guardian*.

Another raved, 'Depp seems permanently drawn to characters on the fringe of society and is perfectly cast as a man who takes boyish delight in the opportunities that life possesses.'

Again it was high praise for another of Johnny's oddball outsider roles, but maybe Johnny was rapidly tiring of playing the oddball outsider. Maybe, too, it was time for that blockbuster action movie that he had so proudly avoided through his previous work. Certainly there were those critics who wanted to make him painfully aware of that. Johnny, however, remained adamant. 'I'm not blockbuster boy. I never wanted to be.'

Besides, he continues, 'you can never predict what's going to be commercial but I have to feel stimulated by the material in order to turn in a good performance. I'm not going to take the dull character for the sake of a big pay cheque. It's very easy to take that road, but there's just ... nothing there, you know. Everything has been done ten zillion times and if you can, at least, try for something a little different, then why not? I just want to do the things I want to do.'

CHAPTER 10

'I'VE NEVER LIKED BEING IN THE PUBLIC EYE.
IT MAKES ME FEEL VERY UNCOMFORTABLE. THAT'S WHY I
LOVE SPENDING TIME IN PARIS SO MUCH. I CAN DO
WHAT I WANT WITHOUT BEING SCRUTINISED, JUDGED
OR STALKED. I'M NOT REALLY INTERESTED IN GLITZ.
I PREFER TO LIVE A LIFE FILLED AS MUCH AS POSSIBLE
WITH UNUSUAL EXPERIENCES.'

THE NICK OF TIME

Johnny and Kate left for the Cannes Film Festival shortly before *Ed Wood* and *Don Juan DeMarco* were released in America in May 1995 to attend the première of his next movie, Jim Jarmusch's *Dead Man*.

Jarmusch, of course, like Tim Burton, could be described as one of the few visionary directors to have established himself in the upper echelons of Hollywood. A former film student, he first came to the public's attention in 1984 with his low-budget black-and-white piece, *Stranger than Paradise*, and then two years later with *Down by Law*. But he is probably best known, however, for his obliquely observed study of foreign tourists adrift after hours in Elvis-haunted Memphis in 1989's *Mystery Train*, and for his stunningly visualised *Night on Earth* three years later. The latter takes his audience on five cab rides in five cities over the course of a single night, linked by the interaction of passengers and drivers, one played by Winona Ryder. Interestingly enough, though, it is perhaps one of his, and Winona's, least-seen movies.

So with that pedigree, it should be no surprise that Johnny wanted to link up with the acclaimed cult director even though the film opened to generally bemused critical reaction. It was, noted some, a hypnotic, slow moving, sometimes astonishing western, that seemed to have much more in common with Ingmar Bergman's *The Seventh Seal* and Sam Shephard's mystical western *Silent Tongue* from 1993 – River Phoenix's last film – than it had with any characteristic Hollywood outing. Maybe that was *Dead Man*'s greatest downfall, in critical terms at least. Derek Malcom thought so when he wrote his review for *The Guardian*; 'What looks like an intriguing short story is stretched by Jarmusch into over two hours of slow burning and effortful watching, with its humour existing side by side with a kind of portentous visual philosophising.'

All the same, its glorious black-and-white photography – stunningly shot by Robert Muller – made the film an intriguing and nicely paced contemporary western epic with a dash of classic *film noir* thrown in for good measure.

For Jarmusch as well as Johnny, it was, according to the press release, the story of a young man's journey, both physically and spiritually, into very familiar territory. William Blake (Johnny) travels to the extreme western frontiers of America some time in the second half of the nineteenth century. Lost and badly wounded, he encounters a very odd, outcast Native American named

Nobody (Gary Farmer), who believes Blake is actually the dead English poet of the same name.

The story, with Nobody's help, leads Blake through situations that are in turn comical and violent. Contrary to his nature, circumstances transform Blake into a hunted outlaw, a killer, and a man whose physical existence is slowly slipping away. Thrown into a world that is cruel and chaotic, his eyes are opened to the fragility that defines the realm of the living. It is as though he passes through the surface of a mirror, and emerges into a previously unknown world that exists on the other side.

Johnny adored the movie, and the character he was playing even more so. At the same time, though, he hoped it was 'the last of these innocents I play. It's a character that is, again, like a naïve young guy who's trying to get his life together. He's trying really hard to make his life work and he ends up slowly dying. And he knows he's dying. It's a beautiful story, though.'

In fact, Jarmusch wrote the part of William Blake with Johnny in mind. Not surprising, really, since he was a friend, and by the time filming got under way, he had been for five years. 'He really is one of the most precise and focused people I've ever worked with,' enthused the director of his star. 'The whole crew was kind of amazed by that. It's a side of him that I'm not really familiar with. I'm more familiar with seeing him fall asleep on the couch with the TV on all night. But it somehow fits; he's full of paradoxes.

'What I love about him as an actor is his subtlety and very interesting physicality, which is underplayed; he has amazing eyes, which he uses to great effect. I didn't appreciate his precision until I worked with him; he doesn't make false moves or overdo it.'

Much the same as Robert Mitchum, one of America's most accomplished actors of the western genre, who had four years earlier returned to the screen for a cameo role in Martin Scorsese's *Cape Fear* – the director's gripping remake of Mitchum's 1962 original.

Johnny was also thoroughly enamoured to be working with him, particularly when he would recall Mitchum's 'Love' and 'Hate' tattooed fingers from Charles Laughton's *The Night of the Hunter*, the same one to which Winona had introduced him, long before it was restored by the British Film Institute in 1999. Today, Johnny still values the experience. 'He was about 7ft tall and in great shape. He's a tough guy.'

That was something Johnny could comprehend, in retrospect at least. Painfully aware of his public profile, he believed that to many people he was a celebrity first and an actor a poor second, and that his career, his work and even his personality were being judged accordingly.

Public perception of Johnny was influenced by such apparently inconsequential remarks as his curiosity with the afterlife. Nowhere was that better expressed than when staying at the Mackay Mansion in Nevada during filming. It was a three-storey Victorian house reputedly haunted by a little girl wearing a silk party dress with a blue sash. 'I want to run into some spirits here,' he told *Première* magazine.

'When I was a kid, I used to have these dreams. But they weren't dreams. I was awake, but I couldn't move. I couldn't speak. And a face would come to me. Someone told me it was the spirit of someone who died that was very close and never got to say something that they wanted to say. And I believe it.' And that wouldn't be the only occasion he would openly admit to such experiences.

'I was staying at this hotel in London that used to be a hospital. This face, like an evil surgeon's face, suddenly came right at me. I was just lying in bed, and I was asleep and wasn't on any sort of drugs. It really scared me, which was cool.'

Not so cool was the time he stayed in Paris, in the room where Oscar Wilde died. 'I didn't see him. It was definitely the bed he died in. I'm not sure if it was the room, but there was all his furniture. I was a little paranoid that I might be buggered by his ghost at 4.00am.'

One of the biggest thrills for Johnny, however, was the time he visited the home of escapologist Harry Houdini, situated above Laurel Canyon. Although now a collection of ruins, 'Canyon residents tell of strange happenings on the hilltop site. There's no house. I bet this was a really romantic place at night. I often think I might have been Houdini myself at one time.' And it's no coincidence that Winona Ryder used to buy him antique locks for what he called his 'Houdini' hobby.

He also thought it was time to extend his range of movie roles. It was a realisation that surfaced towards the end of *Don Juan DeMarco* and now he wanted to make it happen.

John Badham's latest project seemed ideal, and Johnny was hooked when he heard what the director was filming. All the same, it seemed strange that Badham should take on a third remake of Alfred Hitchcock's 1934 *The Man Who Knew Too Much*. Strange, that is, when you consider it was one of Hitchcock's best-loved thrillers, and even spawned another version, updated and colour-enhanced by the director himself 22 years later.

For the Hitchcock audience, the story centred on a young girl kidnapped to prevent her parents from revealing their knowledge of a political assassination plot. But in attempting to find a new angle for Badham's 1995 version, *Nick of Time*, the plot was twisted slightly by turning the central role into a young professional who is forced to carry out the political assassination himself to save his young daughter's life. Even in pre-production, the forthcoming *Nick of Time* promised to be a tantalising remake of the Hitchcock original.

It all starts on a normal afternoon for accountant Gene Watson (Johnny) as time ticks by without incident. But not for long. He is about to become entangled in one of those high-octane dramas that holds the general population gripped when played out on the news. Fate has just dealt him a terrifying hand.

Arriving at Union Station in downtown Los Angeles for an appointment, Gene and his six-year-old daughter Lynn, played by Courtney Chase, are suddenly taken hostage by police impostors Christopher Walken and Roma Maffia (aka Mr Smith and Mr Jones). Gene is told he must commit a murder within the next 90 minutes or his daughter will die. Any effort Watson makes to go to the authorities is stymied by the sure knowledge that the kidnappers will retaliate by carrying out their threat. In his frantic race against the clock, each moment has immediate and deadly consequences.

The fact of being at the wrong place at the wrong time lies at the heart of the movie. Certainly that is true for

Johnny's character Gene Watson. He is confronted with the most profound and frightening situation imaginable. An 'ordinary' accountant and devoted father whose courage and wits are tested in a unique, harrowing ordeal. It appears that the kidnappers' insane and compelling plan will implicate Watson through a home video in which he will appear to be an unhinged loner hell-bent on exacting a terrible revenge.

As John Badham, best known for *Saturday Night Fever* and *Blue Thunder* explains, 'Nearly every day the newspaper reports incredible but true incidents that are as unfathomable as they are tragic. Such stories repeatedly demonstrate that truth is much stranger than fiction. Most people expect each day of the week to unfold much like the one before. Yet every single day there are those who will experience something so unexpected or shocking that they can't even accept the fact that it is happening, and it's happening to them.'

That, he continues, 'is the situation faced by Johnny's character – an ordinary man who gets caught up in extraordinary circumstances that are horrible and beyond his control. This situation could happen to any of us. *Nick of Time* puts before the filmgoer the terrifying question, "What would *you* do if this happened to you?"'

From that point of view, it was easy to understand Johnny's attraction to the role. It not only offered him the opportunity to distance himself from the kind of roles he had played for the last five years – the oddball or kooky – but it could also be seen as a calculated attempt to shake off any last vestiges of what his critics called his 'quirky' typecasting.

Executive producer DJ Caruso agreed. 'His role is very different from what we've seen Johnny do in the past, and the audience will be rooting for him even as they wonder whether he can be the hero.'

That is certainly how Johnny played the part. Even the stunts were 90 per cent his own, everything from the elaborate fight sequences to the daring 90ft cable fall. 'Action actor' was how stunt co-ordinator Shane Dixon acknowledged Johnny's resilience in his determination to succeed – and he did that as well.

There was, however, another factor in Johnny's relish of the role. It tapped perfectly into his intense desire for a family of his own. It was an area of his private life which apparently caused difficulties in his relationship with Kate Moss as much as it had with Winona Ryder.

'To play the role, I drew on what was accessible,' Johnny confirmed. 'Family is very important to me. I have nieces and nephews whom I absolutely worship. If anything happened to them, I would go crazy and do anything to save them.'

Equally intriguing was the idea of teaming Johnny up with Christopher Walken. It was a stroke of genius on Badham's part, and another of Johnny's reasons for accepting the role. It would also help him to overcome any concerns he had for playing an action hero. Up until then, he thought he would 'look goofy as an action man unless I could wear a shirt that had "Action Man" printed on it, then I would do it'.

Shooting commenced on 2 April 1995 at the Westin Bonaventure Hotel in the heart of downtown Los Angeles, just a few blocks away from Union Street. It was commandeered for several scenes, while a hotel shoe-shine stand and near-by plant shop were constructed with transparent glass and clocks were strategically placed to offer stark reminders that time for Johnny's character was running out.

Johnny would, according to Badham, arrive on set at 7.00am, sometimes not looking his best. 'We would start to stage a scene, and I would think he was only propped up by a stage brace. He would stand there looking quite shaken, but totally focused.' The director didn't even ask what Johnny may have been up to the night before. 'Why ask the obvious? What I learned right away was, it didn't matter if he never went to bed the night before, because he was right on top of it.' Evidence enough that this extraordinary young actor was also remarkably instinctive.

Johnny's co-star Gloria Reuben agreed, albeit for different reasons. 'He's a Gemini. Very sensitive, a little shy and very funny. If he wanted to trash a hotel room with me in it, that would be just fine.'

At the same time, Johnny also faced the challenge of filming the story in chronological order, as opposed to the more usual movie technique of shooting out of sequence, and then cutting it together at a later stage. The film, Badham explained, 'was shot as if we just happened upon these people and their circumstances. The actors were filmed without make-up using hand-held cameras to achieve a raw, realistic feeling.'

He elaborates. 'A documentary is shot with the knowledge that you have one shot to get it right, so you can't always put the camera exactly where you would like. You can't always be in focus. Sometimes you're too far or too close to the action. The lighting isn't always perfect or flattering to your subject. That is the illusion we tried to create.'

For Johnny, it was an inspiring and instructive process. 'We did a lot of scenes that involved two or three cameras, which reduced the number of takes and kept a freshness and spontaneity to the acting. You're not bound within frame lines and feel like you can go anywhere and do anything.'

All the same, continued Badham, 'You can't skip or take short cuts through transmissions and mundane aspects of a story, such as when a guy is seen leaving his office in one scene, and then walking through his front door in the next. In this situation, we have to stay with Johnny's character wherever he goes and at the same time, keep the pace moving.'

His enthusiasm for his performance, and his acceptance of the challenges he endured while filming *Nick of Time*, proved that Johnny could hold his own in any company and in any movie. It seemed only natural that having once played in the big action leagues, he would only continue there.

But there were some people, however, who were surprised, even shocked, at the news of his next film project.

Enjoying the freedom of being between movies, Johnny turned his attention to an aspect of his career that he had not yet pursued at any great length – directing his own feature. It was something he had long wanted to do. And nowhere is that desire better expressed than in the clutch of music videos he had directed for and with his own circle of friends and colleagues.

He shared the directing honours, for instance, for Red Hot Chilli Pepper John Frusciante's first album with Gibby

Haynes; he directed another for Shane MacGowan and the Pogues; he appeared alongside them on *Top of the Pops*; and he even found time to direct a couple of film shorts, one a 12-minute journey through a house filled with junk backed by a rock 'n' roll soundtrack, and the other, an eight-minute anti-drug documentary. All of these could be seen as Johnny's yearning for his next project as director, star and writer of *The Brave*.

Well, not exactly *the* writer. Johnny had written the screenplay with his brother Dan, when the two adapted Gregory MacDonald's novel of the same name. 'It's about a man making a sacrifice for his family,' explained Johnny. 'And I play that man, and since I've sponged off and stolen as much as I can from the film-makers I've been fortunate enough to work with – Tim Burton, John Waters, Emir Kusturica, Lasse Hallstrom, Jim Jarmusch – I thought I'd try directing one myself. But I have absolutely no idea why. I felt somehow driven to it.'

Unfortunately, a lot of people disagreed with him intensely. Although Johnny was, by this time, an actor with a well-respected pedigree, this was his first major directorial project, and although it turned out to be a unique look at the sorry state of contemporary American Indian culture, Johnny certainly had his fair share of critics.

His idea, as one of those critics put it, 'was to pose a problem and he does this without once pausing to inject his work with feel-good amphetamines. If anything, *The Brave* is designed to make the viewer feel as though he's sitting on a mat of needles – however much we squirm and shift, we just can't get away from those little points of pain.'

It was the classic, but also timeless, tale of redemption,

about how an American Indian man, Raphael, played by Johnny, out of work and desperate for cash, decides to sell his life to a producer of 'snuff' films, played by Marlon Brando, whose work involves the filming of genuine and horrendously brutal murder scenes, for which he pays huge sums of money. Raphael accepts a 'role', so that his wife (Elpidia Carillo) and his children can have a more comfortable future. He has one week to report back to the set where the movie-makers will torture and kill him. The movie then centres on the seven days Raphael spends with his family, the first and last good days they will ever have together.

With only a few dollars in his pocket and even fewer days to live Raphael springs a number of surprises on his family. Probably the most successful is the scene when he builds a vast fun fair in the middle of the night that is almost unapologetically lifted from Johnny's own *Arizona Dream* movie. The only difference is that this time the construction is not a flying machine.

In another scene, Raphael is confronted by the producer's vile assistant, memorably played by Marshall Bell, who promptly plunges a pick-axe into his hand. Equally daunting is the opening sequence, when Raphael arrives at a deserted warehouse, is interviewed by the same unpleasant character, and is finally ushered to a subterranean chamber where an electric chair, and Brando in a wheelchair puffing on a mouth organ, await him.

Johnny's vision was certainly haunting, with the viewer's discomfort multiplying as the story unfolds. There is, for instance, the inevitable brutality of Raphael's final 'starring' role. It appears that for a down-and-out American Indian, selling his body to die in a snuff movie is the only route available to secure a better way of life for his family. That theme lies at the heart of the movie. Raphael drinks, moves in and out of prison, and can't afford a car. His own family exist in a dilapidated village next to a waste dump in the middle of a deserted nowhere. There, like other similarly deprived sectors of society, they build their homes from pieces of scrap material and rummage through mounds of rubbish each day barely managing to get by.

Once again, Johnny was totally delighted to be working with Marlon Brando, even if he was only playing a cameo role. Far more important, Johnny concedes it was an act of friendship that left him completely floored. 'Marlon coming and doing this film for me was an incredible blessing. It was beyond a dream. I was very fortunate to have worked with him, and maintained a friendship, a relationship with him, so when we went to work together, the process was very enjoyable. We were cackling and laughing together.'

But as far as directing Brando went, Johnny wasn't remotely worried. 'I don't think anyone needs to direct him. You just turn the camera on and capture him, and take what you can take. What he came in and did for me was above and beyond anything I ever expected. He really dug inside.'

Even with Brando, the film seemingly did nothing more than gather dust on a distributor's shelf. But two years later, in May 1997, it was scheduled for its international début at Cannes. With so much conspiring against the film, the first reviews following its première came as a major shock. Many were disappointing. 'Every morbid, sensitive high school kid's dream movie,' wrote one US critic.

Another called it 'oddly haunting' for its eccentricity. 'There's a lot wrong with *The Brave*, with a pace that may be intended to evoke desert languor, but is often plain leaden. It wasn't the most narcisstic film a director has ever made starring himself.'

Some, however, were much kinder. Johnny Depp, wrote *The Guardian* critic Jonathan Romney, 'comes across as wanting to create his own cinematic style. Cannes catcalls not withstanding, he should be encouraged to give directing another go.'

Indeed, as Johnny himself explains, 'I was very naïve. I thought directing would be easy to do, but it's insane. Completely insane. You don't sleep when you're supposed to sleep, and when you're working, you're desperate to sleep. People ask you questions like "What colour would you like the red shoes to be?" when "red" would suffice. It's the most insane thing I've ever done.'

There was, of course, a temptation to draw comparisons with Kevin Costner's *Dances with Wolves*. Indeed, if Costner was praised for his use of ecological imagery, then Johnny had displayed a similar skill. American Indians, it seems, living on recycled material, taking public transportation, giving their children toys they made with their own hands, are an obvious tragedy, mainly because the American Indians 200 years ago were ecologists by choice and tradition. For the same people today, it's a condition enforced by poverty.

It was something Johnny's ex-fiancée Winona Ryder understood as much as Johnny himself. She had, after all, been raised on a Californian commune with Northern California Indians as neighbours. It was, according to Winona, where the two cultures – emphasising community, simplicity and respect for the earth – were so similar that the lines between them often blurred.

'Native American culture is American culture,' Winona believes. 'And we can all learn from it. It's just so profoundly important to preserve all of our country's culture.' It is what led to her involvement with the American Indian College Fund to raise funds and maintain an interest in that same cultural heritage.

She even asked Johnny to show her the movie. According to the December 1997 French *Première* magazine, the last time they saw each other, Winona had been pleading with him. But it was impossible because the film was locked away in a safe.

But Winona also knew that the film had special meaning for Johnny. In a strange way, he was proud. 'I thought it sort of parallelled what happened to the American Indians 100 or more years ago.' Even more convincingly, elements of the movie echoed his own concern that he still considered America a gluttonous society that was all about winning and results, and again accused Andrew Jackson, the former President pictured on $20 bills, of being a genocidal murderer responsible for the death of millions of American Indians.

In fact, it was Johnny's appearance at Cannes that same year that publicly revealed something the Hollywood grapevine had been insisting for weeks – that he and Kate Moss had broken up. Within a month, Britain's *Sun* newspaper was reporting 'Supermodel Kate Moss has finally split from Hollywood hell-raiser Johnny Depp. The couple are going their separate ways after a stormy four-year relationship. A source said they planned to remain friends and Kate will go to Depp's film premières. Kate had once talked about marrying the *Edward Scissorhands* star. Earlier this year, Depp moved into Kate's New York flat. But instead of cementing the relationship, the couple found they got on each other's nerves.'

The *New York Post* said much the same. 'Things were already rocky for the couple back in May at the Cannes Film Festival. They rented separate villas. Kate shared one with her pals from Oasis. And they never visited each other's pad. Friends say Kate wants to keep the relationship alive, but Johnny won't change to suit her. When Depp was in town recently, the pair didn't even see each other once.' Johnny's spokeswoman, at the time, however, wasn't so sure. 'To our knowledge, the break-up is untrue.'

True or not, it didn't stop *People* magazine subsequently suggesting that 'According to friends, Moss wants to continue to date Depp occasionally, but Depp isn't into open relationships.' And in *New York* magazine, 'Kate has told friends that she called it quits with the hot-tempered heart-throb last week because they were having too many fights. They've had small separations before but this was a major break-up. '

Far more dubious was *Star* magazine's revelations by Janet Charlton that Winona Ryder had been calling Johnny because she still cared for him. Winona remained unperturbed by speculation, and the suggestion seemed preposterous.

Another report in the *New York Post*, however, was quick to notice that Kate did not remain alone for long. 'Moss has taken up with 32-year-old Tarka Cordell. Sources say that, for the past year, Cordell has stayed at Moss' apartment in New York whenever he's in town ... "To my knowledge, they've been friends for a while," says Paul Rowland, owner of Moss' agency, "but I don't think there's any romance involved."'

But Johnny was in no hurry to let anyone else into his life. Although Jennifer Love Hewitt of television's *Party of Five* would admit to having a crush on him, it was never suggested that they were a couple. Not even when he turned up on the set of her television series. That was more to do with a fan letter she had sent him years earlier.

'It was one of those days when I was dressed in sweats and wasn't wearing any make-up. I looked hideous. I was in my trailer when all of a sudden I hear the wardrobe girl yell "Johnny Depp is standing right outside." I just couldn't meet him looking so awful. So I ran out of the trailer, screaming at the top of my lungs until he left. I was totally humiliated.'

As for Kate, Johnny concedes, 'We would still be together today if I hadn't behaved like such an idiot. She was the best thing that ever happened to me, but I blew it because I was too moody and too miserable to be around. I hated myself and she couldn't take it any more. I don't blame her one bit. I would give anything to have Kate in my life again. I was sick to my stomach. I think anyone who has ever broken up with a girl he loves understands that. You're lying in bed, staring at your TV, smoking your fifth pack of cigarettes and wondering how you managed to make such a mess of a good thing.

'I still feel that way about Kate. She knows how I feel about her. But we also probably know there's no going back. If I could have taken things more easily and not got so depressed about my work and other garbage, we could have been so happy. I don't know, maybe I just couldn't deal with the fact that things were so good between us and had to act like an idiot and push her away.'

No sooner was his work on *The Brave* complete than Johnny was starting work on yet another movie. Joining Marlon Brando once again, Debra Winger, and *Dead Man* ally John Hurt, he headed out to County Cork, off the Irish coast, to film *Divine Rapture*, Thom Eberhardt's dark satire about religious miracles.

In fact, it was amusingly ironic that Johnny would be playing an investigative journalist looking into an assortment of miracles that Brando's character, the local priest, is apparently involved in. Winger was given the substantial role of a fisherman's wife who dies but is later brought back to life, and Hurt was cast as the local doctor.

Life on the set, however, was not without its dramas. It was barely the eighth week of location filming when the production first hit trouble, from the Irish Catholic Church of all places. Two of their churches, Eberhardt believed, had a sociological resonance essential to the movie's sense of realism. Unfortunately, the local clergy didn't see it that way. Nor did the Bishop of Clyne, who believed that churches were not film sets. As far as he was concerned, Ballycotton's Star of the Sea and Immaculate Conception churches could not be used. Not only that, but Brando's priest character was, in his opinion, an insult to Catholicism.

The locations, however, were not the only problems that Thom Eberhardt had to contend with as the *Divine Rapture* set hit even more trouble. 'I've been over here eight weeks already,' complained the director. 'Most of the time, the weather was glorious. Then as soon as we got under way the rain rolled in.'

Not that anyone could be blamed for thinking things weren't running smoothly. Quite the opposite, in fact. The villagers of Ballycotton welcomed the film crew enthusiastically. For them, the arrival of Hollywood film-makers could only mean one thing – dollars in their pockets. Even Marlon Brando's $4 million fee, they believed, would help the local economy. It did, for a time.

The actor began shopping for a place to stay. By the time production got under way in mid-July 1995, he had found one. A mansion in nearby Shanagarry for which the production would pay the owner $4,000 a week. 'I have never been so happy in my life.' Even when he stepped off the plane, 'I had this rush of emotion. I have never felt so at home in a place as I do here. I am seriously contemplating Irish citizenship.'

Although the shooting of the movie hit snag after snag, Johnny did, nonetheless, manage a couple of day's filming. Between takes, he was happy signing autographs, or at other times, he just sat in his room at the exclusive Ballymaloe House where he would be staying for the duration of the shoot. Although Kate was expected to join him, she didn't. In the end, his friend, and now *Batman* star, Val Kilmer flew out to join him.

Not that he would be staying long. Neither would Johnny for that matter. Three days later, and with only 20 minutes of shot footage, production on the movie was halted completely. The word around the set was that the less than moderate $16 million budget was washed up. Either that, or the film's financial backers Cinefin were deliberately pulling out of the project.

Although Brando had already been paid $1 million up front, Johnny and the rest of the cast and technical crew were less fortunate. Eberhardt was worried. 'Basically, what you have is a roomful of question marks and, upstairs, another roomful of producers where the problem now lies.'

For an entire week, work on *Divine Rapture* was suspended while those problems were thrashed out by the powers-that-be. Unfortunately, in the ensuing battle of wits, there was no winner. Production was officially halted. The cheques paid out the previous week were unlikely to be met and the seven years that Eberhardt had spent in development on the movie collapsed in just one weekend. A statement was issued.

'With deep regret, we have had to cease production of *Divine Rapture*. In spite of continuing assurance of financial backing, the funds have not been forthcoming. Along with cast and crew, we are shocked at the situation and deeply saddened by our inability to continue with this wonderful project. We wish to thank the people of Ballycotton who showed us so much support, and we will be doing everything we can to compensate them for their time and effort.'

But the cast and crew were not the only ones out of pocket. Fishermen, hoteliers and food suppliers all had outstanding bills that needed settlement. The Bay View Hotel, for instance, where much of the cast and crew stayed, was due payments for at least 20 rooms.

Even more damaging, long after the actors went home, was the aftermath of the film's failure. 'We hoped it would keep the hotels and guest houses full for years when the fame of the area spread throughout the world because of the film,' explained hotelier John O'Brien. Even Adrian Knowles, the owner of the Shanagarry mansion, was disappointed. Not only that, but he was another to suffer financially. 'I did receive a cheque that I understand will not be honoured, but I have been assured that I will be paid.'

It was a promise Brando himself made before his departure, long after Johnny had already given up hope on the production when it was first suspended. A weekend trip to France with Kate did not see him return.

'*Divine Rapture*,' Johnny laughs at the memory today. 'You want my experience of it? I had gotten a script from Marlon. He said, "Hey, come over and join me in Ireland. We'll do this thing. It'll be fun." I said, "Sure." I went over. We started shooting and were having a great time. Everything was real good. The next thing we knew, they were saying, "It's over." And that was it. It was like being in the middle of good sex, and then having the lights turned on and 15 people with machine-guns come in and say, "Stop or die."'

Meanwhile, Barry Navidi, one of the producers, predicted years of legal action between the producers and the financiers over the film's collapse. Far more important, he recalls, was the tragedy of it all. 'We have quite amazing rushes of the movie with incredible performances from the stars.' Mark Crowdy, one of the other producers, agreed with that summation.

After *Rapture*, Johnny's next role came knocking just as he was getting used to the freedom of being between movies. His agent thought it was perfect for him as she handed over the script of *Donnie Brasco*, Paul Attanasio's screenplay based on the book by Joseph D Pistone. Johnny quickly agreed.

CHAPTER 11

'THERE'S NOTHING WORSE THAN SOMEONE
WHO CONSIDERS THEMSELF A SERIOUS ACTOR,
BECAUSE AN ACTOR IS ESSENTIALLY A LIAR. I MAKE
A LIVING. I DEFINITELY WOULDN'T CALL MYSELF A
FILM STAR. I'M MUCH MORE "IN THE TRENCHES"
THAN GLITTERY!'

JOHNNY BE GOOD

In less than a week, in February 1997, Johnny Depp's latest movie would be opening. As he read the first reviews, he must have felt incredibly relieved that the test audiences and mass-market reviewers had responded so favourably to the film. Writing in Britain's *Daily Star*, their film critic offered one of the most concise summaries, shared by most reviewers, that Mike Newell's *Donnie Brasco* was 'the finest gangster film since *The Godfather*.'

It was the true story of FBI undercover agent Joe Pistone, aka Donnie Brasco, who, in the late Seventies, infiltrated the Mob in what was to become one of the most successful mole operations in the history of the American Government's crack-down against organised crime. Nonetheless, it was a mission that exacted a devastating personal price on the man who was drawn into an unexpected and revealing friendship with the criminal he was supposed to be destroying, and in the process almost destroyed himself.

The idea that Mike Newell would take on the American mobster myth with a dramatic examination of the emotional and moral core of the tough-guy loyalty that usually goes unquestioned, almost beggared belief. It was as if Quentin Tarantino had announced an adaptation of Danielle Steel. The shock was understandable too, for nowhere in Newell's career to date – from *Four Weddings and a Funeral* to *Enchanted April* and *Into the West* – had he suggested he'd even be interested in filming a true story based on Brasco's undercover life in the Mafia. But he was.

Even more intriguing was producer Lou DiGiaimo's attraction to the project. He had known Pistone in high school and continued to socialise with him as an adult, but he never knew the truth about his friend's job until Pistone hit the headlines.

'I had no idea he was working for the FBI,' confessed DiGiaimo. 'We used to play basketball two or three times a week and then, one day, he just disappeared without a trace. About six or seven years later all the New York papers had a front-page story about this FBI agent who went undercover in the Mob, and they kept using the name Pistone. At first I thought it was a joke. I was thinking, can it really be Joe? A few days later he called me and we had dinner. I told him right then, I thought this story would make an incredible book and possibly a movie. He hadn't thought about that yet and he just said, "Well, we'll have to wait until the trials are over." That took four years.'

About the same time as it took to get the movie into production, producer Mark Johnson recalls, 'We were in the middle of *Rain Man* when Lou DiGiaimo brought us this fascinating book. It seemed very much worth developing into a screenplay.' Johnson's first choice of co-producer was his partner Gail Mutrux; he called him as soon as he had finished the book, who in turn called Paul Attanasio, best known for his screenplay of 1994's *Quiz Show*. And, of course, he jumped at the chance of scripting the movie.

Recruiting Mike Newell as the director was equally instinctive. 'We all felt that very strongly,' said Johnson. 'Mike could understand what was most important about this story; the vibrant characters and the both funny and tragic situation they find themselves in. I also think there's something appropriate about having an Englishman direct this movie because sometimes an outsider can see and reveal things about an American way of life that a native would miss. When I first went with Mike to Brooklyn for location scouting, it was like going on a sociological expedition.'

Yet it could have turned out so differently, Newell explains. 'I spent some time in Brooklyn where these guys are still running the same kind of businesses they always have: gambling and loan sharking and so on. I would go out on the weekends, drink and eat with them and hang around in their social clubs. Obviously, there was a lot they wouldn't show me, but I saw as much as I could. It was like being let into the heart of the tribe. They were very generous to me and I became very fond of them, so I had to remind myself that they also did horrendous things, that these men that I was having such a good time with were also ... well, I didn't really want to know.'

Newell would work with that same sense of vigilance in mind as he set about selecting his cast. Although Johnny may have seemed an unconventional choice to many, he did prove to be the correct one. 'This particular role interested him, I think, because the whole character had to run beneath the surface, as it were,' Newell said later. And although the film buffs may be right when they say no one will ever displace Marlon Brando and Al Pacino as the godfathers of the mobsters, Johnny came as close as anyone. In fact, both *Godfather* veterans called Johnny the best actor of his generation.

'He's very polite, a very gentle person in all sorts of ways,' Newell enthused. 'But I also think he has a devil in him. Underneath this wistfulness, you feel a sanction of violence. So there's this terrific mental energy going into keeping these two mutually antagonistic things in balance. That's what keeps you coming back.'

Asked why he chose Johnny, and not someone like Keanu Reeves, Newell was quick to reply. 'Well, I wanted someone who could act, for a start. And Johnny is one of those actors who acts in a kind of long term. You stay with his characterisations throughout a film because he tells you his story in his own good time, and more important, you are willing to wait for it.'

That is certainly true. All the same, Newell continues, 'Johnny doesn't suffer fools gladly. He tends towards a choice of material that's going to interest him intellectually, and has always said to himself that his career comes second.'

Denise Di Novi, producer of both *Edward Scissorhands* and *Ed Wood*, agreed. 'I was so thrilled to see *Donnie Brasco* because I think it was another level for Johnny. You know, a different character. I think he had really created a niche playing the strange guy, and the Donnie Brascos aren't your average person. I think it was a little broader context – the movie and the character.'

Johnny, however, was astonished when he heard what Brando and Pacino said. 'I don't know why people like that say those things, but I mean, obviously, that's great. I'm lucky to be able to say that they are friends of mine, but they are heroes, too. I have nothing but respect for them.'

Others on the *Donnie Brasco* set were well aware of what he meant. They also knew what it meant for Johnny to be filming in Florida, his own childhood stomping ground. As Jefferson Sage, the art director, would point out, it was the promised land, and an integral part of the filming. 'It's bright and colourful and a new start for the guys in the movie. Here was a whole new turf that was virtually wide open for them to exploit. It was exotic, warm and easy. But then that gets closed off to them and it makes coming back to Brooklyn twice as bad, you know, in the depth of winter and all that.'

The decision to cast Al Pacino in the role of the ageing hit-man Lefty Ruggiero was equally instinctive. As instinctive, in fact, as his acceptance. Besides, how could you go wrong with the actor who had established the archetype mobster as successfully as Bela Lugosi had the vampire.

Working with Al, Johnny continues, 'was everything and a whole lot more than I expected. It was a real treat and an honour. I learnt as much as I could, but it's difficult to pick out specifics. I expected him to be very serious and not very loose and playful, but he wasn't like that at all. He was constantly making jokes and making people laugh.'

The feeling was apparently mutual. 'Al was very, very relaxed and didn't feel that he had to compete in any way whatsoever,' Newell elaborated later. 'Johnny was working with Al very close to the beginning of our shooting and they were in a car. Suddenly, and absolutely unmistakably, there's this huge ripping fart, and Johnny said, "I'm terribly sorry, terribly sorry." A little silence fell, then there was another huge fart. Johnny said, "What can I say, I'm terribly sorry." And Al opened the window. Then there was a third one at which Al kind of looked at him, and then it was a whoopee cushion. And Al thought that was the greatest thing since sliced bread.'

In fact, it was the film's central relationship between Pistone and Ruggiero that most probably attracted Newell to the project in the first place. Certainly, the director focused on this element more than any other. How the undercover FBI agent adopted the identity of Donnie Brasco posing as a small-time Florida jewel thief, and Ruggiero, the lowly, embittered Mafia man who unwittingly vouches for him so that he gains access to the Mob world. It was a relationship that must ultimately be betrayed.

In the time Johnny spent with the former FBI agent months before filming got underway, 'I spoke about that with Joe. He said that there was no way you can hang around with someone for six years solid and not feel something for them. On the one hand, you can hate them and despise them, but on the other, you sort of love the guy.'

But, Johnny continues, 'it's wrong to say that Joe was betraying them. If he had been a Mafia guy from the beginning and then turned on his friends and associates, then that would have been a betrayal. But the fact is that Joe came in as an FBI agent and he was just doing his job. He made an enormous sacrifice. He missed his children growing up, he faced the daily threat to his life, and he had to move his family constantly to protect them. He is maybe the strongest person I ever met in my life.'

Pistone was also thoroughly enamoured with Johnny, particularly when 'all I knew about him was what I'd read in the papers. You know about him trashing hotel rooms and stuff. But we spent a lot of time together, we worked out in the gym, and I took him to the FBI academy in Virginia. He wanted to know everything.

'He would even ring my wife and ask questions. He kept saying, "I want to make this right for you because you have to live with this film for the rest of your life and I want to do it justice." And he did. Captured me to a tee. He absorbs so much, he doesn't try. It just comes to him. And he remembers everything. He's like a sponge. He wouldn't even go to see a screening until I could go with him. Most actors wouldn't care. They would just take the money and run. He's a lovely guy.'

Newell agrees with him. But he also explains it was the 'novel point of view about the Mob' that also attracted him, the idea that Brasco is 'a hard and brutal man' operating in a narrative that offers him no convenient escape clauses, no soft or fanciful evasions of fate. As much as anything else, Newell focused on creating an epic of heartbreak that defies even the most cynical viewer's urge to simply grab the title character by the throat and shout 'Fool!'

He is forced to abandon his real family for his Mob

family. His wife's patience with his absences finally runs out and he must ultimately betray his only real friend in the criminal clan for the law enforcement bureaucrats who show not an ounce of understanding, let alone compassion for the soul Brasco has tortured in their service.

That ability is what lends *Donnie Brasco* its morally estranged edge, a blade that can slice friendship and trust in two. If nothing else, *Brasco* is a portrait of secretiveness, watchfulness, danger, duplicity and disguise.

Even with the movie's scope so sharply focused, there were still times when Pistone was resistant to what was being filmed. One of those occasions, Newell remembers, was when 'we were shooting the scene where Johnny as Pistone hits his wife. Pistone was around on the set and there was a fantastic hoo-hah. It took the producer a whole morning to calm him down. He said he would never have hit his wife, and I believe him. But I insisted this was fiction.'

Another time was while the cast and crew were filming in New York, one of four locations commandeered for several scenes. This time, Newell complains, 'I had a woman come up to me in the street and spit in my face; "You think it's a joke! But it's not a joke. That bastard put my husband away. He stacked all the chips against him. He gave false testimony!" So I asked Pistone, did you? And he said, "Absolutely not, I proved all my cases."'

What must be remembered, however, is that the evidence collected by 'Donnie Brasco' led to over 200 indictments and over 100 convictions, and although Pistone continues to live with his wife under an assumed name in an undisclosed location, there is still a $500,000 open contract on his head.

Not that Pistone was convinced he was in any danger. According to Newell, 'He says he isn't because the guys who would carry it out are either in jail or they're too old. Or it's simply that Mob leadership changes. But what he does feel in danger from – and he travels around in disguise, armed all the time – is that some daft kid will come up to him in a bar and shoot him out of a clear blue sky, as a trophy scalp. Something the kid will get kudos from.'

There were, after all, the mobsters in Brooklyn. The same ones Johnny encountered while preparing for his role. 'I found the majority of them to be good guys – real, real gentlemen, family men, good fathers, good husbands. I had the utmost respect for the guys that I met – not exactly what we've come to know in the movies, that sort of wise-guy persona.'

All the same, Newell added, 'They're like unruly children. They'll do the most charming things and then they'll do the most savage things, sometimes almost in the same breath.'

Johnny elaborates. 'I don't think that they're serial killers. Let's put it this way. I think there's a circle in which they live, and within that circle there's a game of survival. But you can tag this to anyone who is, you know, living and has a pulse. That tag would be, if it's him or me, he's going down. I mean, I can't be any more plain than that. That's just the way it is. If somebody's gonna get ya, you're gonna try and get 'em first.'

As a child, it was something Johnny's mother Betty Sue advised him to do. 'She told me when I was really little that you get in a fight with somebody and they're bigger than you, you pick up the biggest fucking brick you can find, and you lay 'em out, you just fucking knock 'em out. I'll never forget it.' Although he may not have been old enough then to understand exactly what she meant, he does today. That's why,' he added, 'my mom is one of my best friends.'

The other self-defence tactic, of course, was guns. 'I have a few in the house, just in case some nightmare happens. I sometimes go shooting as well. Out into the desert and set up beer cans, because when they get really hot and you hit one, there's an enormous explosion. It's nice. I never shoot moving targets though. And living things are out.' His father, on the other hand, he explained, 'has been trying to get me to hunt with him for years. He hunts wild boar. But I can't kill an animal. I can eat quite a few, but I just can't shoot them.'

Although Pistone would most probably agree with that, he wasn't quite so happy with the suggestion that he betrayed the people he was infiltrating. In reality, he argued, 'it was my job'. Yet when he watched the movie for the first time, Newell added, 'He was in tears, really weeping. And I can only guess what was going on inside him. We presented the ethical and emotional side of this case as sharply as we could, and it got to him. If you live with these guys for seven or eight years and they wind up dying grisly deaths it would get to anybody, but Pistone was brilliant when he talked about living with them.'

Newsweek's Karen Schoemer said Johnny's performance was brilliant, especially, she added, as it was 'from someone who has admitted taking drugs as a teenager and who was arrested three years earlier for trashing a fancy New York hotel room'.

So isn't it surprising that Johnny and, not least, Al Pacino, were completely overlooked by the Golden Globe and Oscar committees even though the word around Hollywood predicted Pacino to be a clear favourite for an Oscar nomination. It just didn't seem feasible that the film could go completely unnoticed in the plethora of the two award shows.

Still, it wasn't the first time that Johnny's work had gone completely unappreciated. But he hadn't, *Newsweek* continued to acknowledge, 'become one of the best actors of his generation by playing nice, normal, aw-shucks guys next door. Peers like Brad Pitt and Keanu Reeves may have better track records at the box-office, but Depp has one up on them. He takes chances and he's created a body of work that actually makes sense when taken as a whole.

'The fractured fairytale boy in *Edward Scissorhands*; the beleaguered family caretaker in *What's Eating Gilbert Grape?*; even the morally estranged FBI agent in *Donnie Brasco* share a common bond – they're good-hearted people who find themselves unable to connect with the ones they love.' It was one of the things his characters did best.

CHAPTER 12

'MAYBE ONE DAY I'LL MAKE A MOVIE THAT REALLY
BLOWS PEOPLE AWAY. THE SORT OF MOVIE THAT
I CAN POINT TO ONE NIGHT WHEN I'M REAL OLD AND
WATCHING TV AND SAY TO MY GRANDCHILDREN:
"HEY, GUYS, GRANDPOP WAS PRETTY COOL IN THIS
FILM DON'T YOU THINK?" YEAH – I'D LIKE TO
BE ABLE TO SAY THAT ABOUT MYSELF ONE DAY.'

IN LOVE WITH LOATHING

Five days into his stay with Hunter S Thompson, Johnny longs to sleep. Thompson, the self-styled King of Gonzo journalism and noted author of 1971's *Fear and Loathing In Las Vegas* is not a man noted for keeping regular hours. Like some kind of nocturnal vampire, he would live by night and then, finally, in the late afternoon, trail off to bed for a few hours before rising again. At that moment, Johnny would escape to the basement room, or 'the dungeon' as it was known, at Thompson's isolated Aspen retreat, still exhausted from Hunter's display of tireless excess, knowing that in a very short time the writer would be hammering on the door, yelling for him to get up.

After a couple of days, Johnny recalls, 'I began to appreciate more and more that sleep was my friend. I was staying in the dungeon and it was the darkest room in the house. I'd go down there and lie on the bed, just rest up and read a book and smoke a cigarette. I really needed that time just to recharge before facing Hunter again.'

All the same, Johnny continues, 'He was incredibly generous to let me live in his basement. I spent the first week absorbing as much as I could by staying holed up with nothing but his books and my roll-ups for company. On the sixth day, I suddenly realised the room was packed with gunpowder kegs and I was smoking. I was lucky not to have blown the whole house up. Hunter just laughed when I told him.'

That was two years after the two men first met at the Woody Creek Tavern in Aspen, Colorado, Thompson's favourite drinking haunt. It was Johnny's, too. During his Christmas stay when taking a break from filming, he journeyed out to the ski resort with Kate, her mother and some others for a few days off. What he didn't expect was for Thompson to walk in, Johnny recalls, 'with a Taser gun in his left hand and a huge cattle prod in his right hand, swinging them around getting people out of his way.'

Neither did he expect him to take a seat at Johnny's table, to swap tales about their Kentucky roots; Johnny on Owensboro, Thompson on Louisville. He was even more surprised when he invited Johnny and his party back to his 'fortified compound' to carry on drinking. That compound, it turns out, had enough explosives, small fire-arms, canned food, bottled water and alcohol to survive even the aftermath of a nuclear war.

It was where Johnny's intense interest in the nickel-plated shotgun hanging on Thompson's wall turned to sheer delight. Surprisingly, Johnny recalls, 'He took it down and led me into the kitchen. He had a couple of big tanks of propane in there and handed me some nitro-glycerine capsules. We taped them to the side of the tank, took it out back, and I shot it. I've shot guns since I was eight years old, so I knew I could hit something.

'The target itself – a tube of nitro-glycerine – was pretty small, but the shotgun sprays, so I knew I'd hit something near. But I was kind of like, "I hope I don't miss." And bang! Boof! Bullseye! I got it first shot. There was this 75ft burst of fire, an enormous explosion. It was great fun. I was a little worried about shrapnel, but no one got caught, thank God. Mrs Moss was a little freaked out, but she did well. She hung in there, and when we left, she was kinda like, "Who is that man?"'

That man, it turned out, would be the basis for Johnny's next character on screen, or rather Thompson's alter-ego, Raoul Duke, in the movie version of *Fear and Loathing in Las Vegas*, the Thompson novel that was also Johnny's favourite book.

It was based on a journey that Thompson took with a friend, lawyer Oscar Zeta Acosta, to cover a road race, the Mint 400, for *Sports Illustrated*. 'My idea,' Thompson explained later, 'was to buy a fat notebook and record the whole thing as it happened, then send in the notebook for publication, without editing. But this is a hard thing to do and in the end I found myself imposing an essentially fictional framework on what began as a piece of straight/crazy journalism. As true "Gonzo" journalism, [a style of reporting based on William Faulkner's idea that the best fiction is far more true than any kind of other journalism] this doesn't work at all, and even if it did, I couldn't possibly admit it. Only a goddamned lunatic would write a thing like this and claim it was true.'

First published in *Rolling Stone* magazine under Raoul Duke's name, the magazine promptly gave the game away by revealing Thompson as the author. The initial piece, and the book that followed, was a landmark. A dark and idiosyncratic commentary on what Thompson called 'The Foul Year of Our Lord, 1971'.

By this time, of course, the Sixties had already ended. Nixon was in the White House, the war in Vietnam was still grinding on, the aftermath of the Beatles break-up was prolonged by one of the most disruptive earthquakes in the history of southern California, and it seemed the spirit of free thinking, free love and free drugs, once the buzzwords of a generation, were dead and buried.

Indeed, the Seventies had already begun to undo everything its predecessor had fought so hard for. The spirit of peace and love was pronounced dead at Altamont during a free Rolling Stones concert at a motor speedway arena just outside San Francisco, where a young black man was stabbed to death by Hell's Angels, stage centre, to the tune of 'Sympathy for the Devil', and captured in *Gimme Shelter*, a movie 'coming to a theatre near you' in 1971. The peace, love and innocence of Woodstock was history.

Dead, too, were Jimi Hendrix, Janis Joplin and Jim Morrison, three 27-year-old icons of rock 'n' roll, gone within the space of a year, all attributed to drug overdoses, and in a secret meeting with President Nixon, Elvis Presley offered his personal services as an undercover narcotics agent.

Good news for many was the death sentence for Charles Manson and three of his girl-gang members for the

Tate–LaBianca murders, which had augured the apocalyptic end of flower power in 1969. Sixties' idealism had fast turned to cynicism, and the American dream was swiftly becoming the American nightmare.

Johnny agreed about the themes of Thompson's writing. 'What America was, what it might have been, what it's become now. Although the book is hysterically funny, it's written totally seriously; it's kind of melancholy. It's about the death of the American dream, the death of hope. At that time, Martin Luther King had been murdered, Robert and John F Kennedy had been murdered, there was a gangster in the White House. It was a really weird time. And it's only gotten weirder. I mean, we've recently been scrutinising the specifics of what the President has done with his penis.'

And he was right. Just as it must have seemed right that the only sane direction for Thompson to go was the one he took. Straight over the top and call it 'Gonzo'. That's certainly the route he took when he wrote *Fear and Loathing in Las Vegas* in 1971.

'That's when it all started,' recalls Thompson, 'when I left Vegas for the first time, skipping the hotel bill, driving off in the red convertible all alone, drunk and crazy, back to LA. That's exactly what I felt. Fear and loathing.'

Although critically acclaimed for its literary success for nearly a quarter of a century, it had strangely remained untouched by Hollywood ever since. Strange, that is, when you consider the number of other great works that Hollywood has been involved with, but it could be that the money men considered Thompson's *Fear and Loathing* more difficult than most to bring to the screen. After all, just how do you translate page after page of drug-fuelled madness and paranoia, and bring it to life on celluloid? More important, of course, was finding the right film-maker to do it.

Almost 25 years later, British director Alex Cox, best known for *Repo Man* and *Sid and Nancy*, thought he had the answer. Armed with script and a respectable $5 million budget, he initially approached Johnny to ask him if he was interested in playing the part of Duke/Thompson. He was. Far more important for Johnny, of course, was the seal of approval from Thompson himself. He got that as well.

Cox also got Benicio Del Toro, best known for his role in *The Usual Suspects*, to play Thompson's road companion, Dr Gonzo. He then left for Aspen to meet with Thompson himself. That meeting, however, soon fell on stony ground. Thompson's idea of a fun-filled day that included placing a blow-up sex doll covered in film blood near the side of the road to mark the turning to his house didn't enthral Cox at all. Neither did the sausages Thompson cooked, or the ball game he wanted to watch on TV. 'Jesus Christ,' recalls the author. 'It was a classic example of how not to work, as a director, with writers. First he hated football, refused to watch it, and then I cooked really good sausages, which I prize, and he complained that he was vegetarian.'

Not long after, Cox surrendered his role as director over what the industry deemed as artistic differences of opinion, but another version credited Johnny with the coup. It wasn't until the arrival of Terry Gilliam taking over the director's seat that things improved.

From the outset, Gilliam seemed perfect. The choice was understandable, too, for his career path endorsed his credibility. He had been an audacious interpreter of twentieth, and other, century manners, from *12 Monkeys* to *The Fisher King*, and from *The Adventures of Baron Munchausen* to *Brazil*, *The Time Bandits*, and the Monty Python trilogy.

More importantly, he had the ability to create the impossible on film with a vision that seemed to echo Tim Burton's same defiance of logic. On that point alone, it should be no surprise that Gilliam wanted to work with Johnny, and Johnny with Gilliam.

In fact, it turned out to be the prime reason the director accepted the project in the first place. 'I think Johnny is the best actor of his generation,' he confirmed. 'It was really a combination of the subject matter and Johnny that drove me to it. I don't think there's anything that Johnny can't do. He's very inventive, fast on his feet, funny and incredibly hard working.'

The feeling was apparently mutual. 'Terry came in, grabbed it, shook it around and did it right. He's one of the best directors I've ever worked with, one of the most inventive, pure, organic experiences that I've had. He'll give you a piece of direction, it sparks something in you, and boom, there's a huge explosion or flurry of creativity.'

Still, it was strange the way it came together, Gilliam continues. 'They were basically going to make a $5 million film with Alex Cox directing it. Then Johnny got involved and said, "This isn't enough money to make this film." So the budget crept up to $7 million.

'So they had a script, they had Johnny, and they had $7 million, but they didn't have a director, and so they came to me. I said, "OK. I'll come on. But we'll write a new script and I think you had better double the budget." I think we made it for about $18.5 million in the end.'

Johnny was thrilled. He had found a movie he was interested in, and a director he was interested in making it with. Now, he determined, he would observe Thompson at work and at play by spending three months with the writer at his Colorado home in Woody Creek. On one occasion, he even became 'Ray', his road manager and head of security for a book tour. Not so captivating, however, was arranging the bottle of Chivas and ice, which were required at every stop among other things. Afterwards, Johnny concedes, 'I wouldn't wish it on my worst enemy, trying to wake Hunter Thompson up.'

But that didn't stop Thompson playing a gig at The Viper Room, much the same as Johnny's other personal heroes had done in the past; Johnny Cash, Winona's godfather Timothy Leary, and counter-culture luminary Allen Ginsberg, another friend of Winona's father, Michael Horowitz.

'I felt under tremendous pressure,' Johnny would confess later. 'I was so freaked out by the idea of disappointing Hunter. So I did my best to absorb him. My goal was to steal his soul. That's what I wanted to do, to try and take as much of him as possible and put him into my body.'

He elaborates, 'I know it sounds really goofy and all that stuff, but I felt like him, especially when we were doing it. I found it hard to find Johnny in a way because I felt more like Hunter. Even when I was not working, at the weekends, I felt like Hunter.'

But he felt no reservations about accepting the part.

Afterwards, he raved how the whole thing from beginning to end had been simply exhilarating. So much so that he was still enamoured with Thompson for months after completing the filming, when he was preparing to join the set of his next movie.

But, then again, he wasn't quite so sure about that. 'Maybe I spent too much time with him. Maybe it had gone too deep. I don't know. It was strange. Hunter's an incredible animal, he's really something to watch. On the one hand, he's this great Southern gentlemen, very sensitive, very caring. But on the other he's very sharp and very cutting. He's a great observer. I mean, the fact that Hunter is still around is a miracle. The way he has lived, the life he has built is like no one else I have ever known.'

It probably didn't help that during filming Johnny was calling Thompson up every day, talking with him for four hours at a time. Gilliam, on the other hand, recalls, 'I had as little to do with Hunter as possible. He has this incredible energy and intelligence. But he also makes you crazy. I was like, "Stay away!" I wanted to get it right, but I did not want to sit there and be constantly aware of what he may or may not be thinking. I just had to go my own way.'

The most pressing issue, of course, would be whether the film could misinterpret the use of drugs. In the book, Duke and Dr Gonzo use ferocious amounts of every drug known to man as they encounter real and imagined characters on their surreal, hallucinogenic journey to Vegas. Could, asked some critics, *Fear and Loathing* be seen as a glorification of drug use?

'Absolutely not,' Johnny sighed, and didn't believe for one moment that the movie would do that. 'I mean, when you see this film, and you see what these guys ingest, and then feel, and go through, and then expel from their being, it's not like I watch it and go, "Jesus, what a great idea! Let's get really high and puke," or I'd love to see people wandering around with six hairy tits on their back. I mean, come on, this is like a drug nightmare. What were people expecting – *Peter Pan?* This is *Fear and Loathing.*'

At the other end of the spectrum, of course, those same journalists were itching to ask whether he felt the need to experience personally the effects of several drugs to prepare for the role. 'There are people who don't have to do that, I find acting a little more fun.'

But he also knew exactly what they were getting at. A lot of that he put down to speaking too openly with the press about his past. Sure, 'I have dabbled a bit in my youth,' he reflected years later. 'Experimented in various heinous substances. I know what some of them feel like.'

Unfortunately, he concedes, 'There was a time when I was kind of self-destructive. The brain goes weird on you and I don't know whether it was shock of fame, or just part of growing up. You can't be anonymous any more and you don't get used to that – at least, I don't.'

Maybe as a result of those experiences, continues producer Laila Nabulsi, 'he understood the sensitivity of Hunter that a lot of people can't or don't want to see. The basic image of Hunter, all of the craziness and madness and macho stuff, is just part of the story. Hunter is also a very sensitive, deep, thoughtful person, and Johnny has all those qualities. He has those same eyes, that same deep soul.'

Still, it must have been strange for Johnny to play someone who, in another lifetime, or at least another movie, could easily have turned out to be himself. It had, he explains, 'been screaming to be made into a film since it was published 27 years ago. The book came out of the beginning of the death of the American dream. But Hunter was still out there searching for it, searching madly, hoping that the dream still existed, and all he found was madness in every direction, and tragedy and greed. This book represented a great quest for Hunter, and a kind of exorcism at the same time. It is about hope, it's about insanity, it's about trying to find something out there to believe in.'

One can only imagine what Johnny's parents thought as they watched Johnny playing Raoul Duke, chasing the same dream that they themselves had chased.

Johnny says, 'I think it's a great story that will make people laugh, that will make people think, that will also scare and appal. Some people will see Duke and Dr Gonzo as just a couple of nutcases filling their bodies with heinous chemicals. But it's not about recreation. It's about need.'

All the same, there was an immediate connection between Johnny and Hunter. 'I remember laughing constantly,' recalls Johnny. 'He zeros in on faults and good points immediately. I was with Kate, and I think he went straight for the romantic jugular shit like whether I beat her enough. I probably told him jokingly, "Yeah, she gets a severe beating."'

Johnny also read 'pretty much everything of Hunter's writing that's been published and also lots of stuff that hasn't. I think one of the things that helped with the initial meeting between us was that we're both from Kentucky. Hunter is, beneath it all, a real Southern gentleman.'

The greatest challenge for Johnny, however, was to bond not only emotionally but also physically with his character. 'I tried to make myself look as much like him as possible,' he said. 'I shaved my head on top and just left a kind of short-haired chinchilla around the sides. Hunter's ears are larger than mine, so I wore small devices to make mine poke out a little more. And there's a unique body language that Hunter has, and I could feel myself clicking into that once we started.'

In fact, it was the body language that allowed Johnny to hook into the physical likeness much more easily. His constant bobbing and weaving motion, for instance, and his ever-present cigarette holder functioning almost like an antenna was comparable, some say, to a graceful, if highly offbeat, dancer who is constantly in danger of falling off the stage. Johnny captured that perfectly.

Yet it could have turned out very differently. 'Having Hunter on set for the first time was very intimidating,' explained Johnny. As much, in fact, as it was when Ed Wood's real-life wife visited him on the set during the making of that movie. It was scary, continued Johnny, because 'I was afraid that it might be upsetting for him. But he was great.' Not only that, but he was also very supportive throughout the entire project. 'To allow me to, in a way, become his shadow, in his home, and on the road, 24 hours a day, for months. I was very blessed to have that.

'I really did become him in this film; in fact, too much. He is all the things I want to be – sensitive, cutting, sharp, observant. When I lived with him I wanted to swallow his thoughts and emotions. Actor Bill Murray (who played Thompson in 1980's *Where the Buffalo Roam*) called me up before we started filming and said, "This is your warning call. Hunter never leaves you. It will take years to shake him off." And he was right.'

Fear and Loathing in Las Vegas was scheduled for a May 1998 release in the States, and for September in Britain following its première at the Cannes Film Festival. It was among the competition entries judged by Martin Scorsese's jury, that interestingly enough included Winona Ryder.

The critical reaction was muted, if a little bemused. The movie, like the book, lacked plot, the general consensus ran, even if praise for Johnny's performance far exceeded the expectations of the film itself.

There was, however, a sting in the tail. Johnny's performance, no matter how good or bad it was, was seen by many as 'another of his quirky roles in a career that has studiously avoided the mainstream'.

But why, asked those same critics, does he avoid the mainstream? 'It could be ignorance,' Johnny attempted to explain. But then again, 'It could be that I'm just incredibly thick and dumb. But it takes commitment. I feel deeply committed to these characters I've chosen because I have an interest in them. I find them stimulating and I think it's something I can do that's maybe a little different. I think it's very easy to take the paved road, and I think it's very boring.'

He even blamed that commitment to his break-up with Kate Moss. Their on-off-on romance now seemed off for good, and Johnny knew exactly where the blame should lie. 'I let my career get in the way and I didn't give her the attention I should have done. We had so much going for us, but I've just been very stupid. I was a horrific pain in the butt to live with. Trust me, I'm a total moron at times.

'We ended up living apart and only talking on the phone every two weeks. I really feel like I blew it with Kate. There's a big part of me that really misses her and I keep wondering why we aren't together, thinking about starting a family.'

But maybe that was another reason why his relationship with Kate didn't really work out, as much as it hadn't worked out with Winona. Both had burgeoning careers in their respective fields, and perhaps children did not rank quite so highly in their personal ambitions as they did in Johnny's.

All the same, that didn't stop Kate joining him at Cannes, or at the Las Vegas première. It even sparked new speculation of a reconciliation. It probably didn't help that Johnny was still wearing the huge silver skull ring she once gave him. They were, after all, nothing more than just good friends, Johnny insisted. 'She was in town and she was going to be seeing the movie anyway. Everyone's thinking, "Oh my God, they're back together." But we're not.'

Three months before Cannes, Johnny and Kate's appearance at the 1998 Rolling Stones Madison Square Garden gig with Ethan Hawke and Uma Thurman did much the same. 'Johnny Depp and Kate Moss appear to be back together,' shouted the *New York Daily News*. On leaving the concert, the paper continued, 'Depp was in high spirits. When *paparrazzo* John Barrett dropped his house keys, Depp picked them up, then asked Barrett to "prove" they belonged to him. Barrett did, prompting Depp to toss them back on the sidewalk.'

Johnny's next role appeared just as he was wrapping up work on *Fear and Loathing in Las Vegas*. His agent, Tracy Jacobs, probably thought it was perfect for him. Or at least, that it would make a welcome change.

Rand Ravitch's *The Astronaut's Wife* would commence filming on 14 January 1998 for release late the following year. Even in pre-production it sounded promising.

Imagine it, 'Johnny Depp hunted by aliens,' warned one of many journalists visiting the location filming in New York. 'Shades, black coat, cigarillo in his mouth, hair short as never before, this is the cool look in which Depp is hurrying through the streets of New York. At the top of a subway staircase he stops quickly and grabs a black attaché case which a young woman has put on the railing only seconds before. Carrying the explosive documents under his arm he disappears in the crowd.'

It was, according to production company New Line's advance information, a spine chilling, psychological thriller about a woman driven to the brink of madness by the terrifying suspicion that the father of her unborn twins is not the man she married – he may not even be human.

Jillian and Spencer Armacost, played by Charlize Theron and Johnny, are the perfect couple, living the American dream, until one fateful day when Spencer, an astronaut on a routine Shuttle mission, mysteriously loses contact for two minutes with mission control. What happened in those eerie two minutes of silence Jillian will never know.

Although Spencer returns home alive and is decorated by the President as a hero, Jillian begins to realise that she is witness to a terrifying metamorphosis. When Spencer announces that he is quitting the space programme for a job as a defence contractor in New York, a city that he has always hated, Jillian reluctantly agrees to his decision.

Once settled in New York, Jillian and Spencer resume a normal life – on the surface. When Jillian discovers she is pregnant with twins, Spencer is thrilled. Yet the happy news is overshadowed by haunting visions of outer space and strange sounds that creep into Jillian's dreams. She is confused and scared – her dreams seem like reality and her life with Spencer has dissolved into strange days of loneliness and confusion.

Her fears and suspicions increase when Sherman Reese, a NASA official who was fired for 'paranoid delusions' about the incident in space, tracks her down and shares his findings that something did indeed occur during those missing two minutes, something horrifying that has changed Spencer and made him an unwilling participant in an other-worldly attempt to invade earth.

With Spencer becoming increasingly deranged and his actions and whereabouts a complete mystery, Jillian knows she is in a race against time to find the truth about her husband before he changes the future of mankind for ever.

With his work on *The Astronaut's Wife* completed, maybe Johnny should have taken a break. But he had already committed himself to another movie, and he was damned if he was going to pull out.

Empire magazine, in its countdown to future films, would suggest that for *The Ninth Gate*, 'Depp remains in similar territory as the upcoming *Astronaut's Wife* for this follow-up. Cutting back on his usual fee for the chance to work with Roman Polanski, the film, based on the 1997 novel *The Club Dumas* by Arturo Perez-Reverte will see Depp as a rare books expert who, while attempting to track down two copies of an ancient demonic text, becomes embroiled in a supernatural conspiracy over which he has no control. Add the Polanski trademarks of a multi-million dollar cast, including Frank Langella, Emmanuelle Seigner and Lena Nolin, and some picturesque continental settings for the unexplained events, the outlook is decidedly rosy – especially for those who prefer their horror on the intelligent side.'

It was here, during location filming in Paris, that Johnny would first clap eyes on Vanessa Paradis without even knowing who she was. Twelve years earlier, Vanessa's first single, 'Joe Le Taxi', had stormed the international charts when she was just 14 years old.

By then she was about to make her mark on French cinema with her début in 1989's *Noce Blanch*, and over the next ten years would feature in another four features with the much acclaimed *The Girl on the Bridge* in 1998. With her Lolita-esque looks she also made her mark in the world of fashion and photography as the new face for Chanel's Coco perfume and the body for Jean-Paul Goude's pictures.

But when Johnny spotted her at the bar of the Hotel Costes, he knew little about her. But that didn't stop him buying her a drink, and in an echo of his meeting Kate Moss, invited her over to his table. Even if he wasn't quite ready to dive into a new relationship, he certainly underestimated the strength of his own emotions.

Only a few months after they met, they were sharing a flat in the upstate Montmartre district of Paris, and a few months after that she was pregnant with his child. And if everything went according to plan, Johnny and Vanessa's daughter, Lily-Rose Melody Depp, would be born on 27 May 1999, in Paris, France. She was.

'I want to carry a child, to conceive it and to feed it,' she had said in an interview the previous year. Johnny, too, had said much the same at Cannes just over a year earlier. 'There's a part of me that would love to settle down and have a couple of kids, a wife and goldfish and watch television every night till eleven. I want to be an old man with a beer belly sitting on a porch. A part of me would love that, but another part of me needs to roll round in the mud.'

Even Vanessa's parents were delighted. 'She has introduced Johnny to the whole family and they find him charming,' revealed one of their friends. 'He obviously dotes on her.' But according to some, the news would be more than heartbreaking to Kate Moss, who at the time was recovering from exhaustion at London's Priory clinic, where patients are treated for depression, eating disorders, and drug and alcohol abuse.

It was from where Kate, shortly before her discharge, would almost burn the place down, just as Winona had almost done five years earlier in her Portugal hotel room, when she fell asleep with a burning cigarette between her fingers.

But according to Jess Hallett of Kate's agency, Storm Models, 'The fire was out before the three fire engines arrived. It was all over very quickly and it was no big deal. Kate certainly wasn't embarrassed by it. More than anything else, she thought it was amusing.'

That is probably true. At the same time, though, the

press couldn't help writing about how the incident had seemingly been sparked off by Johnny himself. He apparently decided to cheer Kate up with a 'get well soon' BMW. She was so excited, noted New York's *Daily Post*, 'that she asked the chauffeur to take her for a spin around the grounds'. He did. The trouble was, Kate had placed one of her meditating candles too close to the scarf her mother had given her, and it went up in flames. So did her room. It was, observed London's *Evening Standard*, the second of 'Depp's ex-girlfriends to accidentally start a fire on breaking up with the actor'.

It would even invite rumours that the couple were back together. According to Dominic Mohan writing in the *Sun* less than a month later, 'They spent an intimate evening together at a private party in Notting Hill, West London, where my sources tell me they were nattering for hours. And although they left separately, Johnny's car and driver were spotted minutes later outside Kate's nearby home despite Johnny's impending fatherhood with Vanessa Paradis.'

Johnny, of course, let the speculation drift over his head, but still the stories of a reconciliation rattled on. Another in America's *National Enquirer* went even further when it suggested, 'There's no doubt about it, Johnny's still in love with Kate and she with him.' According to one insider talking to the same tabloid, 'When Vanessa read British news reports about Johnny and Kate getting back together she was hopping mad.'

It was the same when Johnny and Winona were together. Rumours abounded that both had been stepping out with other young stars. Now, as then, Johnny, Kate and

Vanessa ignored the tattle, refusing even to dignify the tales with a response.

Whatever else, Johnny, now barely 36, still had kids on his mind. 'I thought the time was right. I'm getting broody. What scares me is the thought of not having kids some day. I'm ready to have a young 'un. But I also have a traditional idea of marriage, too – a home in the country, a picket fence, a couple of dogs. It's a big dream of mine.'

Less than a month after he had fininshed *The Ninth Gate*, Johnny boarded a plane for London. Tim Burton, his old ally from *Edward Scissorhands* and *Ed Wood*, would be waiting for him when he got there, and having worked with Johnny twice before, he knew exactly what he would be getting – one of America's most respected actors.

Once again, it was no surprise that Johnny agreed to join forces with Burton, this time for Andrew Kevin Walker's adaptation of Washington Irving's classic story, *The Legend of Sleepy Hollow*.With its original unwieldy title changed to the snappier *Sleepy Hollow*, the movie would, according to *Entertainment Weekly*, be a huge departure from the original tale. In many ways, it picks up where the classic left off, and there would be far more focus on blood and guts. A sort of direct homage to the Hammer horror films of the late fifties and early sixties.

Although Hammer was a small British film production company that had turned out routine B-movies for almost twenty years since the 1930s, it was not until the late fifties when *The Curse of Frankenstein* and *Dracula* had ushered in a whole new era of the horror movie with a style and panache that made Hammer Films world famous. With more than seventy horror, science fiction, prehistoric adventure and thriller films over the next two decades, Hammer firmly established themselves as the master of all the above genres.

With that in mind, and huge fans of anything Hammer, it is probably true to say that the most exciting cast member for both Burton and Johnny was Christopher Lee, the British actor who to this day is one of cinema's favourite villains, especially from his early Hammer horror days and his most famous role as Count Dracula. With his more recent outing as Saruman in *Lord of The Rings*, he has both terrified and delighted cinema audiences in a career spanning fifty-six years and three hundred screen credits. But it was *Sleepy Hollow* that brought him back to the fore, out of retirement, and according to the *Guardian*, was now the coolest actor on the planet.

In his 2003 autobiography, Lee recalls that Burton wanted him to appear for five minutes at the beginning of the film. And that was enough, it seemed, 'to prefigure a roll of luck' that has lasted him to the present day. In the opening scene in the town hall, Lee's message as Burgomaster to Constable Crane, was to proceed to a faraway town, called Sleepy Hollow in the mountains where several people have had their heads lopped off, 'clean as dandelions', and bend his scientific intellect to resolving the mystery.

'The story is comic gothic' says Lee. 'And Johnny, who became a lasting friend, made an excellent job of dealing with the weird phenomenon of the headless horseman who erupted from a tree and hunted terrified members of the Dutch community. The legend was spun around the idea of the restless corpse of a Hessian soldier left over from the Revolutionary War. Hessians apparently filed their teeth to points, as shown in the head when discovered, and this in my view, was as alarming as the absence of a head. '

Even if the film was Burton's personal tribute to Hammer, the setting, according to one observer, still embodied the Burton trademark. That unexpected strangeness that is strangely expected from a Burton movie. 'Imagine the old scary forest you used to hang out in as a kid. Imagine digging this whole forest up – trees, hills and all – and planting it in the middle of a studio. Well, that's sort of what it was like. But better. You see whilst I was convinced that it was real, there was something unreal about it.

'You know the opening of *Beetlejuice* – the way there is something unsettling about the landscape? Well, that's just what they got here. The trees were devoid of leaves, and were painted to look quite ghostly. The backdrops were all quite impressionistic, and mainly monochrome. The more you looked at this forest, the more unsettling it became.'

Certainly that was the opinion of the clutch of actors recruited for the other parts. Johnny had already agreed to appear as Ichabod Crane long before the rest of the cast was assembled. Christopher Walken played the grisly galloping apparition with his own head tucked out of sight. Michael Gambon and Miranda Richardson played Baltus Van Tassel and the Old Crone respectively.

Although not credited for his performance as a frightened coach passenger being chased by the headless horseman was Martin Landau, the distinguished American actor who had, of course, played Bela Lugosi, regarded by many a film buff as the only true King of the Count Dracula's, in Burton's *Ed Wood* – and quickly becoming a veteran of Burton movies (and Johnny's).

Michael Gough, another Hammer regular, just a few years older than Christopher Lee also came out of retirement for another cameo. The decision to cast Christina Ricci, Johnny's co-star from *Fear and Loathing*, as the leading lady, Katrina Van Tassel, was equally instinctive. She remembers her first meeting with Johnny on the set of *Mermaids* very well, mainly because he was with Winona at the time.

'I was nine years old and didn't know what "gay" was, and when I asked Winona, she said, "I can't tell you, ask Johnny". Johnny explained how there were different theories about why people were gay, what it was to be gay, and – this is what I couldn't figure out – how gay people have sex. He was amazing like that. Eight years later, I'm going into rehearsal on *Fear and Loathing* and he remembered me, our discussions, and my mother, Sarah. He said to her, "Hi, Sarah, how are you?" and asked about my brothers. He was really sweet, kind and gentle.'

Even as he worked on the Tim Burton movie, and awaited the release of his 1998 cameo as himself in the French art house movie *LA Without A Map*, Johnny was being tentatively linked opposite his old flame Winona Ryder in Michaelangelo Antonioni's latest film *Just To Be Together*. Johnny's publicist, however, had not even heard of it. Nor had Winona's. But according to *Now* magazine, Matt Damon, Winona's then current boyfriend, was more concerned than most.

He adores Winona, confided one of those convenient 'friends' who always seem to be on hand to comment about showbiz affairs of the heart. 'Johnny has always protested that he still loves Winona, while she has always held a special place for him in her heart because he was her first real love.'

Such a premise was not altogether to anyone's benefit, least of all the tabloids. 'It's not as if Johnny and I are buddy-buddy,' affirmed Winona. 'But it's nice to know we can have a friendship. It's good to be able to think about him without having a horrible feeling in the pit of my stomach, or cringing or feeling heartbroken or like he hates me. After you break up, you go through all those feelings.'

But break-ups, Winona elaborates, are 'hard for anybody, but it's particularly tough when your life is being documented and you see the person's picture everywhere. Most people don't have that added problem when they break up. Our break-up was like the never-ending story because it was such a public thing. We didn't know how to break up. I had my first real relationship with Johnny. It was a fiercely deep love that I don't know that I'll ever .... the first love is like that, isn't it? It was a wild time back then.'

Not so wild was the fact that both stars had been linked to projects before that never came to anything. And still are to this day. Most recent was the rumour of the leading lady role in Tim Burton's *Sleepy Hollow* that was eventually taken by Christina Ricci. If those rumours were true, and Winona did actually pass on the role, it would have been for no other reason than she had latched onto *Girl Interrupted* as both star and producer, and didn't want anything to conflict with the movie that, some say, had simply become an obsession to her.

Another that had been doing the Hollywood rounds ever since Johnny and Winona had made *Edward Scissorhands* together was a film version of *Dream Lovers*, the true story of Bobby Darin and Sandra Dee, based on the book by Barry Levinson, Darin's son, and at the time, linked Johnny alongside Winona in the title roles. According to the Internet, eight years later, Johnny was still in the running for the part. And interestingly enough, Winona had been reading the book when she was shooting *Boys* two years earlier.

And another biopic, *Empire: The Life, Legend and Madness of Howard Hughes*, also linked Johnny to the title role for what many believed would be his most challenging part.

A millionaire since age 18 years of age, Hughes was a celebrity playboy made famous by producing such films as *Hells Angels* and *The Outlaw*. Above all, he was made famous for his love of flying. As much, if not more than Charles Lindberg was. His romances with some of Hollywood's most beautiful women were equally notorious. Jean Harlow and Katharine Hepburn among them. More tragically, of course, he was best known for his descent into isolation. It began after he survived a near-fatal air crash and became dependent on prescription drugs, much the same as Elvis Presley would decades later.

At the time of his death, he was long-haired, long finger-nailed and confined to his bedroom for much of the time. Not only that, but he had developed a debilitating fear of infection and disease. According to the book, on which the film would be based, his arms were spotted with broken ends of hypodermic needles embedded in his skin.

There were even plans of Johnny linking again with Terry Gilliam, his director from *Fear and Loathing in Las Vegas*, for a film version of Miguel de Cervantes classic,

Don Quixote. He would be cast as a modern day man who is sent back to the seventeenth century where Quixote mistakes him for his sidekick, Sancho Panza. With a working title of *The Man Who Killed Don Quixote*, the film was eventually green lighted for production in early 2001 by the French arm of Britain's Studio Canal Plus with a reported thirty-two million dollar budget.

But sadly, the film, the first that would have placed Johnny and Vanessa side by side in the starring roles seemed almost doomed from the start. It wasn't only the chance to work together but also the added bonus for Johnny and Vanessa to be with Lily-Rose while working. Although looking back, without shooting any scenes together, Vanessa says she 'would have been scared to play in the same movie.' She didn't, she admits, want to disappoint the one man she most wanted to impress with her acting. 'He is much more experienced than I am. And I want him to be proud of me in all fields.'

Proud or not, the practical similarities to *Divine Rapture* six years before were many. Once again, production was halted and suspended after only five days of shooting. French actor, Jean Rochefort, cast as Quixote, was forced out of the production after suffering a double herniated disc, and apparently, could not be replaced.

That and an apparent myriad of other reasons. Not least the financial uncertainty that now seemed to relegate the project to the back burner. Although many claimed shooting would restart two months later, with or without Rochefort, from watching Keith Fulton and Louis Pepe's documentary made about the making and unmaking of the movie, *Lost in La Mancha*, it seemed unlikely. Having so firmly established his vision for the film, Gilliam had already spent years raising the required funding from European sources to pass over Hollywood and produce a film without feeling divorced from it or to have it recut and buried by the time the film was released. An experience many a director has put up with in the past. One of those was Gillian Armstrong, who last worked in Hollywood on 1991's *Fires Within*, which turned out to be a disaster. Today Armstrong sighs philosophically any time she discusses the project. 'It was the old Hollywood story. It's part of the game. They put up the money and then they tell the director who's made them a hundred-million-dollar success that she doesn't have the final cut. It's the luck of the draw, really.' And Gilliam did want to take that chance.

If Johnny and Vanessa were feeling as disappointed about the setback as Gilliam was, they didn't have long to mourn. Roman Polanski, Johnny's director from *The Ninth Gate* presented him with the Cesar, the French equivalent of the Oscar that honoured his contribution to the arts. Johnny responded with sheer delight and a taped message he prepared because his French, he openly admitted, wasn't that great.

'I don't really understand the concept of praise in general and I hate the idea of competition. The only person against whom I'm fighting is me, to go as far as possible each time in my work. Nobody is better, we are just all different. But it's a great honour to receive this present from France because I love and respect your country which gives the chance to art to stay alive. To everyone who followed me on this road, I'm deeply grateful. Thanks very much.'

Enjoying the freedom of weekends away from filming, Johnny and Vanessa continued spending time together, unaware of what was about to hit them that February 1999 evening when they left London's Mirabelle restaurant. Neither for that matter, did the photographers waiting outside to snap their pictures.

'We had been tipped off that Depp was at the restaurant and when we arrived, he was already there,' explained one of the photographers. 'He came to one of the side doors and wanted one of the cameras, and kept saying he didn't want his picture taken. He said if we took a picture he'd smash our heads in. He'd kill us. We just thought he was being over-dramatic. Shortly afterwards, his girlfriend came out covered up and one of the photographers took a couple of pictures.'

That was it, continued the photographer, 'Depp said, "Do you want a fucking mess? I'll fucking kill you." Then he came out with a piece of wood in his hand that had been propping up the door. He must have picked it up inside. He threatened to smash our heads in and muscled up to each of us and chased us, threatening us with this piece of wood. He chased us down the road. All the time, none of us took a single picture.

'We called the police after this had gone on for five minutes. Then the guy with him came up and pushed my camera into my face, cutting my head. I had started to walk back towards the restaurant as the flashing lights appeared. Depp chased me again with the wood tucked under his arm, and became very nasty. Within seconds, the police jumped out and grabbed him. He still had the wood in his possession. Even as he was being shoved into the back of a police van, he kept lashing out until the police grabbed the wood from him.'

Whatever the reasons for Johnny's outburst, and they were probably to do with his rebuttal of media exposure, Johnny would not make any comments about the incident afterwards. That was left to his spokesperson and Scotland Yard. 'A 35-year-old man was cautioned and released without charge. He is not on bail and does not have to report back to us.'

Unfortunately, there were a lot of people who roundly criticised Johnny's behaviour. Not even the headlines of HOLLYWOOD WILDMAN'S NIGHT OF SHAME could help his defence. More fatefully, of course, were the pictures of his arrest adorning the tabloids the following morning that did nothing more than add fuel to the fire.

But according to Winona Ryder, 'He's such a nice guy. Certainly some of the things I hear about him I know aren't true, you know, some of the rumours. All the bad boy stuff. He's not a bad boy, he's a good boy, and he never causes any real damage. He's a really wonderful guy.'

And she was probably right. Although he would join Dawn French for a Comic Relief sketch from *The Vicar of Dibley*, and also play a cameo role in the last ever episode of his other favourite British television comedy, *The Fast Show*, he decided to maintain a comparatively lower profile than he had of late. Although to some, his recent behaviour with the London paparazzi encouraged an onslaught of criticism from those who didn't care much for celebrities behaving badly, it did encourage Johnny to perhaps reconsider the key to his success. Although he made his living in Hollywood, he didn't have to live his life there as well.

CHAPTER 13

'I'D LIKE TO HAVE THE OPPORTUNITY TO KEEP WORKING. I'M STILL A LITTLE SHOCKED THAT I KEEP GETTING GIGS, KEEP GETTING JOBS. I FEEL VERY FORTUNATE, VERY LUCKY, THAT PEOPLE STILL HIRE ME.'

A CAREER ON THE
RISE AGAIN

When Winona was sentenced to 480 hours of community service, three years' probation and charged thousands of dollars in fines in October 2002, almost one year after she was caught shoplifting at Saks Fifth Avenue in Beverly Hills, Johnny, no stranger to tabloid scrutiny, was horrified by the way the media handled and targeted her during the heavily over-publicised trial. Although he hadn't spoken with Winona for a while, and despite her being dragged over what Johnny termed 'broken glass', he was sure his ex-fiancée would bounce back in no time. 'She's a good girl and she's also very strong. She'll make her way through it.'

Although she still has to do that, Johnny was no less reticent about adding his name to Winona's fight to have three convicted murderers released simply because she was convinced of their innocence. She had even taken to wearing a bracelet honouring the trio. Known as The Memphis Three, Damien Echols, Jason Baldwin and Jessie Miskelley were teenagers when they were arrested for the ritualistic murder of three eight-year-old boys in West Memphis, Arkansas, in 1993. This happened in the same year that Winona had crusaded to find kidnapped child Polly Klaas's killer. It was probably the 1996 televised documentary *Paradise Lost: The Child Murders At Robin Hood Hills* that raised questions about the guilt of the three men and prompted a number of stars, including Johnny, to join Winona's campaign.

At this time Johnny was enjoying his most successful run of top-line successes. That run had started at the 2000 Venice Film Festival, when the first of those successes, *Before Night Falls*, had its first outing on the big screen and went on to win the Grand Jury Prize. It was the second feature film from New York artist turned filmmaker Julian Schnabel, who had made his name with his 1996 directional debut, *Basquiat*, about the Manhattan graffiti artist who rose from homelessness to fame before sinking into madness.

Much the same territory is covered in *Before Night Falls*. Based on the posthumously published memoir by Cuban poet Reinaldo Arenas, the film is an episodic examination of the exiled author's life, from his childhood to his death in New York City.

Arenas was born into crushing poverty in pre-Castro Cuba and, from a young age had, according to his teacher, a gift for poetry. When his grandfather heard of this, he beat the boy, which more or less set the pattern for Arenas's life. Despite his attempts to exercise his gift as a poet and novelist, society continually slapped him down. It probably didn't help that he was also homosexual.

In the film and in real life, Arenas believed the great betrayal in his life was Fidel Castro. As a teenager, he had hitchhiked to the hills and joined the revolution, but once Castro came to power and spread his anti-intellectual and anti-homosexual message, Arenas became an outcast, and found himself a stranger in his own country. Finally, he was thrown into a Cuban prison for seven years until 1980. It was only then he took advantage of the boat exodus for criminals, gays, the mentally ill and others considered unfit to be Cubans. Ten years on, in Manhattan and dying of AIDS, he committed suicide with pills and, just to be sure of success, a plastic "I Love NY" bag over his head.

As film critic Roger Ebert wrote in his review, *Before Night Falls* tells the story of Arenas life through the words of his work and the images of Schnabel's imagination. 'Schnabel, the painter, makes his screen a rich canvas of dream sequences, fragmented childhood memories and the wild Cuban demimonde inhabited by Arenas and others who do not conform. There is no sequence more startling than one where Arenas stumbles onto a ragtag commune of refuseniks and find that, in the roofless ruin of an old cathedral, they are building a hot air balloon with which they hope to float to Florida.'

Playing Arenas on film was Javier Bardem, a Spanish actor with a speciality in macho heterosexuality. 'But he doesn't play Arenas as a gay man, so much as a man whose body fits like the wrong suit of clothes,' Ebert's review continues. 'The audience do, of course, accept Arenas as gay in the movie simply because the story says he is, and because there are, after all, no rules about how a homosexual should look or behave, but there is somehow the feeling that the movie's

Arenas is not gay from the inside out, but has chosen the lifestyle as part of a compulsion to defy Castro in every possible way.'

The film contains two more convincing homosexual characters, both played by Johnny. Lieutenant Victor, a sleek, tight trousered military officer, and 'Bon Bon', a flamboyant transvestite who struts through Castro's prison and proves incredibly useful by smuggling out one of Arenas's manuscripts, concealing it in a place where most of us would be most inconvenienced by a novel.

According to the film production notes, Bardem was thrilled to work alongside Johnny. 'I think he did amazing work and he was very generous, very helpful. He really got into the mood of the character, Bon Bon, and that scene with him as Lieutenant Victor is something that will stay in my memory. I admire him a great deal, as an actor and a human being.'

Despite his cameo performance alongside an almost recognisable Sean Penn and French heartthrob Olivier Martinez, best known for his role opposite Diane Ladd in Richard Gere's *Unfaithful*, and current beau of Kylie Minogue, Schnabel was equally thrilled to have Johnny on board. As he told television's *Reel to Real* host Christopher Heard, at the Toronto Film Festival, 'Johnny could not have been cooler about the whole thing. I told him what I wanted him to do, and he did it. I really admire him for it and really am grateful that he took the time to work with me on this.'

Even though a relatively small cameo role, it wasn't the only cameo Johnny was playing. Before shooting *Before Night Falls*, he had played a small part in *The Man Who Cried*, which, to this day, is perhaps Johnny's least seen film.

Set in Paris on the eve of World War II, the film is a romantic drama about the diverse lives of four strangers that intersect as a result of the choices each is forced to make in order to survive. Suzie, a young Jewish singer played by Christina Ricci, is befriended by a glamorous Russian dancer who helps her to find her voice and guides her through the magical city of lights. She also finds the joy of love as she is captivated by the mysterious ways of an enigmatic gypsy, played by Johnny, and danger in the deception of a wilful Italian opera singer. As history unfolds around her, Suzie is forced to choose between staying with her only love or escaping Paris as her only hope of survival. It is out of this bitter crucible that Suzie finally finds the strength to achieve her dreams and end up in Hollywood.

So enjoyable was the experience of playing two cameos, that Johnny decided to repeat the experience when he moved into shooting his next movie, *Chocolat* – a comic fable about how just one taste of life's pleasures can change a person, a relationship and a town. It is a tale of temptation, repression and the liberating powers of the senses, a comedic story of an escalating small town war, sparked by the passions and fears aroused by the arrival of a mysterious chocolate shop.

At the heart of the story is Vianne Rocher, a woman possessed with special powers, who arrives in the French village of Lansquenet to open a chocolaterie purveying luscious candies that can, in addition to tantalising the tongue, cure lost hopes and awaken unexpected emotions. Her effect on the village is immediate and extraordinary. The elderly find themselves re-experiencing young love; troubled couples regain their spark and sniping neighbours become happy friends.

But Vianne's sumptuous candies also arouse something else – an escalating battle between passion and moral indignation. As some in the village begin to let go, others clamp down, led by the righteous Comte de Reynaud, who also declares Vianne to be public enemy number one. Just as she is about to raise the white flag, an unexpected romance with a stranger forces her to choose between leaving her hostile surroundings or making a true difference to the townsfolk.

Based on novelist Joanne Harris's 1999 novel, *Chocolat* is also the story of the battles that the free-spirited Vianne undertakes in the name of living life without denial. As with the novel, critics and readers alike were swept up by the dramatic use of chocolate as a metaphor for the liberating powers of pleasure.

One of those drawn to Harris's tale was Swedish director Lasse Hallström, the original exiting director of Cher and Winona's *Mermaids*. At that time he was probably best known for 1985's *My Life As A Dog*. Since then, of course, he has won unlimited acclaim for the multiple Oscar nominated *The Cider House Rules* starring Michael Caine and, in between, for taking the directional seat for Johnny's 1993 *What's Eating Gilbert Grape?*

What Hallström found so fascinating in Harris's unusual fable was a quality he always looks for in his cinematic storytelling. That is, the celebration of the funny, eccentric and wonderfully unpredictable ways human beings behave with one another.

More importantly, perhaps, he found himself enchanted by the story's exploration of life's most delectable moments and how they can arise from the bitter, the dark and the semi-sweet. In many ways, the story advocates not just tolerance of indulgent pleasures like chocolate, but also calls for a deeper appreciation of the wide expanse of human foibles and quirks. 'To me it is a very funny fable about temptation and the importance of not denying oneself the good things in life. It's about the constant conflict in life between tradition and change. And at its very centre it is about tolerance and the consequences of not letting other people live out their own lives and beliefs.'

Even more intriguing to Hallström was the multi-layered tone, which has the magical essence of a fairytale, and presents a series of characters whose emotions and concerns, from marital mistakes to family dishonesties, are palpably, often humorously real. But what interested him most was the 'broad range of elements in the story; the dramatic, comedic, at times farcical, the poetic, a comic fable that doesn't simplify its character portraits but is rooted in reality.

'I think a noticeable common thread in all my movies is a fascination with depicting human irrationality in all its wondrous, endearing forms. *Chocolat* offered the opportunity to explore yet another set of character eccentricities. In this story, the characters are full of contradictions and therefore come alive and enter our hearts. The heroine of the story is Vianne, a truly free spirit but at the same time a prisoner to her destiny. Her nemesis, the Comte de Reynaud, appears in control but is a prisoner to his sense of tradition. He looks through the town and sees sinners and failures. Vianne sees only human beings with flaws that might be forgiven.'

Producer Kit Golden knew that there was only one contender for directing it – and that was Hallström. In fact, he was the first one she thought of. Neither could she quite believe her luck when she asked Juliette Binoche if she was interested in the role of Vianne. She was, and jumped at the opportunity. For Golden, it was 'like a dream come true.'

Interestingly, it was Binoche that Hallström had also thought of. 'Juliette was always the first choice, and it was an absolute treat to have this chance to work with her. Her character is the centre of the story and Vianne must stand for kindness, tolerance and the free-spiritedness of love. Juliette was able to capture this because her approach to her work is to always be emotionally present in the scene. She respects the camera and knows just how little you need to convey a deep emotion. I think she was really able to expand in this role, which is different from anything she's done before.'

Another first choice was Johnny for the role of the vagabond traveller, Roux. Even so, as the film's romantic lead, it was a role he has rarely been seen in. All the same, he was drawn both to the movie's iconoclastic love story and to working with Hallström for a second time. 'I would do just about anything Lasse asked of me,' Johnny admits. 'This was such a beautifully written script, and it fits so well with Lasse and his interest in telling stories that actually try to say something in an entertaining, funny and different way.'

It also offered Johnny the chance to create a rough-and-tumble traveller with a Django Reindhardt-like passion for the steel guitar blues, which sat with Johnny perfectly. Enthusiastically explaining the attraction to his character, Johnny said, 'I thought Roux would be really into old blues, and this is the first time I've actually played the guitar on film.' But another inspiration, he admits, was Juliette Binoche. 'She's so beautiful and deep, she makes you fall instantly in love with her. She's an intensely committed actress and if art is possible in cinema, I think she comes as close as anyone can.'

Even though Johnny had only seventeen minutes of on-screen time, he still bought a wonderful presence and a true leading man quality to the film, raves Hallström. 'I'm always impressed by what he does. His choices are always very tasteful and very accurate and beyond that, he is a wonderful, kind man.'

Another of Johnny's tasteful choices, and more proof that he was indeed a reliable actor who always chose interesting projects, was *Blow*. Premiered in London in May 2001, for which Johnny travelled from France via Eurotunnel, it was the true story of George Jung, an average small-town American boy who decided to pursue the American Dream by becoming the first American to import cocaine into the United States on a large scale.

In just a few short years during the 1970s, powder cocaine turned from being a relatively obscure illegal drug into a multi-billion dollar international business with the power to make and break nations. Most people know that behind the surge in cocaine's popularity were powerful Colombian drug cartels determined to make money no matter what the cost. What most people don't know is that the Colombian narco-lords had an American connection who made it all possible.

In no time at all, Jung was sleeping, breathing and eating money, living out a fantastic, no-rules lifestyle that many dream of. But, no matter what he did, he could never get the only thing he truly wanted – a love that wouldn't be taken from him.

So how did the typical boy next door become Pablo Escobar's right-hand man, one who played a key role in the importation of cocaine to the States during the 70s and 80s? *Blow* set out to answer this question. It also revealed the riveting inside story of George Jung's rise and fall. The story of how one man used every last bit of his ingenuity, ambition, courage and savvy only to blow all of his dreams on greed. By providing an intimate look at the border crossings, illicit fights, ruthless negotiations, brutal executions, extensive money laundering and all-out war with the justice system that let the party go on, the film set out to reveal the other side of 1970s glitz and glamour. At a time when drug use and addiction continue to grab headlines in America, *Blow* provided a moving and human look at how we got to where we are today, and what the price has been.

As far as Demme, the director, was concerned, he set out to bring to the screen the combination of an intimate portrait of human yearning mixed with an epic story of American crime and culture over the last three decades. 'This is an amazingly tragic story, yet it's also exciting and sexy and fun because the backdrop is always sex and drugs and rock 'n' roll. It's about a period of time in America that was all about transformation, from innocence to cynicism, from pot to cocaine. But it's also a very personal story to me because so many friends of mine have been touched by the effects of the drug trade and what happened during those flush days for George Jung.'

But in the film, Jung is not just portrayed as a drug trafficker, nor simply one of the first to recognise the profit-making potential of turning cocaine into a major recreational pastime, but also as a man of his times. Like America itself, he journeys from the innocence of the 1960s, to the decadence of the 1970s, to the retribution and redemption of the 1980s and beyond. To play such a shifting role, Demme wanted an actor with a reputation for originality and the ability to delve into the darkest spaces of human experience, and he could think of only one.

Johnny Depp is a very unique actor, noted Demme. 'No matter what, he never gives a dishonest take, from day one, he became George Jung and the nuances he brought to the part never ceased to amaze me. His instincts are impeccable, not just as an actor but as a person.'

Producer Joel Stillerman agreed. 'We knew the key to the success of the role of George Jung would lie in the subtlety and intelligence an actor could bring to it. Somebody had to make him much more than a drug dealer, and that's exactly what Johnny did. He brings a cerebral quality to his roles that takes them in unexpected directions.'

'He really saw himself as a modern day pirate,' exclaimed Johnny enthusiastically. 'He didn't believe in the system or politics or rules or bosses. He just wanted to go out there and really live. He didn't want to end up in a cookie-cutter job like everybody else, he had a real vision of freedom. He just wanted to do it and go out there and live in a very intense way. But it swooped him up, and he lost everything, including the people he loved.'

Perhaps, above all else, Johnny could relate to Jung's dizzying rise to fame and fortune. Playing him 'reminded me of when I started acting because I didn't want to be this at all when I first started out. But I started making money like I'd never seen before in my life. And I think that's what happened to George. He was just going into business, the way he saw it. It was like Coca-Cola or McDonald's to him at first, just marketing a new product. And it was even being supported by the government, by very high-level politicians. I know that George sees now that he did some very bad things, but he was just following what looked at first a promising future.'

Throughout playing the role, Johnny remained cognisant of the fact that he was playing a living human being who actually experienced what he was dramatising. Never one to miss an opportunity to delve deeper into his characterisations, he even went to the prison where Jung is serving time on drug charges until 2014, mainly to absorb the man's vast inside knowledge about the temptations and tribulations of his drug smuggling and unpredictable existence.

After meeting him several times, Johnny felt a deep responsibility to George Jung 'because, bless him, he's in a prison cell without the possibility of parole for a long time. I didn't get to spend that much time with him, but one day I just felt the character click into place. It's an exciting moment when you feel yourself thinking and moving and talking like another person. That was the most exciting thing to me.'

Equally exciting, for everyone involved with the making of the film, was to watch Johnny transform himself into the character he was playing. 'He really got his body language,' recalls producer Georgia Kacandes. 'He even started to look like him in a weird way. There was a whole subtle shift in Johnny between the time George is in his prime to when he is actively deteriorating under the stress and doing too much coke. His body just collapses into itself and it's amazing. He physicalizes the role without makeup or wardrobe. It's all in his psyche.'

But that subtlety came from Johnny's research into Jung's

incredible story of dodging not only the FBI but also the deadly Colombian cartels. 'I wondered how he could have done it all, but I think it came down to the adrenaline. He needed the rush. The excitement and the danger became the high for him. The drugs were just incidental. He just liked being a pirate, doing things his way. He never thought of himself as a bad guy. He was just making money on his own terms, giving the people what they wanted.' But as Johnny notes, perhaps Jung has now served enough time. Certainly it is something Johnny feels very strongly about. 'I hope that people see that he's just a human being who got caught up in something bad. Right now, he won't get out of prison until he's seventy-two. Other people involved in the same bust got out in three years. I think he's paid his debt.'

Joining Johnny in bringing Jung's story to life was an accomplished cast playing the assortment of colourful and unconventional characters that surround him on his journey to becoming a cocaine king.

Penelope Cruz was recruited to play Jung's ravishing, demanding, high-living wife. A major star in her native Spain, Cruz had been coming to the fore in Hollywood since her role opposite Matt Damon in *All The Pretty Horses*. For a couple of years before filming got underway, Damon had been dating Winona Ryder. During the filming he fell for Cruz, broke up with Winona, and he and Cruz became an item.

If Winona being dumped for his leading lady concerned Johnny, he didn't let it show, and if, despite all of that heresay, he was impressed by Cruz as an actress, the feeling was mutual. Cruz said, 'Johnny is one of the most special people I've ever met. He has that magic charisma and he doesn't force it and I don't know if someone's born with that quality or if you have to work at it, but it's very rare.'

Equally intriguing to her was the role she would be playing. Mirtha, she says, was 'a woman who goes through so many changes and is so extreme. Someone who for a while lived in a fantasy world that took her far from the pain of reality. She created a world of money, power, drugs and fashion and, when she lost it all, she thought she had lost everything. But she actually grows from that.'

Playing Johnny's parents was a task that fell to Ray Liotta and Rachel Griffiths, who portray Fred and Ermine Jung, an argumentative, working class New England couple who thought they were raising a nice, small-town boy. It is Fred Jung who first tells George, 'sometimes you're flush and sometimes you're bust.' A lesson it takes George a tumultuous lifetime to learn.

'It was fun to play Johnny's dad,' laughed Liotta. 'But actually Fred Jung was a big influence on George. He was a hard-working guy who played by the rules and never amounted to much. George sees his father struggling and knows he doesn't ever want to live like that. Johnny plays it that George really loved his dad but he couldn't stand to see him so brow-beaten by life.'

Although never deemed a flop, there were some critics who found the whole thing rather tedious. The movie reviewer in *Film Review* was particularly chastening. Having already admitted that he missed out by not growing up in the seventies, and therefore perhaps didn't 'get it', he still opined that '*Blow*, for the most part, really isn't that great of a movie. It's pretty much a rehash of every other rise to the top of the drug heap movie I've ever seen.' He did, however, admit that Johnny was a good choice for the role and 'really pulls together an otherwise weak movie and makes it work.'

Elsewhere, things were slightly better. But only just. The *Rolling Stone* review called it 'ambitious, messy and bursting with feelings for which it can't always find coherent expression.' In the *San Francisco Chronicle*, Edward Guthmann thought that when 'the film finally winds down after two hours, and tags on a photograph of the real George Jung in prison, looking ravaged and older than his years, the chill that we're supposed to feel just isn't there.' And, perhaps being even more unnecessarily critical, was Peter Bradshaw in Britain's *Guardian*. 'Johnny Depp in a blond wig makes him look like a permanently hung-over Francis Rossi look-alike in a Quo tribute band.' And as for Penelope Cruz, he continued, she 'gives the most embarrassingly bad performance of her career, perennially caking her face with white powder and screeching lines like "Let's have some motherfucking fun you motherfuckers!"...'

But sometimes it doesn't matter what the critics think – the cinema-going public is perfectly capable of making up its own mind. With a respectable $52 million dollar gross taken in American cinemas alone, it could hardly be called a flop. Whether the critics hated it or not, it really didn't matter.

In the same month that *Blow* was released in America, Vanessa returned to performing live music in her first concerts since 1993, and only her second tour ever. It was to promote her new album, *Bliss*, on which Johnny had played lead guitar on a track called *Firmaman*, and on another titled *St. Germain*. Johnny had co-music writing credits for the title track, which some noted was an obvious love song from

Vanessa to Johnny. He had also shot the photograph that decorated the front cover.

That was, Vanessa confesses, because 'I wanted to distance myself from the usual glamour shoot. This one is very honest, and shows me as I am. Johnny took it and touched it up on his computer. The fuzzy effect gives the feeling my dreams are engraved in it. It is a declaration of love for the man in my life, Johnny. I'm sure of that; we are made for each other. I have often been in love, but I've never had a relation as intense as with Johnny. I want to spend the rest of my life with him. And without him, I could never have recorded this CD. For the first time, I wrote and produced a big part of the songs by myself. His faith in me was so strong that I didn't want to disappoint him.'

And disappointment, it wasn't. Neither was the series of intensive rehearsals in Cannes, nor the tour that kicked off in the Paris suburbs at Rueil-Malmaison and then went onto to play another 30 dates between then and the end of June. The highlight of the tour was the Parisian leg, which included five consecutive appearances at the Olympia. Johnny attended every one and, on the last night, with guitar in hand, joined her onstage for an encore.

CHAPTER 14

'I'M NOT SURE I'M CAPABLE OF LEAVING BEHIND
A PERSONAL MESSAGE. BUT IF I DID, I HOPE IT WOULD
BE THAT IT'S OKAY TO BE DIFFERENT FROM THE CROWD.
IN FACT, IT'S REALLY GOOD TO BE DIFFERENT FROM
THE CROWD, AND THAT WE SHOULD REALLY QUESTION
OURSELVES BEFORE WE PASS JUDGEMENT ON
SOMEONE WHO IS DIFFERENT TO US.'

ONCE UPON A TIME
IN HOLLYWOOD

During the period following his sharing in Vanessa's successful return to music and enjoying what he would later describe as 'living a simple life,' perhaps Johnny was somewhat reluctant to return to work. When he finally did, it would be on the Prague set of *From Hell* – a movie that advance reports insisted would prove as gripping as its predecessor was compelling.

Released in the US in October 2001, and in Britain the following February, just two months before Johnny and Vanessa would celebrate the birth of their second child, Jack John Christopher Depp III, the film was a re-examination of the infamous and unsolved Jack the Ripper murders in Whitechapel. To this day, he remains the most notorious and enigmatic serial killer in history. Over 100 years after he committed five heinous, ritualistic murders during a ten-week span in the fall of 1888, creating a frenzied atmosphere of gossip, rumour and terror, our continued fascination with him should not that surprising, when you consider that his legend ushered in a new era of pulp press. Before Jack the Ripper, Johnny reminds us, 'there were a few hundred newspapers in London. At the height of his murder spree, thousands of additional papers emerged.' Jack the Ripper, created in part by the press, became its first 'tabloid star.'

But, like Dracula, perhaps no one could imagine the story returning to the screens for the umpteenth time with anything approaching success. And like Dracula, hadn't Jack the Ripper been done to death? So why do a remake?

In their own assessment, directors Allen and Albert Hughes had an affinity for the Ripper story that stemmed from the climate of 1880s East London. The city's vast disparity of wealth produced masses of poor and destitute people, many of whom congregated in the area in which the murders took place. The dirty seamy slum was a haven for drug use, prostitution, alcoholism and random street crime.

As with most of their previous inner-city dramas, and in particular their 1993 debut, *Menace II Society*, this was a ghetto story, confirmed one the Hughes brothers, Allen. 'It concerns poverty, violence and corruption, which are themes we deal with in our movies because they fascinate us. What also intrigued us was the psychology of Jack the Ripper, his behaviour and the hysteria he incited.' Not only that, but 'previous accounts of this story have been antiseptic, told from the eyes of the prim upper class. We're revealing it from the perspective of the people who lived in squalor, in the neighbourhood where this terror was inflicted.'

Although claimed in many quarters to have been influenced by Bob Clarke's 1979 *Murder By Decree*, and following an almost identical trail, *From Hell*, based on Alan Moore and Eddie Campbell's graphic novel of the same name, the movie offers a different take on the whole thing by primarily focusing on people trying to survive the grimmest of circumstances. It is the story of five impoverished prostitutes who share a desperate friendship, who are drawn closer together as their ranks are terrorised by a gruesome murderer. They exist by earning a meagre living with their bodies in a society that on the one hand dishonours them, and on the other feeds upon them. Owning virtually nothing of value, they are under threat from the very thing that would steal their only personal possession. And that is life.

Johnny's co-star Heather Graham confirmed that impression, and explained how her character Mary Kelly 'and her friends live on the edge of starvation in this horrible slum. Each day is a struggle. Having a place to sleep is luxury. The only thing that sustains Mary is her dream of returning to Ireland, where she lived as a young girl.'

The theme of hardship lies at the heart of one of the establishing scenes in the movie. The women awake after a fitful night's sleep tied together on a bench, which is the only uncomfortable option for those unable to afford a bed. The landlord arrives in the morning to untie the rope and return them to the streets where they must earn money for food and shelter for the coming night. It is a harsh, unrelenting circle of survival.

Actress Lesley Sharp, who played one of Heather Graham's street mates, agreed with Graham. 'The lives of these women are gruesome and dark. Their day-to-day existence is always under threat from pimps, violent johns, street criminals, disease and addictions.'

In *From Hell*, the sole authority seemingly concerned with protecting these 'unfortunates', otherwise viewed as expendable, is Fred Abberline, the real-life Inspector played by Johnny. But Abberline himself is equally aggrieved. Tormented by unendurable memories, he seeks temporary escape with opium. Like Sherlock Holmes before him who, according to *The Seven Per Cent Solution*, was addicted to cocaine, it is an addiction that heightens him to the spells of clairvoyance that bring both insight and incapacity.

'He has been beaten up by life,' Johnny says of his character in the film. 'He lost his wife and child, and relies on self-medication to get through the day.' Indeed the Inspector, promoted out of Whitechapel after years of service, once again finds himself assigned to the seedy district to lead the Ripper investigation.

Aiding him in his troubled investigation is Sergeant Peter Godley, played by Robbie Coltrane, who first found fame as a comedian before landing his most famous role as television's forensic psychologist *Cracker*, and more recently, playing Valentin Zukovsky, a James Bond villian in *Goldeneye*, the film that re-established the Bond movie with box-office receipts far exceeding any of its predecessors. And again, in 1999, returning to reprise that role in *The World Is Not Enough*. Godley is a loyal friend who takes a strong hand in caring for Abberline when influenced from his substance habits. 'He is a straightforward Scottish cop who draws conclusions from concrete evidence,' adds Coltrane, 'such as a blood-stained knife and eyewitness accounts. He's intrigued by Abberline's intuition and unorthodox methods. It's contrary to Godley's nature, but he accepts Abberline's visions as genuine and feels compelled to act on them.'

That is certainly how Johnny would best describe him. 'He is the only person in the world that Abberline listens to and respects. Godley keeps him alive, watches over him. He's his closest friend.'

But, as the Whitechapel murders escalate, the two men are thwarted by superiors more interested in sweeping the crimes under the carpet than finding the killer. The sole exception is the renowned Sir William Gull, played by Ian Holm, a physician to the royal family, and a powerful enough figure to assist the shunned Inspector, who knows the murders are being committed by someone with medical knowledge. Certainly the killer possesses surgical skills beyond those of a butcher or labourer. His killings involve a bizarre and terrible ritual.

With Gull's guidance, Abberline is able to deduce that the killings were part of a menacing conspiracy involving the Order of Freemasons, who in turn were acting on behalf of the monarchy itself.

The Freemasons are an enigmatic, cult-like organisation whose members have included some of the wealthiest, most powerful men in the world. They have been the subject of numerous conspiracy theories, owing to their mysterious initiation ceremonies and sworn oaths of secrecy.

With this in mind, the idea of the Crown being linked to the Jack the Ripper murders comes to seem less far-fetched. Indeed, it is a theory held by many throughout Europe, where the case holds as much fascination for the

British as does the John F Kennedy assassination does for the Americans.

'Whether the British monarchy was literally involved in the Ripper murders doesn't diminish the power of the accusation levelled at the ruling class,' notes screenwriter Rafael Yglesias. 'That the authorities refused to even consider the possibility that the suspect might be wealthy speaks volumes about the Victorian era. Society's ills were viewed exclusively as the fault of the poor and the lower class.'

Perhaps above all else, though, the Ripper case also advanced police forensics that were still in their infancy during the 1880s. As Allen Hughes puts it, 'At that time, if the police didn't catch you near the body with blood on your hands, they couldn't likely convict you. There were no standard procedures for fingerprinting or blood tests. But this case helped bring about the development of new scientific procedures and tools for apprehending criminals.'

Jack the Ripper was never apprehended. It is the mystery of his identity, his daring to commit heinous murders in public places, and his ability to slip back into the night that has intrigued the public for more than a century. In the eyes of Robbie Coltrane, 'he's the prefect nemesis for a movie.'

For the Hughes brothers, 'the challenge and attraction was taking a well-known mystery, rich with legend, and using our imagination to give it added dimension.' This dimension is the relationship that develops between Mary Kelly and Abberline. 'As a member of that lower class as well as a prostitute, Mary Kelly is unaccustomed to the company of respectable men, at least when she's not working. Distrustful and wary of being used, she initially rebukes

Abberline's investigation. Girls working the streets had their guard up. Mary views Abberline as just another guy who wants to use her. His decency and sincerity eventually breaks down her defences as she begins to trust him'

But as their relationship deepens, a far more threatening barrier than social mores and class distinctions stands between them. A dagger of conspiracy and ruthless intent is pointed at their hearts, and it is held by the hand of a butchering madman destined for the pages of history.

Even with naked bodies stretched out dead and alive, barbaric practices extending to the medical theatre, and a brief scientific observation of the 'elephant man' John Merrick, the film still fell short of its promise as far as the critics were concerned. The bulk of critical objection focused on Heather Graham. Writing in *The Guardian*, Peter Bradshaw condemned the actress for being implausible as a prostitute. 'She is not merely the most glamorous, but the one with the most access to expensive makeup, style and skin care.' Nor was he too overwhelmed by Johnny's cockney accent. But then again, that is be like criticising Winona Ryder's English accent in *Bram Stoker's Dracula*, because she said 'toe-*may*-toe' when she ought to say 'toe-*mah*-toe'. It's like damning Rembrandt because he painted one nostril larger than the other. It simply doesn't matter.

Although the general consensus was pretty poor, and despite its gothic look, Hammer horror, or slasher movie it wasn't, said Roger Ebert of the *Chicago-Sun Times*. 'It's a movie catering to no clear demographic.' This was much the same verdict elsewhere, and the *Village Voice* thought it was 'more stylish than gruesome.' It still had 'the lush decrepitude of an autumn compost heap or an old Hammer werewolf flick.' The *BBC Film Review* by Nev Pierce wasn't much better. 'A whodunit where the who is bloody obvious and the characters disposable. It has the odd chilling moment, but no amount of blood 'n' guts can compensate for a lack of heart.'

If *From Hell* created a general feeling of disappointment, perhaps Johnny's next role, in Robert Rodriquez's *Once Upon A Time in Mexico*, would improve things. After all, it was a sequel of sorts to *Desperado*, which itself was a remake, or expanded version of his breakout film, *El Mariachi*.

The new adventure was set against a backdrop of revolution, greed and revenge. Haunted and scarred by tragedy, El Mariachi has retreated into a life of isolation, and is only forced out of hiding when a corrupt CIA agent recruits the reclusive hero to sabotage an assassination plot against the president of Mexico, which has been conceived by cartel kingpin Barillo. But, of course, Mariachi has his own reasons for returning.

Although modestly budgeted and shot in Mexico over a seven-week shooting schedule, on high-definition video, the film was seen by many as a tribute to the kind of movies that inspired Rodriguez to become a filmmaker in the first place. Films like those of Sergio Leone, who brought the classic spaghetti western to the screen through Clint Eastwood's 'Dollar' films: *A Fistful of Dollars*, *For A Few Dollars More*, and most notably, *The Good, The Bad, And The Ugly*.

The El Mariachi legend, of course, had already had an interesting and unique history, and no one is more surprised at its evolution than Rodriguez himself. Speaking of the first film, he says 'I wanted to come up with an idea that was a little off-kilter and kind of fun, so I thought of making the hero, a guitar player with a guitar case full of guns. It was very off the cuff.'

Interestingly, the first film was shot for a mere $7,000 and catapulted the young filmmaker to prominence, earning him the coveted Audience Award for best dramatic film at the Sundance Film Festival. The second movie, *Desperado*, began as a bigger budget remake of the first movie, but grew into a sequel of sorts, incorporating more elaborate action sequences than the director had been able to execute in *El Mariachi* and making international stars of its two leads, Antonio Banderas and Salma Hayek.

In many ways, the idea of making a third movie was down to Amy Pascal, then an executive vice president of production at Columbia who discussed the project with Rodriguez, pointing out that *Desperado* had gained a cult status and, on that basis, suggesting a sequel. In the end, remembering what Quentin Tarantino had once told him to make the Mexican equivalent of the Dollar films, Rodriguez agreed, but only on the condition that the film be more epic and titled *Once Upon A Time In Mexico*. Amy agreed, and according to Rodriguez, 'off we went.'

Once again, the cast Rodriguez selected was stellar. Antonio Banderas and Salma Hayek both returned to reprise the roles they had made famous – or been made famous by – over a decade before. Ruben Blades, Eva Mendes, Willem Dafoe and Mickey Rourke took substantial supporting roles, and playing the corrupt CIA agent, Sands, Johnny was probably facing his most unlikely role yet.

With a long standing desire to work with Rodriguez,

Johnny jumped at the chance, even if it was playing 'a guy who's a little against the grain of what you'd expect to see in a CIA agent. He wasn't someone who was clichéd or who I felt I had seen before. It was an interesting idea for Robert to create a man who's in the CIA, but stationed somewhere he doesn't want to be because no one likes him. He is a man who has no regard for human life. I've never played someone like that before, who's not a good guy in any way.'

Perhaps outside his own circle of colleagues, Johnny was considered an odd choice for the part. But not as far as the director was concerned. Johnny was one of the few stars Rodriguez knew who would allow themselves to take on the role. 'Johnny's character is very edgy, and you have to have an actor who's willing to embrace that, because so many actors don't want to come in and be unlikeable.'

But Johnny, he continues, 'didn't seem to care about that as long as the character was interesting. What's funny is that, no matter how vile we made him, Johnny still has this incredibly likeable nature, so the character stills end up being sympathetic. I don't think you can really hate a Johnny Depp character, no matter how rotten he may be, and Sands is rotten to the core. He was my favourite written part in the script, and the first character I began developing for this movie. He's the character who orchestrated the entire assassination plan in the movie and slowly watched it fall apart. Then Johnny came in and took Sands to a whole other level.'

Released in September 2003, the film was received as well as could be expected, and the general consensus was that Johnny stole 'every scene that he's in as a rogue CIA agent who doesn't let a small thing like getting his eyes gouged out stop him from a gunfight. He slips on a pair of shades to hide the blood dripping from his peepers and hires a kid to tell him where to aim. You don't want to miss Depp in this movie, he knocks it out of the park.'

Again it was high praise, but there was a sting in the tail. When Johnny attended the première in New York, practically everyone there was asking him about the recent anti-American comments he had reportedly made to a German magazine during an interview. But Johnny made it clear that he loved America and would never disrespect his country or its people.

The whole thing had exploded into the open when *Stern* magazine printed an interview with Johnny in which he had apparently hit out, comparing America to 'a stupid, out of control puppy dog,' and insisted that he would not be returning to his home country, especially after the war on Iraq proved all his worst fears. According to the magazine, Johnny said that 'America is dumb, it's like a dumb puppy that has big teeth that can bite and hurt you, aggressive. My daughter is four, my boy is one. I'd like them to see America as a toy, a broken toy. Investigate it a little, check it out, get this feeling and then get out.' Also, in the same interview, he had apparently slammed President George Bush's administration for its criticism of French opposition to the war in Iraq, saying that politicians had shown themselves as 'idiots'.

Right or wrong, his explanation of his comments at the première told a very different story. 'Taken in context, what I was saying was that, compared to Europe, America is a very young country and we are still growing as a nation. It is a shame that the metaphor I used was taken so radically out of context and slung about irresponsibly by the news media. In fact, it was just the opposite. I am an American. I love my country and have great hopes for it. It is for this reason that I speak candidly and sometimes critically about it. I have benefited greatly from this freedom that exists in my country and for this I am eternally grateful.'

But perhaps everyone was missing the point. As Vanessa explained, 'we don't want to raise our children in America. There's too much violence.' Maybe that is why they split their time between the home Johnny still has in Los Angeles, his Paris apartment in the fashionable Montmarte district and their new £500,000 villa near St. Tropez.

Although preferring to maintain a comparatively low profile, whether in France or America, Johnny remains grateful that he is so much in demand as an actor. He was particularly thrilled the day he was handed the screenplay for *Secret Window*, a film that had begun its journey to the screen when executives at Columbia became intrigued by Stephen King's suspense thriller *Secret Window, Secret Garden*. It was part of King's *Four Past Midnight* collection that had already prompted one reviewer to literally rave over how these 'four spellbinding tales of evil are can't-tear-your-eyes away stories that burn your imagination.'

According to a synopsis of the film, long before the production notes had been given out to the movie reviewers, it was the story of successful author Mort Rainey, who knows that, although he should be at his computer writing another book, or at least walking his dog along the sparkling lake outside his dingy cabin, he was sleeping on his favourite sofa for up to 16 hours a day. He is in the midst of a painful divorce and everything about the break-up has turned messy and unpleasant. It has sapped his energy and siphoned away his creativity, leaving him with a monumental case of writer's block that renders him incapable of ever stringing a simple sentence together.

Then, when it seems as if things can't possibly get any worse, a psychotic stranger named John Shooter shows up at his doorstep, accuses Rainey of plagiarizing his story and demands satisfaction. Despite Rainey's efforts to placate him, Shooter becomes increasingly insistent and hostile, intimating a twisted sort of justice that could include cold-blooded murder.

Forced into a mind-bending game of cat and mouse, Rainey discovers that he has more cunningness and gritty determination than he ever imagined. But in the end, he realises that the elusive Shooter may know him better than he knows himself.

'I like guy-in-a-house-going-crazy movies,' laughs writer and director David Koepp. 'I enjoy the challenge of working out a story that takes place in a confined place. Even though there are some outdoor scenes, the story is really about Mort Rainey's living space. It's about somebody who's in a really bad place in his life where he is just spending way too much time alone at home. I wanted to explore the confinement and paranoia themes, which have always interested me. Confinement can be really scary, and having bad things happen in your living space can be truly unsettling.'

It was this that also intrigued and attracted Johnny to the project. But what really sold him on the part was the quality of Koepp's writing. 'What I remember most was reading the screenplay, getting ten to fifteen pages into it and thinking, wow, this is incredibly well-written. The dialogue is real and not forced, with an interesting train-of-thought quality to it. The situations felt true. As I kept reading, I got to the point where I was totally invested emotionally in Mort and his dilemma. And then, when I got to the ingenious plot twist, I was completely shocked. I really didn't see it coming, which is very satisfying for a reader and I knew it would be for audiences as well.'

But then again, Johnny seems to have an affinity with and for writers. He befriended and played the legendary journalist and raconteur Hunter S. Thompson in Terry Gilliam's *Fear and Loathing in Las Vegas* and, although it was then yet to be seen, he had already portrayed another legendary scribe, J. M. Barrie, author of Peter Pan, in Marc Forster's *Finding Neverland*. But asking Johnny's co-star Kate Winslet about it, she had no idea when it would be released. 'I honestly don't know. I saw the final cut of the film well over a year ago. It's fantastic, I'm so excited about it. It's just timing. They're choosing when to release it I guess. I play Sylvia Llewellyn Davies, who had some kind of affair with J M Barrie. It's a story about how he conceived the idea of Peter Pan through the relationship he had with Sylvia and her four sons. It was the time that he spent with them that inspired him to create Peter Pan. And one of Sylvia's sons is called Peter, so it's almost about that little boy.'

But, as Johnny continues, 'I think for anyone in the creative arts, but especially for a writer, your imagination is your best friend. It can also be your worst enemy if you are plagued by too much thought, an overload of information in your head. That's Morty's problem. He's definitely a recluse. He's uncomfortable around people and just wants to be left alone. Unfortunately, he can't leave himself alone.'

And that is what Koepp sensed Johnny would innately understand in the character he was creating for the screen, and today, he admits that he wrote it specifically with him in mind. While Johnny was filming *The Pirates of the Caribbean* on location in the Caribbean, and before travelling out there to woo him for the role of Mort Rainey, Koepp sat down and composed a letter to take to Johnny.

'I wrote that I was hoping to cast him in *Secret Window*, that he was the guy I thought about when creating this character. He's one of our great actors, so inventive and so different every time. I've found him totally accessible as an actor throughout his career. There is an old saying that if you aim for the general, you hit nothing, but if you aim for the specific, you might hit the universal. That sums up the body of Johnny's work. He is very meticulous and he draws us in by finding little moments of truth and behaviour that people recognise and identify with. Therefore, they ultimately identify with the character. His choices are spontaneous and often unconventional, but they always work. He is also a completely fearless actor. In terms of this character in particular, it's rare to find a movie star who is as unafraid as Johnny to play fear. Needless to say, I was thrilled when he agreed to take the part.'

In fact, Koepp's good fortune continued throughout the casting process. 'I feel incredibly lucky. We got everyone we wanted, and that rarely happens. Once all the actors had fallen into place, it was a great relief. It was like having a great car and all I had to do was drive it and try not to crash it into a tree.'

Prominent among his casting coups was snaring John Turturro for the role of John Shooter. Johnny, of course had worked with him previously during the making of *The Man Who Cried*, and at the time, Turturro was probably best known for his role as Adam Sandler's unusual personal butler, Emilio, in Steven Brill's 2002 blockbuster, *Mr Deeds*. He's one of those actors, confirm Koepp, 'who really becomes the part, who creates a fully realised, credible person. And that was especially important in the case of Shooter. Because John is such a chameleon, audiences can't always quite put their finger on him, which is great for the role - a man who shows up out of nowhere and has an intangible, mysterious quality about him.'

It was a quality that was recognised from the first reviews when the film opened in America in March 2004. As usual, Roger Ebert was one of the first to comment. 'The movie stars Johnny Depp in another of those performances where he brings a musing eccentricity to an otherwise straight-forward role.' But it was in the opening scenes that Ebert was most enamoured. 'The first shot after the credits is an elaborate one. It begins with a view across a lake to a rustic cabin. Then the camera moves smoothly in to the shore, and across the grounds, and in through a window of the cabin, and it regards various rooms before closing in on a large mirror that reflects a man asleep on a couch.'

Much of that was down to cinematographer Fred Murphy. In preparation for production, Koepp and Murphy watched several notable suspense films, including Roman Polanski's *Rosemary's Baby* and *The Tenant* and John Boorman's *Deliverance*. Taking a cue from the latter film, Murphy opted to shoot *Secret Window* in the wide screen Super 35 format, an interesting choice for a movie that, on some levels, is about confined spaces and the intimate, inner workings of the protagonists mind.

'I like the wide screen for close-ups, says Murphy, 'because it allows you to add more to the background. It also opens things up more, so the movie doesn't feel so claustrophobic. We had several scenes at the lake near Mort's cabin, and the wide screen allowed us to take advantage of the great scenery.'

The danger of shooting in widescreen, however, is that it's hard to conceal any mistakes, and there were plenty of opportunities for error, since Koepp was interested in employing a recurrent theme of reflections. 'Much of the movie is about a guy in his house by himself. That's very interior, but Fred opened it up by including multiple reflections. This is really a mirror movie. At one point Fred said he had never had as many mirrors in a film as in this one. Because it is about reflection – looking at yourself and seeing things you may not like – mirrors are a major element, particularly the large one over Mort's fireplace. A mirror also makes the set look bigger, providing for some interesting shots. But you have to be so careful because the actors aren't the only thing that's reflected. The crew and the equipment can show up too. It was hard to work with, but the film definitely looked better and was more visually compelling.'

CHAPTER 15

*'IF ANYTHING, MINE HAS BEEN A CAREER OF FAILURES.
I THINK I'M GETTING ALL THIS ATTENTION RIGHT NOW
BECAUSE PEOPLE FEEL SORRY FOR ME. I'M AN
UNDERDOG. OTHER ACTORS LOOK AT ME AND THINK,
THAT POOR BASTARD IS STILL HACKING AWAY AT IT.'*

A LOST SOUL NO MORE

Johnny left for London shortly after the 2004 Oscars ceremony to begin work on Laurence Dunmore's *The Libertine*, a biopic of John Wilmot, the 17th-century poet and second Earl of Rochester, described by Samuel Johnson as having 'contempt of decency and order, a total disregard to every moral and a resolute denial of every religious observation. He lived worthless and useless and blazed out his youth and health in lavish voluptuousness.'

The independent film, adapted by Stephen Jeffreys from his own play, was set to start production in late February outside London, but suffered a quite unexpected setback from the British government, who announced changes to the tax laws closing a loophole to prevent what the Inland Revenue called 'complex and abusive schemes to avoid paying tax being drawn up by film investors'. The announcement – which went on to confirm that 'the government has been consistent in closing these kinds of abusive schemes in the past, and will do so again in the future' – sent shock waves through the British film industry and jeopardised the production of a great many films, including *The Libertine*.

In fact, so devastating was the news that production on *Tulip Fever* starring Jude Law and Johnny's *Pirates of the Caribbean* co-star Keira Knightley was halted altogether.

According to BBC News Online, 'The UK Film Council handed the government a list of another forty films that could be affected, hoping for temporary measures to save productions from collapse.' But the government stood firm, saying that it 'simply cannot be expected to stand by' while people abuse the tax system at the expense of honest taxpayers.

But all was not lost. Isle of Man Film, production company Mr Mudd and First Choice Films agreed to co-finance Johnny's movie. In a statement, Dan Taylor of First Choice affirmed that, 'as was always the case, our primary motivation is to ensure that a commercial British film gets made in Britain. It has been commonly misunderstood that our use of tax relief to manage the risk of film investment reflected a disregard for the success of the film. This couldn't be further from the truth.' All the same, the future of the movie was seriously threatened by the 2004 changes.

But perhaps it was because the filming schedule was changed that Johnny was able to join other academic bookworms at the British Library lost in research. It was in the legendary reading room that Johnny pored over every spit and comma on the subject of the remarkable maverick he was about to bring back to life. John Wilmot, the devil-may-care second Earl of Rochester, was the Pete Doherty of the 17th century. An astonishingly depraved rock star of his time, Rochester lived life according to his own rules.

He was the original libertine, a ne'er-do-well who was the inspiration for Doherty's now defunct band The Libertines. And now this amazing man was to be the subject of a British film that, more than four centuries after his death, was still expected to test the limits of public decency.

Visitors to the controversial production's set during filming in England, Wales and on the Isle of Man would find themselves staring at huge phallic symbols, instruments of sexual bondage and all manner of hedonistic accessories for unbridled pleasure.

Johnny, of course, excelled at playing Rochester, delivering a tour de force as the debauched Earl falls spectacularly from grace. Actor John Malkovich had first approached him about the project more than ten years earlier and Johnny was simply thrilled to see what had become a grand obsession for him finally come to fruition.

'I tried to track down every available piece of information on the Earl of Rochester and found these incredible books that were the basis for everything. The thing that was the key for me was learning as much as I could about Rochester and knowing that, for a lot of people, there is this surface impression that he is just a debauched, hedonistic, lunatic drunk. I had the opportunity to go to the British Library and read his letters – the actual letters – in his own hand. Letters to his wife, letters to his mother, letters to his children. They gave me volumes about him and I was able to see that underneath the surface there were layers of this hypersensitive genius with an unbelievable gift. Also, his poetry was just beautiful.'

Rochester's unbelievably wild existence was dedicated to exploring every possible avenue of lust, greed and glory. 'If you want a modern comparison, he was as famous as Mick Jagger,' says producer Russell Smith. 'But I suppose he was more like a punk because he put the finger up at everybody.'

Poet, wit, war hero and sexual adventurer – Rochester was all these things and more. Born in 1647, the son of the first Earl of Rochester, John Wilmot was a shining light of the new England that was emerging from the Middle Ages. His first brush with the debauchery that was to become a way of life came when – as a veritable child prodigy – he went up to Oxford University at the age of 12. After graduating, he set off to sea where he became a famed hero in the battles against the Dutch.

His reputation spread across Europe at breakneck speed, swept along by his literary brilliance, his unique cutting-edge personality and his penchant for dangerous blasphemy. Fortunately for this unique character, he served at the court of the enlightened, fun-loving and charismatic King Charles II, who loved bawdiness. But even Charles's laidback approach was tested to the extreme by Rochester's apparent mission to infuriate his long-suffering monarch.

The outrageous Earl wrote poems and plays that at the time were seen as totally libellous and – not to put too fine a point on it – absolutely filthy. He even broke the sacred code by criticising the King. And randy Rochester's successions of sexual dalliances were internationally notorious.

When he did finally fall in love, naturally, his method of seduction was a little out of the ordinary. He didn't so much capture the heart of teenage heiress Elizabeth Malet as her entire body. He kidnapped her.

Pushed too far by such unacceptable behaviour, Charles imprisoned Rochester in the Tower of London. Then, in his typical manner of extraditing himself from deep trouble, the promiscuous peer successfully begged his seething sovereign for forgiveness. Rochester was released. Even more incredibly, he went on to persuade his kidnap victim to marry him. But all good things must pass and, in the end, the original loveable rogue's sexual abandonment proved to be his downfall. He died of syphilis when he was just 33.

'The more I read about Rochester, the more I researched him, I just fell in love with him,' Johnny admits. 'Of course, there was this fun surface side to him, but he was an incredibly complicated man and a horribly pained soul.'

It was writer Stephen Jeffreys who saw the potential of tapping into Rochester's explosive life story. Probing the connection between genius, decadence, freedom, danger, lust and love, his play *The Libertine* was staged at Chicago's famous Steppenwolf Theater with John Malkovich in the title role. It was where he asked Johnny to come and see the production and told him of his plan to turn it into a movie.

For the big-screen version, Malkovich switched to the role of King Charles with Johnny in the title role. Johnny was literally beside himself with excitement. 'When I first read and saw the play with John on stage ten years ago, I didn't know how they could translate it from stage to cinema. But Stephen has done a beautiful job. When I read his words, I said to myself, "You only get one opportunity for something as good as this." Something like this only comes around once in an actor's life. The words are spectacular.'

Looking back at Johnny's history, it would be easy to understand why director Dunmore might have seen him as the perfect person to play the Earl. 'I definitely had a phase in my life when Rochester and I would have spent the night together. He is a character I know in a lot of ways. Guys that are parallel to him are Jack Kerouac – great writer, but horribly misunderstood; Shane MacGowan – one of the greatest poets of the 20th century but he imbibed to a degree where we would all be in the gutter. And Hunter Thompson – a great hero and a great friend of mine. All these guys came into my mind.'

But Johnny also saw closer parallels between himself and Rochester. 'I recognised something that I had gone through. I quit drinking spirits because I wouldn't stop. I would just keep going until a black screen came down where you can't see anything any more and you don't know if you're around.'

Johnny quit drinking, thinking it was 'wasting time', and in the same period he stopped doing drugs. 'Trying to numb and medicate myself was never about recreation. It was existing without living. If I'd done this part ten years ago when John Malkovich first approached me and I agreed, it would have been very different. I would have made a dangerous mistake of trying to live it. Not necessarily going out and shagging everything that had a pulse, but drinking, and I would never have got through it. Ten years later, I have a solid foundation to stand on.'

Of course, the Johnny Depp of ten years earlier was a more destructive soul. It was about that time that he had his raging, destructive, on-off relationship with Kate Moss. At the suggestion that he and Kate and all their tumult seemed to prove that true love exists, he becomes very wistful and says, 'I don't think I was good for Kate.' And as for the stories you may have read in the tabloids claiming that he had taken an interest in Kate's troubles, invited Pete Doherty out for lunch and warned him to lay off the drugs, telling him that he should be nice to Kate, he denies it ever happened. 'I've never met him. I like him in that I like his music very much. I think he has a great talent and it seems to me that he and Kate could be great together because she's a great girl. She's got a great brain on her and I think she's a good mummy.'

But he remains shocked at the bad time that some journalists give her, believing it's not fair to 'drag her through the mud like that. Kate's growing up, we all are. Let her be. But I never took Pete Doherty aside and I never sent her a mirror, as has been written. They said I sent a mirror to the place where she was getting straight because it is supposed to be an old Indian custom: look in the mirror and find your own strength to abstain. But I would never have thought a mirror would be the right thing to send her. I feel so bad for her.' Although, just as when he had spoken out in defence of Winona during her shoplifting trial, he had not spoken to Kate directly recently, but still remained a firm supporter. 'The press are trying to crucify her, and all that's gonna do is give her more power. She should take that and run with it. Ultimately, I know she's very strong and very smart. She'll be fine.'

In a reflective mood, he would even set the record straight about the Mirabelle restaurant incident in London in 1999 when he was arrested and held in a police cell for four hours after he chased a photographer outside with a piece of wood. 'I'm not sure they would want me back, but they do have a terrific wine list and I do like a good claret. The incident at the Mirabelle was because the paparazzi wanted to get a photograph of Vanessa and me and her tummy. She was about to burst and I thought, I am not going to allow fatherhood to commence as a novelty. I was already protective of my kiddies.'

But he showed how gracious he could be when a journalist presented him with an elegantly carved dildo similar to the ones that appear in *The Libertine*. The sex-toy is now named after him and is available from a chic Los Angeles emporium. Receiving the gift with glee, he was genuinely ecstatic and started waving it around. 'I haven't had one of these for 20 years. It's gorgeous.' He claimed that he was going to put it in a frame similar to the ones fire extinguishers are held in. 'It'll have a sign. Break only in an emergency.'

The movie reviewer in the *Hollywood Reporter* was probably more interested in Johnny's latest film role than in the dildo he had been given, and pondered whether, having admitted he had created an indelible rogues' gallery of lovable freaks and nonconformists, was Johnny now venturing into the realm of the monstrous? No, he wasn't. What he was doing, however, was delivering 'a haunting portrait of the 17th-century poet, provocateur and debauchee John Wilmot, second Earl of Rochester, who achieved literary acclaim only after his lingering death at 33, ravaged by syphilis and alcohol. One of the achievements of director Laurence Dunmore's insistently gritty first feature is that his protagonist, a repellent creature of rapacious sensual appetites, grows more recognisable the more physically grotesque he becomes. A dark cousin to such screen rapscallions as Raoul Duke, Jack Sparrow and, yes, the upcoming Willy Wonka, Depp's dissolute Earl possesses a staggering allure beneath the blood-chilling sneer.'

But not everyone liked *The Libertine* or even Johnny's performance in it. One of those was *Entertainment Weekly*'s Owen Gleiberman. In fact, he was particularly disparaging about the entire film. 'At the beginning of *The Libertine*, Johnny Depp, in long black Renaissance curls that make him resemble a debauched rock-star musketeer, sneers into the camera as he describes his ability to seduce women and men alike – a boast masquerading as a confession. "You will not like me," he declares, spitting out the words with ice-blooded disdain, and it's easy to think, "That's all well and good as long as we get to see you indulge in a bit of nasty sexy gamesmanship."

'In *The Libertine*, however, it's all downhill following the terse misanthropy of that opening monologue. As John Wilmot, the Second Earl of Rochester, a 17th-century poet, wit, and drunk who was celebrated and reviled for the single-mindedness of his depravity, Depp singes away his sweetness, making himself a cross between Casanova and Richard III. The movie, though, in a singular feat of perversity, never shows him doing anything even remotely pleasurable, like, you know, sleeping with someone. This may be the most sexless film about a seducer ever made.

'So what does the Earl do? Why, he talks. That's all anyone in *The Libertine* does. On top of that, what comes out of their mouths isn't what you might call, except in the most loose technical sense, "dialogue". It is gibberish, verbiage, ghastly faux-literate conversational diarrhoea. The Earl forms one quasi-attachment to an actress (Samantha Morton) who's too naive to save him, and he writes a play mocking Charles II (John Malkovich), which propels him on a downward spiral that culminates in an icky death by syphilis. *The Libertine* is such a torturous mess that it winds up doing something I hadn't thought possible: it renders Johnny Depp charmless.'

Just two weeks before *The Libertine* was released, *Finding Neverland* opened on 324 screens across Great Britain at the end of September, and took £776,124 at the box office on its opening weekend. Its release had been delayed by a year, due to a conflict with Columbia Pictures. They owned the rights to the play for their own *Peter Pan* movie, and they had refused Miramax permission to use certain scenes if the films were released at the same time.

Unlike Columbia's *Peter Pan* in 2003, which would tread the familiar territory of one of the most charming children's stories ever conceived, which has enthralled audience imaginations for nearly a century, *Finding Neverland* took a completely different approach with its semi-fictional account of the experiences of the story's author J M Barrie that led him to write the children's classic in the first place.

It is the story of how successful Scottish playwright J M Barrie, played by Johnny, watches his latest play open to a lukewarm reception among the polite society of Edwardian England, and, although a literary genius of his time, he is bored with the same old themes, and soon comes to realise that he is clearly in need of some serious inspiration. Unexpectedly, he finds it during his daily walk with his St Bernard Porthos in London's Kensington Gardens, where he encounters the Llewelyn Davies family: four fatherless boys and their beautiful, recently widowed mother, played by Kate Winslet.

Despite the disapproval of the boys' steely grandmother Emma du Maurier and the resentment of his own wife, Barrie befriends the family, engaging the boys in tricks, disguises, games and sheer mischief, creating play-worlds of castles and kings, cowboys and Indians, pirates and castaways. He transforms hillsides into galleon ships, sticks into mighty swords, kites into enchanted fairies and the Llewelyn Davies boys into 'The Lost Boys of Neverland'.

From the sheer thrills and adventurousness of childhood, Barrie sets about writing his most daring and renowned masterpiece, *Peter Pan*. At first, his theatrical company is sceptical. And, even though his loyal producer Charles Frohman worries he'll lose his shirt on this children's fantasy, Barrie begins rehearsals only to shock his actors with such unprecedented requests as asking them to fly across the stage, talk to fairies made out of light and don dog and crocodile costumes. But, just as Barrie is ready to introduce the world to *Peter Pan*, a tragic twist of fate makes him and those he loves most understand just what it really means to believe.

And it was that theme that director Marc Forster was looking for when producer Richard Gladstein handed him David Magee's screenplay for the film. Forster was immediately drawn to the story, which imagined the circumstances and emotions behind the creation and evolution of *Peter Pan*, a tale that has touched millions all over the world.

According to the film's production notes, J M Barrie's real-life friendship with the Llewelyn Davies family was the inspiration for the very themes that made Barrie's play so resonant: the wonder of the imagination, the nostalgia for childhood innocence and the longing to believe in something more enchanted than everyday life.

'I saw the film as a story about the power of a man's creativity to take people to another world, and about the deep human need for illusions, dreams and beliefs that inspire us even in the face of tragedy. For me, it is about the transformative power of imagination. Being able to transform yourself into something greater than you are, even if nobody believes in you.'

Gladstein agreed. *Finding Neverland* presented 'a unique opportunity to create a film combining intimate personal and emotional drama with incredible bursts of imagination and invention. It's a story for the child and adult in all of us.'

The idea of making a movie version of *Finding Neverland* – then under a working title of *J M Barrie's Neverland* – really started with Allan Knee's stage play *The Man Who Was Peter Pan*, an imaginary series of conversations between Barrie and the Llewelyn Davies boys. Producer Nellie Bellflower had seen the play at a local theatre workshop and immediately optioned it and gave it to screenwriter David Magee for adaptation. 'Allan Knee's play was an incredibly moving story of a man who becomes a father figure to these young boys and then guides them through terrible tragedy. I had always loved *Peter Pan* and Allan's play was a fantastic jumping-off point for exploring the creation of *Peter Pan* and its universal themes.'

But, as Magee admits, his screenplay was 'not a factual retelling of what happened to James Barrie when he wrote *Peter Pan*. I wanted to tell a story about what it means to grow up and become responsible for those around you. I hope people see the film as a respectful tribute to Barrie's creative genius and come away with a feeling that, as human beings, we can grow up without losing all aspects of childhood innocence and wonder.' Magee also found that the story became ever more emotional and personal as he wrote. 'My first child was about to be born when I started working on this material, and my father was coming to the end of his life after a long battle with cancer, so I was really thinking intensely about what it means to grow up and to become aware that time really is chasing after all of us. For me, this story is about a man who is starting to face these issues in his own life.'

Not only that, he continues, but, 'as a writer, I was also interested in exploring how one's own life inspires art and how art in turn informs our lives. There is this notion that creative people hold on to their childhoods longer than the rest of us, but there are moments throughout our lives that weigh on us heavily that we need to explore through storytelling and art. Barrie's brilliance in *Peter Pan* is that he expressed both the joy in childhood and just how bittersweet it is when you have to leave it behind. He took this very real and universal experience and made it something magnificent and special.'

At the suggestion of Miramax executive Michelle Sy, Bellflower sent a draft of the screenplay to producer Richard Gladstein. At this point, Sy contacted Gladstein and the project was set up at Miramax. The screenplay was developed and the search for the right director began. The search took a fateful turn in 2001 when Gladstein saw an early screening of Marc Forster's award-winning *Monster's Ball*, which told the harrowing love story of a prison guard and a criminal's widow with tenderness and raw emotion, and sent Halle Berry to the Academy Awards ceremony to collect the Best Actress Oscar for her role in the film. Says Gladstein, 'The depth of character and subtlety in all the performances convinced me that Marc would bring something unique and special to the project.'

As they developed the screenplay and began to search for a cast, Gladstein noted that the filmmakers found inspiration in some of Barrie's own words. 'Barrie wrote an important bit of direction to his actors, saying, "All characters, whether grown-ups or babes must wear a child's outlook as their only important adornment." This principle guided us in the creation of the film, and we even wrote it, as a sort of prologue, into several drafts of the screenplay so that all the actors and crew understood the intention.'

Of course, central to *Finding Neverland* was the casting of Johnny as Barrie, who, according to Forster, as much as any leading modern actor seems to have kept his own childlike spirit vibrantly alive. 'Johnny is perfect to represent a man who never wants to grow up because you can see that he has this very accessible child inside him from the choices of movie roles he makes. He brought something very special to the role, underplaying it in a way that really pays homage to the man we both believe Barrie wanted to be.'

Johnny also found his way into his role by working with a voice coach on an authentic Scottish brogue, which he employs with the quiet air of a man who on some levels will always remain an enigma. As Gladstein would note, 'Johnny brings out a natural sense of mystery in his portrayal of Barrie, sparking the audience's curiosity about what's happening in Barrie's mind.'

Johnny particularly enjoyed how the story of *Finding*

Neverland was propelled by the undercurrent of unspoken love between his character and Kate Winslet's – a love that never becomes a typical romance. 'The film never seems to go quite where you expect it go,' he says. 'It never turns into a sentimental love story of two people destined to be together or that sort of thing. Instead, it's a much more complicated and moving relationship between two people who need each other on a level that's really beyond explanation or words.'

At the heart of the film was the innocent yet at the time scandalous relationship between Winslet and Johnny, who, according to most reviewers, weren't an obvious screen pairing, but which is precisely why Forster chose them. 'Kate has a real earthiness to her, a strength of will power, and Johnny has this very creative spirit, out there and floating and everything. So the two of them juxtaposed I think makes an interesting match.'

To retain that sense of innocence, there was a scene that was taken out, explains Winslet. 'When we first arrive at the cottage in the country, and we're sitting outside drinking tea and Johnny's smoking a pipe, there's a line that I say to Johnny, something along the lines of "Sometimes I wonder if you realise how much you've come to mean to us all." And he says, "Well, the boys are young." And I say, "Yes, but for me." If that scene had been kept in, the suggestion of something more intimate between the two of them would have been much, much bigger. I love the fact that, in the film, there's never the clinch or the kiss or the moment.'

Perhaps that is also what attracted Johnny to the project. But, perhaps most of all, he was drawn to the role by the magic of the *Peter Pan* story itself. 'It's truly a work of genius.

It's a masterpiece of imagination, and the result of the most remarkable inspiration. It's one of those rare perfect things in the world that will always be with us and this was a wonderful opportunity to explore where such a powerful story might have come from.'

Of course, there was another reason that Johnny was attracted to the role. Playing the part of the man who created *Peter Pan*, he says, finally gave him the childhood he never had. He openly confesses that he lost so much of his life to his wild lifestyle, and has famously admitted to having underage sex, drinking and starting on drugs by the age of 14. So taking on the role of the man who refused to grow up was like a dream come true after his own troubled youth. 'I think I lived the first 35 years of my life in a fog. I didn't really know what I wanted or who I was. I used to feel really lonely and I poisoned myself constantly: drinking, not eating right, no sleep, lots of cigarettes. If I had kept on going in that direction, I could have killed myself.

'My parents divorced when I was 15. We moved probably 30 times. I started smoking at 12, lost my virginity at 13 and did every kind of drug there was by 14. I swiped a few six-packs, broke into a few classrooms, just to see what was on the other side of that locked door. I did my share of despicable stuff.' But that, he now says, is all in the past.

Still enjoying the love of Vanessa and a settled family life with their two children in his adoptive home of Paris, Johnny insisted in 2004 that he is happier now than ever before with his life and his career. 'It's only because of my family that I am a better person and I'm much more centred than I've ever been. Meeting Vanessa changed all that. My kids gave me life. They are the greatest thing that's ever

Glenn in *Nightmare on Elm Street* was Johnny's movie debut when he was literally swallowed up by a bed in the first of Wes Craven's slasher movies.

Johnny's boyish charm in *21 Jump Street* made him an overnight pin-up.

Top: For *Cry Baby*, Johnny collaborated with famed director John Waters, for a role which satirised his own teen idol image. His performance drew comparisons to fifties rebels Marlon Brando, James Dean and Elvis Presley.

Bottom: Despite a lukewarm reception to *Dead Man* at Cannes 1995, Johnny valued the experience of working with co-star Robert Mitchum and director Jim Jarmusch.

Although it is not evident from his performance, much of Johnny's time shooting *What's Eating Gilbert Grape?* was plagued by emotional upheaval following his split from Winona Ryder. He is shown here with co-stars Leonardo di Caprio and Juliette Lewis.

According to director Tim Burton, starring in *Edward Scissorhands* together presented no problems for Johnny and Winona: 'They were very professional and didn't bring any weird stuff to the set.'

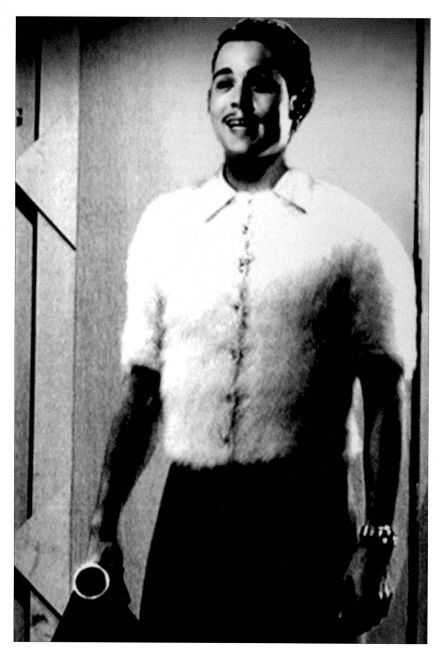

After the success of *Edward Scissorhands*, Johnny welcomed the opportunity to work with Tim Burton again on *Ed Wood*, an eponymous biopic of the occasional transvestite and worst B-movie director of all time.

Al Pacino and Johnny received critical acclaim for their roles in the mobster film *Donnie Brasco*. Many credited it as the finest film of its genre since *The Godfather*.

Posing for a London photocall before a rare appearance on *Top of the Pops* in September 1994. He played alongside The Pogues.

happened. I've lost most of the confusion that dominated my life. I didn't know what happiness was.'

Part of that happiness, he continues, was coming across *Finding Neverland*. In fact, it is one of the most satisfying projects he says he has worked on – even given the hard work it took to perfect the Scottish accent. 'Musically, rhythmically, I initially couldn't quite get a hold of it. Luckily, I found this dialect coach who helped me out a great deal. Also, we had a couple of crew guys who were Scottish and they picked up the falsities.

'*Peter Pan* is a masterpiece of imagination. It's one of those rare perfect things in the world that will always be with us, and, one has to wonder, with such a powerful story, where in the world did it come from? From what I gather, Barrie was only truly comfortable around children. I think he didn't know how to love or be loved in an adult way, and he was always looking for approval and maybe even for a mother figure. I created him from bits and pieces of observations from people who saw him as quite a dark figure – yet mixed together with the flashes of light and happiness that surely led him to write *Peter Pan*.'

Despite Johnny's pin-up status, he has usually avoided mainstream movies in favour of more interesting character parts. 'I never wanted to be a movie star. I've always wanted to be a character actor. I take roles because I fall in love with the character. It was never my goal to become a big box-office star. I built my career on failure. Before now, my movies never seemed to make any money. It's been tempting to accept a big paycheque, but I never saw the point of doing something that has been done thousands of times.

'The constant theme in things I do seems to be that they deal with people who are considered "freaks" by so-called "normal" people. I've never been bothered with the way I look as long as it's right for the character. Ugliness is better than beauty. It lasts longer and, in the end, gravity will get us all. I've had the opportunity to do all the things I wanted to do and work with all the people I wanted to work with. When I was asked to do *Finding Neverland*, it was certainly a big plus that it was a film my kids could watch. I had the same reason for doing *Pirates of the Caribbean*. I enjoy making films my kids can see. I think the idea of staying a child forever is beautiful, and I think you can. I've known plenty of people in their later years who were like little kids, had the energy of little children, the curiosity and fascination. But I think it's great fun growing old.'

And to play a character as playful and fatherly as J M Barrie must have been a dream come true. Just as he had found inspiration for Jack Sparrow in *Pirates of the Caribbean* from Keith Richards, Johnny turned to another unlikely source for his character in *Neverland*. This time to the Osbournes. 'There's an innocence to Ozzy Osbourne,' he told *The New York Times*. 'He's mingling, but he's somewhat detached.'

Certainly for Kate Winslet, working with Johnny really drove home the film's idea that anyone can tap into the spontaneity and adventure of being a child again. 'Johnny was so able to be a child on the set that it was sort of like working with five children for me! He made me and the boys constantly laugh with his cleverness which is exactly what we needed to create the spirit of the story.'

Winslet, of course, was no stranger to *Peter Pan*. She had

played Wendy in a theatre production when she was just 15 years old and has always been intrigued by the fantastical universe of Neverland. When she read the script for the movie, it was Sylvia Llewelyn Davies, the fiery bohemian mother of a brood of charming young boys in a time of great formality, who captured her fascination.

'The character is such an interesting person, because she's a very modern mother in an era when the view of children was just starting to change. Most people still believed children should be seen and not heard, and children were typically kept away from the adult life in the household. Sylvia does things differently, and she reflects a change in how children were raised. She's very involved in her children's upbringing and she encourages them to be free spirits. I love the fact that she's such a nonconformist.

'But Sylvia is also a recent widow, so there's a lot of buried grief and anger in her, and I think that's part of what makes James M Barrie so intriguing to her. He's this larger-than-life character who couldn't be more different from most of the men she meets in her social circle. She's really magnetically drawn to this man, not because he seduces her, but because he welcomes her into his incredible fantasy world. I do believe, at the end of the day, this is a love story, but it's about the love between Barrie and a whole family.'

Even though there aren't volumes written about Sylvia Llewelyn Davies's life, as there are with Barrie, some of the real Sylvia's letters and writings have survived. And from these Winslet was moved to learn that one aspect of her story that is entirely true is her decision not to be treated for her cancer. Sylvia wanted to protect her sons by shielding them from her debilitating illness and keep them from seeing her suffer through drawn-out and painful treatments. 'I think it was the most extraordinary act of bravery. She wanted life to continue as normal and she wanted to slip away quietly. It's an amazing sacrifice to have made for her children.'

For Forster, Winslet was a revelation in the role. 'She's a mother herself so she has this wonderful ability with the kids to embrace them and yet also be very down-to-earth. There's a real physicality to her as a mother that was very important to me; especially because, when she ultimately passes, you really feel the children's immense sense of loss.'

Another person who played a unique role in Barrie's creation of *Peter Pan* was Charles Frohman, the wealthy American impresario who stood by Barrie through much of his career, and found himself backing an entirely unconventional fantasy play he feared would be a failure. The real Charles Frohman, also known as 'the Napoleon of drama', was famed for his ability to develop new talent and was associated not only with Barrie but also with such major writers as Oscar Wilde and W Somerset Maugham. He was also noted for bringing to the fore such Broadway stars as John Drew, Ethel Barrymore, E H Sothern, Julia Marlowe, Maude Adams, and Henry Miller. (Tragically, Frohman died at the height of his career when the ocean-liner on which he was travelling, the *Lusitania*, was sunk by a German submarine. Echoing *Peter Pan*, his final words were reported to have been: 'Why fear death? It is the most beautiful adventure in life.')

Dustin Hoffman was recruited to play Frohman. Ever since he had seen *Monster's Ball*, he had wanted to work with Forster. And when he discovered that James Barrie was going to be played by Johnny, it was simply a bonus for Hoffman, who had long wanted to work with him as well. 'I think he's one of our greatest young actors. He has a quality that I highly admire. He tries everything in his power not to be a star. He takes chances on the roles he chooses and eludes being a pin-up, despite being so handsome.'

Hoffman was also intrigued by Frohman's profound commitment to making an artist's dreams come true, no matter how risky. 'What interested me about Frohman is that he's quite hesitant and reluctant to produce *Peter Pan*, a play with fairies, pirates and crocodiles that he can't imagine will be accepted by sophisticated London theatre-goers. Yet Frohman was the rarefied producer who had the ability to sense genius and who understood that, by definition, genius is excelling at doing something that hasn't been done yet, something in which the artist goes out on a limb. He let Barrie take a risk, and it paid off for the whole world.'

According to one reviewer, Roger Ebert of the *Chicago Sun-Times*, Johnny's performance as the soft-spoken, gentle, inward J M Barrie was remarkable. As remarkable, in fact, Ebert noted, as the performance given by newcomer Freddie Highmore, who was only nine years old when he started filming his role as the emotionally traumatised Peter Llewelyn Davies. Of course, the question on most journalists' lips was how did he come up with his astonishingly powerful performance? 'Well, you just sort of think about what the character's thinking,' he told them, 'and then you're in the character.'

With a vulnerability and focus unlike any child actor since Haley Joel Osment in *The Sixth Sense*, as far as most critics were concerned, Highmore provided an unforgettable portrait of an introverted young boy drawn further inward by the death of his father and the declining health of his mother. 'When there were scenes with Freddie,' Johnny recalls, 'Kate and I just stood back and let him go. It's unbelievably compelling.'

Winslet agreed. 'He has the most terrifying instincts, they're just bang-on. And he has no idea that he has that.'

So good was he, in fact, that both Johnny and Kate each recommended him for the title role in Tim Burton's *Charlie and the Chocolate Factory*, the movie that would reunite Johnny with Burton for a fourth time.

Overall, *Finding Neverland* was received as 'a joyfully unexpected film', so it was little wonder that it entered 2005 with a fistful of award nominations in the plethora of award shows with which both Hollywood and London now seem to abound. More importantly, of course, it would become Johnny's second successive movie to earn him an Oscar nomination for Best Actor.

CHAPTER 16

'AS AN ACTOR I THINK YOU OWE IT TO THE AUDIENCE TO TRY SOMETHING DIFFERENT EACH TIME. IT IS IMPORTANT TO KEEP EXPLORING. IF YOU KEEP DOING THE SAME OLD THING, IT IS LIKE THURSDAY, FRIDAY, SATURDAY – MEATLOAF. I JUST TRY TO DO DIFFERENT THINGS EACH TIME. FRANKLY IT'S A MIRACLE THAT I KEEP GETTING JOBS.'

PICTURE PERFECT

When Tim Burton offered Johnny the role of Willy Wonka, he was barely able to get the words out before Johnny said that he would love to do it. Johnny remembers, 'We were having dinner and he said, "I want to talk to you about something. You know that story *Charlie and the Chocolate Factory*? Well, I'm going to do it and I'm wondering if you'd want to play ..." and I couldn't even wait for him to finish the sentence. I said, "I'm in. Absolutely. I'm there." No question about it. To be chosen to play Willy Wonka in itself is a great honour, but to be chosen by Tim Burton is double, triple the honour. His vision is always amazing, beyond anything you expect. Just the fact that he was involved meant I didn't need to see a script before committing. If Tim wanted to shoot 18 million feet of film of me staring into a light bulb and I couldn't blink for three months, I'd do it.'

In no time at all, the two friends and collaborators were poring over Burton's preliminary sketches, discussing Wonka's look and the themes of the story, falling into the familiar creative rhythm that had begun when the director first cast Johnny as the lead in *Edward Scissorhands*, and had carried on in *Ed Wood* and *Sleepy Hollow*.

Besides, asserts Burton, 'Johnny is a great character actor in many ways. He's a character actor in the form of a leading man. That's what struck me about him from the very beginning and it's what makes him such an intriguing actor, the fact that he's not necessarily interested in his image but more in becoming a character and trying different things. He's willing to take risks. Each time I work with him he's something different.'

Producer Brad Grey agreed. 'He's a tremendously insightful actor. He came to the project with respect for the book and also a sense of how he could do something very special with this character. I can't think of anyone we'd rather have in the role. Sometimes the right magical combination comes together and I believe that's what we have here: Roald, Tim and Johnny.'

Published in 1964, *Charlie and the Chocolate Factory* is still one of the best-loved books of the past four decades by both children and adults, and has now sold well over 13 million copies worldwide and been translated into 32 languages. Its enduring popularity indicates how well the author understood, appreciated and communicated to children. As Grey observed, Roald Dahl 'never talked down to his readers or underestimated their intelligence'.

Certainly, Johnny would agree. He particularly appreciates the unexpected twists in Dahl's writing. 'You think it's going in one direction and then it slams you with another alternative, another route and makes you think. At its centre, *Charlie and the Chocolate Factory* is a great morality tale. But there's also a lot of magic and fun.'

Although the book remains hugely popular with children, the consensus of adult fans is that it's more than just a children's book. It's a wild ride, a fun-house candy fantasyland, but, of course, it has deeper emotional implications. The character of Wonka, who he is and who he becomes at the end of the story through his connection with young Charlie, is a very moving one. It's a fantasy that touches everyone.

'One of the interesting aspects of the book is that it's so vivid in mood and feeling and so specific, yet it still leaves room for interpretation,' says Burton. 'It leaves room for your own imagination, which, I think, is one of Dahl's strengths as a storyteller. Some adults forget what it was like to be a kid, Roald didn't. So you have characters that remind you of people in your own life and kids you went to school with, but at the same time it harkens back to age-old archetypes of mythology and fairytales. It's a mix of emotion and humour and adventure that's absolutely timeless and I think that's why it stays with you. He remembers vividly what it was like to be that age but he also layers his work with an adult perspective. That's why you can revisit this book at any time and get different things from it no matter what your age.'

And this is probably the same feeling that Burton wanted to create for his new movie version. In his retelling of the story, the film remained as faithful to the story as possible, but, in flashbacks that are not in the book, we learn that Willy's life is a complete reaction to an overly strict father, a candy-hating dentist, played by another Burton regular Christopher Lee.

It tells of how Wonka is forced to open his beloved factory for the first time in 15 years to find an heir, and is uncomfortable with the unfamiliar human contact. So he puts on his game face in front of people but underneath he has a great anxiety about actual contact or closeness, Johnny explained. 'I believe he's a germophobe, which is why he wears gloves, and in addition to the gloves it's as if he's wearing a mask. There are moments during the tour when we catch Wonka acting, and acting badly, literally reading off cue cards. I don't think he really wants to spend any time with these people. I think he's struggling, from the first second, to put on an act for them and keep a smile. At the same time, a part of him is genuinely excited about being the grand showman, like P T Barnum, pointing out everything he's created and saying, "Hey, look at this! Look what I've done, isn't this wonderful?"'

Willy Wonka is an eccentric, continued co-producer Richard Zanuck. 'He's odd, he's funny, he's aloof yet terribly vulnerable; it's an interesting composite, both childlike and deep at the same time. No other actor could give this character the kind of depth, range and spin it requires. Johnny has an incredible gift.'

Equally gifted was Freddie Highmore, who was reunited with Johnny for the first time since sharing the screen with him in *Finding Neverland* three years previously. He was 12 years old when *Charlie* began production, and couldn't have been more pleased to be playing the role of Charlie Bucket, a good-hearted boy from a poor family who lives in the shadow of Wonka's extraordinary factory.

Most nights in the Bucket home, dinner is a watered-down bowl of cabbage soup, which young Charlie gladly shares with his father, both pairs of grandparents and, of course, his mother, played by Burton's partner Helena Bonham Carter. They had started a relationship while they were working together on Burton's *Planet of the Apes*, and Helena has appeared in all of Burton's subsequent work.

The Buckets' home is a tiny, tumbledown drafty old house but it is filled with love. Every night, the last thing Charlie sees from his window is the great factory, and he drifts off to sleep dreaming about what might be inside. For nearly fifteen years, no one has seen a single worker going in or coming out of the factory, or caught a glimpse of Willy Wonka himself, yet, mysteriously, great quantities of chocolate are still being made and shipped to shops all over the word.

One day Willy Wonka makes a momentous announcement. He will open his famous factory and reveal 'all of its secrets and magic' to five lucky children who find golden tickets hidden inside five randomly selected Wonka chocolate bars. Nothing would make Charlie's family happier than to see him win but the odds are very much against him as they can only afford to buy one chocolate bar a year for his birthday. Indeed, as, one by one, news breaks around the world about the children finding golden tickets, Charlie's hope grows dimmer.

First, there is gluttonous Augustus Gloop who thinks of nothing but stuffing sweets into his mouth all day, followed by spoiled Veruca Salt, who throws fits if her father doesn't buy her everything she wants. Next comes Violet Beauregarde, a champion gum chewer who cares only for the trophies in her display case, and finally surly Mike Teavee, who's always showing off how much smarter he is than anyone else.

But then something wonderful happens. Charlie finds some money on the snowy street and takes it to the nearest store for a Wonka Whipple-Scrumptious Fudgemallow Delight thinking only of how hungry he is and how good it will taste. There under the wrapper is a flash of gold. It's the *last ticket*. Charlie is going to the factory! His Grandpa Joe is so excited by the news that he springs out of bed as if suddenly years younger, remembering a happier time when he used to work in the factory, before Willy Wonka closed its gates to the town forever. The family decides that Grandpa Joe should be the one to accompany Charlie on this once-in-a-lifetime adventure.

Once inside, Charlie is dazzled by one amazing sight after another. Wondrous gleaming contraptions of Wonka's own invention churn, pop and whistle, producing ever new and different edible delights. Crews of merry Oompa-Loompas mine mountains of fudge beside a frothy chocolate waterfall or ride a translucent, spun-sugar, dragon-headed boat down a chocolate river past crops of twisted candy trees and edible mint-sugar grass. Marshmallow cherry cream glows on shrubs, ripe and sweet. Elsewhere, a hundred trained squirrels on a hundred tiny stools shell nuts for chocolate bars faster than any machine, and Wonka himself pilots an impossible glass elevator that rockets sideways, slantways and every which way you can think of through the vast and fantastic factory.

Almost as intriguing as his fanciful inventions is Willy
Wonka himself, a gracious but most unconventional host.
He thinks about almost nothing but candy – except, every
once in a while, when he suddenly seems to be thinking
about something that happened long ago, something he
can't quite talk about. It's been said that Wonka hasn't
stepped outside of the factory for years. Who he truly is and
why he has devoted his life to making sweets Charlie can
only guess.

Meanwhile, the other children prove to be a rotten
bunch, so consumed with themselves that they scarcely
appreciate the wonder of Wonka's creations. One by one,
their greedy, spoiled, mean-spirited or know-it-all
personalities lead them into all kinds of trouble that force
them off the tour before it's even finished.

When only little Charlie is left, Willy Wonka reveals the
final secret, the grandest prize of all: the keys to the factory
itself. Long isolated from his family, Wonka feels it is time to
find an heir to his candy empire, someone he can trust to
carry on with his life's work, and so has devised this
elaborate contest to select that one special child. What he
never expects is that his act of immeasurable generosity
might bring him an even more valuable gift in return.

Charlie and the Chocolate Factory opened to both
impressive critical and box-office success in July 2005, and,
as Kirk Honeycutt wrote in his review of the film in the
Hollywood Reporter, it was 'a whimsical, magical mystery
tour of the world's greatest chocolate factory that has all the
gorgeousness of hard dark chocolate that melts ever-so-
slowly in your mouth. What a treat coming from Tim
Burton, who has recovered his imaginative touch after a few

missteps, and from his frequent collaborator Johnny Depp, an actor who resolutely embodies Burton's fanciful vision.'

Johnny would probably agree. 'Working with Tim is like arriving home. There is a kind of built-in language from having other experiences together. It is a very comfortable place to be.' There are times, though, Johnny admits, when he dreams of a little payback. That he might consider dabbling in directing again if he could get Burton to appear. 'If the tables were turned, I could do some of the things to him that he has done to me. Like squirting blood on my face off camera on *Sleepy Hollow* and giggling like an infant. Then there were these two horses. They were dragging me along and they had really bad flatulence. They'd had curry for lunch and I was the recipient.'

Payback or not, he continues, 'as an actor, for any character you play, you have to bring as much of your own truth to it as possible. But there is something to be said for it. It is very therapeutic to go and make an ass of yourself.' To play Wonka, he considered he was lucky to have the original source material of the book, rather than just the script, to draw upon. 'It was an amazing help in building the character. Then I had various conversations with Tim and we talked about the memories we had growing up of children's show hosts and that strange cadence in which they spoke to children. While I am reading a script, I get images and ideas in my head and I write everything down. The hairdo somehow I saw early on but it took a long time before I could see or hear Wonka. I just started building this guy layer by layer. Even when we started shooting I think it took me probably ten days to feel that I had really clicked with the guy.'

As *Charlie* was a film that is ostensibly aimed at children, so Johnny felt more at liberty than he usually does to try things out on his then six-year-old daughter, Lily Rose, and three-year-old son, Jack. What could be better, he asked. 'I would test the voice out on my daughter and it seemed to work with her so I kind of ran with it. They saw *Charlie and the Chocolate Factory*, which made me really nervous. I was scared they were going to come home and go, "No, Dad, no. Maybe next time." But they came home quoting it.'

But it was unlikely they would be quoting any lines from Johnny's next project, again with Burton. With echoes of Burton's previous foray into the craft of stop-motion animation, *Corpse Bride* looked certain to repeat the success of his 1993 masterpiece *The Nightmare Before Christmas*.

'What I love about stop-motion animation is that it's so tactile,' says Burton. 'There's something wonderful about being able to physically touch and move the characters, and to see their world actually exist. It's similar to making a live-action film – if you're doing it all on blue screen, it doesn't give you the feeling of actually being there, which the stop-motion process does.

'After doing *The Nightmare Before Christmas*, I was looking for something else to do in the same medium, because I love stop-motion animation. It's such a special art form. Joe Ranft, a friend of mine, gave me a little short story, a couple of paragraphs from an old folk tale, and it seemed right for this particular type of animation. It's like casting – you want to marry the medium with the material. And this seemed like a good match.'

Producer Allison Abbate was thrilled with the idea from the start. 'It's extraordinarily clever and it's a story that you haven't seen a hundred times before. It certainly has the Tim Burton look, the darkness of the humour and the quirkiness of the characters. What drew me most to the script was the fact that it's such a heartbreakingly beautiful story.' And it was.

In a small, gloomily repressed Victorian town, two shy young people are set to be married – although they've never met. Crass, social-climbing canned-fish tycoons Nell and William Van Dort have always dreamed of joining high society – but, while they're not lacking in wealth, they're sorely lacking in requisite class.

Conversely, old-money aristocrats Maudeline and Finis Everglot, direct descendants of the Duke of Everglot – as they freely profess to anyone who will listen – are full of class but drained of cash. Their money has long since dried up, and all they have left of worth is their name and social standing… and, as it turns out, their daughter Victoria. While they've never seen much worth in her, she may just be their ticket back up the social ladder, as it seems the Van Dorts have a bachelor son, Victor.

The Everglots are willing to hold their noses and grudgingly marry off Victoria to the son of the dreadful Van Dorts – nouveau-riche is still riche, after all. The deal is made and the two families are quickly in a tizzy, as everyone becomes excited about the impending nuptials… except the bride and groom. But everybody knows that marriage isn't about love anyway – just ask Maudeline and Finis.

Victor and Victoria first set eyes on each other on the eve of their wedding, when the families gather for a proper introduction between the soon-to-be newlyweds, to be immediately followed by a wedding rehearsal. While it's difficult to say who is shyer, upon their first meeting it seems possible that, against all odds, Victor and Victoria's chance for true love may not have been lost. But, at the rehearsal, Victor bungles his vows so badly – even before he accidentally lights his future mother-in-law's dress on fire – that Pastor Galswells sends him away until he can manage to learn his lines correctly.

Humiliated, he wanders off into the dark forest surrounding the village. Once he is alone, he is able to recite his vows perfectly, even going as far as gently placing the wedding ring on the root of a tree as a finishing touch. But it isn't a root after all.

Terrifyingly, the strange and beautiful decaying corpse of a woman wearing the tattered remains of a wedding gown rises up from the ground, wearing Victoria's ring on her bony finger. It seems that Victor has unwittingly betrothed himself to the Corpse Bride.

Ever since she was mysteriously murdered on her wedding night, the Corpse Bride has waited, heartbroken, for her groom to come and claim her. While her heart may have stopped beating long ago, her search for true love, and a husband to share her eternal rest with, has never ended. Victor mistakenly becomes that groom, and is dragged down beneath the earth to the Land of the Dead, a rowdy reversal of the staid life he has always known – in the Land of the Dead, the pubs are always open and corpses are more lively than anything you will find above ground in the dull and sombre Land of the Living.

Victor tries in vain to find his way back to Victoria, who is waiting bereft in the Land of the Living, somehow unable to convince anyone that a dead woman has dragged her fiancé off to the underworld. Instead of helping their daughter, the Everglots hastily arrange a second wedding, this time to the mysterious and sinister Barkis Bittern who just happens to be in the right place at the right time to take Victoria's hand...

While the Corpse Bride is determined not to let him escape the bonds of their unholy matrimony, Victor must find a way to return from the Land of the Dead and back into the arms of the love of his life.

What is perhaps interesting about the making of *Corpse Bride* is that it was while Johnny and Burton were filming *Charlie and the Chocolate Factory* that Johnny was called upon to create the voice of Victor on short notice. So, after shooting a scene earlier in the day as Wonka, Johnny would then have to rush over to the *Corpse Bride* recording studio and, as he puts it, cobble together a persona based on a 15-minute grilling session with Burton.

Johnny says, 'Victor was born in that little bit of time, and I didn't hear him for the first time until they were recording. So the preparation for this, I was remiss basically. I should be flogged. But I read it and loved it, but it somehow didn't occur to me that we were going to be doing it at the same time. I thought it was going to be like months down the road so I would have some time later to prepare for the character. So you could imagine my surprise when, as I was very, very focused on Wonka, Tim arrives on set and says, "Hey, you know, maybe tonight we'll go and record some of *Corpse Bride*. I was like, sure, of course we can. I have no character. I didn't know what the guy was going to sound like or anything.'

Although Johnny hastily conceived Victor's voice, 'he felt

like a guy that I knew. He didn't feel all that dissimilar to other characters that I've played for Tim. It was just the base emotional feeling. Along the lines of *Scissorhands* is what I felt. Tim was so helpful as he always is. He's a character that's not so far away from other characters that I've played in the past for Tim like *Edward Scissorhands*, a little bit of an outsider. A bumbling, deeply insecure nervous character. A lot like me in life.

'It's like Victor is represented in the same way as *Edward Scissorhands*, of not feeling comfortable in life. That universal feeling we all drag around with us for the rest of our days, of being inept, unable to be understood. The funny thing is I didn't expect to get to a point where I as a reader or I as a viewer would step outside of the actor in me and go, "Well, man, he should stay with the Corpse Bride." I really found myself in that dilemma which helped a lot when we were recording it. I felt, Man, I know Victoria Everglot is fantastic and everything and thank God they fell in love, but the Corpse Bride is so magnificent. She is wildly sexy and beautiful.'

Not only that, Johnny continues, but 'I was very lucky in that I got to meet Victor the puppet just before the session. So, just as I was finding out who he might be, I walked into the recording studio and there he was in his glory, and there was the Corpse Bride and everyone, so that was very helpful. The amazing thing is, and people have said it, there is some degree of resemblance. But the funny thing is they came up with those designs a year before.'

Something Johnny doesn't necessarily fear is the afterlife, which is depicted as a colourful, rollicking and jazzy place in the film. He doesn't claim to know what death will bring, but he has an idea of what he'd like to see in the next world. 'I think it would be great if you one day just went to sleep and woke up and it was 1920s Paris. That would be excellent. But I don't know, because there could be just dirt and worms.'

Corpse Bride was released in September 2005, the same month that Johnny teamed up with BBC Radio 2 in London to present a documentary about James Dean, someone he considered a personal hero. He had been commissioned to present the show by Bob Geldof, whose company Ten Alps Radio produced the programme. In the show, Johnny explored how Dean was perceived as an icon for a generation of rock musicians, including Elvis Presley, who according to David Bret's *Elvis: The Hollywood Years*, was 'obsessed with Dean during his formative years as an actor. He later confessed how he had seen *Rebel Without A Cause* 44 times before stepping on to a film set, and had purchased an original copy of the script so he could learn Jimmy's lines by heart. He subsequently became involved with two of the late stars' friends, Nick Adams and Natalie Wood.'

In fact, the book brings suggestions that Presley's manager Colonel Tom Parker held secret information about a gay affair between Elvis and Nick Adams, the actor who was sexually linked to Dean, over his head like a sword. He made it clear that, if Elvis didn't toe the line, he'd let it get out. At that time, it could well have ruined his career. That's why Parker had so much control over him. Bret says, 'Adams claimed that he had a brief affair with Elvis after Elvis "agreed to be his date" for a preview of Adams's 1956 film *The Last Wagon*.' Presley, by then a sex symbol sending legions of women swooning, became smitten with Adams and even tried unsuccessfully to get him a part in his first movie *Love Me Tender*, says Bret. In 1958, 'Nick Adams and Elvis stayed in the same room of the same hotel in New Orleans while Elvis was filming *King Creole* there.' And, although it sounds preposterous, the many journalists who had apparently attempted to 'out' the star in the past were thwarted by Parker.

Although the documentary didn't touch on such matters, it did commemorate the 50th anniversary of Dean's death on 30 September 1955 when Dean's car was involved in a head-on collision with another vehicle in California. Although Dean took a leading role in only three films – *East of Eden*, *Rebel Without A Cause* and *Giant* – his image was made synonymous with rebellious youth. He became a pin-up for many Western teenagers.

Dean counted many pop musicians among his fans, including Presley, Bob Dylan and John Lennon, who once said, 'Without James Dean, the Beatles would never have existed.'

In addition to presenting the show, Johnny also interviewed Dean enthusiasts, including Morrissey, Sir Paul McCartney, David Bailey and Dennis Hopper.

The show's producer, Des Shaw, said, 'One of the main things Johnny and Bob are looking at is how James Dean was enormously influential to music. He never heard rock 'n' roll and he died before Elvis, Buddy Holly or Eddie Cochrane had their first hits, but he was one of the biggest influences on the music.'

CHAPTER 17

'FIRST OF ALL, JOHNNY IS A PIRATE IN REAL LIFE.
IT'S THE CLOSEST PART HE'S EVER PLAYED TO HIS
REAL SELF, BUT THE FACT THAT HE PLAYED IT KIND
OF NELLY WAS A BIG RISK. IF ONLY REAL GAY
PIRATES WERE THAT MUCH FUN.'
JOHN WATERS

THE PIRATE KING

Just six months before the James Dean radio documentary aired in Britain, Johnny turned his attention back to his film work, and in particular, to reprising the most popular role of his career as Captain Jack Sparrow, for the second and third *Pirates of the Caribbean* movies that were about to be shot back-to-back, and set for release in the same way that the *Lords of the Rings* trilogy had been. One year apart, with the first, *Dead Man's Chest*, promised for a summer 2006 release and the second sequel, *At World's End*, for exactly one year later.

According to a synopsis that appeared on the internet while the third and final instalment was still in post-production, *At World's End* would see Will Turner and Elizabeth Swann team up with Captain Barbossa in a desperate quest to free Captain Jack from his trap in Davy

Jones's locker, while the ghost ship *The Flying Dutchman* and Davy Jones, now under the control of the East India Trading Company, wreak havoc across the Seven Seas. Navigating through treachery, betrayal and wild waters, they must forge their way to exotic Singapore and confront the cunning Chinese pirate Sao Feng. Headed beyond the very ends of the earth, each must ultimately choose a side in a final titanic battle, as not only their lives and fortunes are at stake, but also their entire futures to live the pirate way of freedom they have enjoyed so far.

As one would expect, the story picks up from where *Dead Man's Chest* left off, in which Captain Jack had discovered that he owed a blood debt to the legendary Davy Jones, Ruler of the Ocean Depths, who captains the ghostly *Flying Dutchman*, which no other ship can match for speed and stealth. And, unless the ever-crafty Jack can figure a cunning way out of his dilemma, he will be cursed to an afterlife of eternal servitude and damnation in the service of Jones.

Making matters worse, of course, is how Jack's problems manage to interrupt the wedding plans of Orlando Bloom and Keira Knightley, who also returned to reprise their roles as Will Turner and Elizabeth Swann, and who are forced to join Jack, on his confrontations with sea monsters, unfriendly islanders, a flamboyant soothsayer and even the mysterious appearance of Will's long-lost father, Bootstrap Bill.

Another new character was Lord Cutler Beckett of the East India Trading Company, who sets his sights on retrieving the fabled Dead Man's Chest. According to legend, whoever possesses it will gain control of Davy Jones, and, as soon as Beckett can get his hands on it, he intends to use it to destroy every last Pirate of the Caribbean once and for all.

If there was any criticism about the film, it was the amount of time taken to get all the pieces in play, which many considered a little too drawn out. It made the plot seem more complicated than it actually was. 'Once everything is established, though,' wrote one reviewer, 'the movie offers plenty of what made the first one so popular, but there's a sense that it doesn't need to be as long as it is.'

True or not, it didn't seem to bother *Rolling Stone* journalist Peter Travers. He was one of many critics that simply raved about the whole thing from beginning to end. 'The important thing is that it works. And what works most devilishly of all is Davy Jones, the squid-faced captain of *The Flying Dutchman* who bargains for the souls of those he captures. Davy and his crew of the undead have lived underwater so long they look like something out of an aquarium. I don't have a clue how the computer wizards accomplished the visual miracles – just wait till you see the Kraken, a giant sea monster who sucks entire ships down into Davy's locker – but Bill Nighy's performance as the buccaneer Jack calls "fish face" brims over with mirth and menace. With slimy tentacles wiggling around his head, Nighy blows away every other villain this summer. Not since Disney killed Bambi's mother (Nemo's too) has the studio built up the jolt ante so high on PG-13 entertainment. Kids may wet their pants, but so what? It's the triumphant rogue in Depp that keeps this pirate ship afloat and actually makes the third voyage a trip worth booking.'

Elsewhere, critics echoed much the same sentiment as Travers. One was Baz Bamigboye in the *Daily Mail*. 'There's a lot to enjoy in this high-priced piece of popcorn. Mind you, it's the best popcorn you're likely to find this summer. It's wall-to-wall fun, full of pure silliness.'

The BBC's Nev Pierce shared the same opinion: 'Brace the mainsail and shiver those timbers, etc., for this is a superb swashbuckler – rousing, funny and spectacular.'

Steve Rose, writing in the *Guardian*, was one of those who thought the beginning was too slow, but still joined in with what was now becoming predictable praise. 'It takes a tortuously long time to get all the narrative plates spinning, and, despite all the fits, starts, and flaws, there's enough invention and energy here to make you want to see the next instalment.'

Pirates of the Caribbean: Dead Man's Chest was released in July 2006 and, perhaps as expected, enjoyed both the biggest opening-day and single-day record of the year taking a more-than-respectable $55 million and, on its first weekend, another $135 million. Like the Disney park ride itself, the movies seemed to have appealed to the little bit of pirate that lives within us all, the desire for freedom, adventure and a small amount of mischief. If it's true to say that *Pirates 1* and *2* both sailed into entirely new cinematic territory, breaking with tradition by linking its high-seas tale with lashings of irreverent humour, as typified by Johnny's original and brilliantly inspired creation of Captain Jack Sparrow, then it would also be true to say that the likes of Johnny's own thought-out pirate is something that audiences had never seen before.

It is perhaps interesting to debate whether there could

have been another actor who could have turned Captain Jack into what seems like the only true iconic screen character to have come out of the new millennium. A wholly original and thrillingly eccentric creation conjured up by Johnny. Who, after all, would have thought of playing him like some sort of ducking, weaving, highly superstitious pirate captain of equally dubious morality and personal hygiene to become the screen anti-hero for a new century? But maybe Johnny was surprised too at how popular his character has actually become.

With his long dreadlocks and braided beard adorned with a wild assortment of beads and baubles, various and sundry amulets hanging from his attire, and teeth studded with gold and silver, Captain Jack, like the film itself, appealed to audiences that ran the gamut in age, gender and nationality. In fact, Johnny's performance as Jack Sparrow was so memorable in the first movie that it was named as one of the 100 greatest performances of all time in the May 2006 edition of *Premiere* magazine.

'If you ask most people what they loved most about the first movie,' explains executive producer Mike Stenson, 'it's usually this completely iconoclastic Jack Sparrow character. In a 500-channel universe, where you have so many different opportunities to be entertained in so many ways, you have to give the audience something that's unique and different. That's exactly what Johnny did with Captain Jack Sparrow in *The Curse of the Black Pearl*. He created this character and had absolutely committed to it, and both producer Jerry Bruckheimer and director Gore Verbinski had to tell the powers that be to trust them on it after they saw the first dailies. At the end of the day, Johnny took a risk, and Jerry and Gore backed him 100 per cent.'

Certainly, confirms Bruckheimer, 'Johnny is one of our greatest actors. He invented Jack Sparrow in the first movie, and he's not somebody who wants to rest on his laurels for the second and third. He takes a character to even newer heights. None of us would be back if Johnny had not wanted to play this character again. He loved making the first movie, and audiences loved him right back.'

As for Johnny, he himself claims that 'it is beyond me how such a character has sort of taken root in some people's hearts. It's still shocking to me. I was handed this opportunity to make something of this character, and I had pretty solid ideas about who he was and what he should be like. There were a number of people who thought I was nuts. But I was committed to the guy, and I think that's what happened to me in terms of finding the character. What I set out to do was to try and make Captain Jack appeal to little kids as well as the most hardened adult intellectuals.'

But as screenwriter Terry Rossio notes, 'One of the archetypes that is really underused in American cinema is the trickster character. Most American movies tend to celebrate the warrior who does the right thing at the right time. But the fun thing about Jack, who is definitely a trickster, is that he's not particularly good at avoiding getting caught. He will get caught… you just can't hold on to him for very long. Jack knows that, if he can just bide his time, eventually the world will come over to his side, and that gives him this sort of supreme confidence that he can handle just about any situation.'

The other fun thing about the trickster character, adds

Ted Elliott, Rossio's writing partner, 'is that he basically is just out to have his own good time. He's following his own self interests. The things he does will affect other people – the mortals, if you will – and sometimes it will be to good benefit, and sometimes it will be to their detriment. So that goes back to the whole question posed in the first movie: is Jack Sparrow a good guy or is he a bad guy? Is he a pirate hero or pirate villain? Well, it really kind of depends on the perspective you have.'

Of course, no one ever thought that there would be a sequel, let alone two. The success of the first movie, probably took everyone by surprise. As Bruckheimer now admits, 'There were limited expectations for the first *Pirates*. Lots of people thought we were making a Disney ride movie for toddlers, and, what's more, the pirate genre had been dead for 40 years, and every attempt to revive it had bombed miserably. But then *The Curse of the Black Pearl* was released and caught everybody by surprise, which is the best way to do it. The artistry that Gore and the writers brought to it, and the performances by Johnny, Orlando, Keira and Geoffrey, just captured everybody's imagination and it became a huge success internationally.

'Everything that we set up in the first movie gets pushed forward in the second,' Bruckheimer continues, 'and of course we have the same creative team. Gore is such a brilliant director, with a wonderful sense of humour and a great visual sense. Often, strongly visual directors aren't great storytellers because they focus so much on the physical look of the movie. But Gore has both the visual acumen and the understanding of storytelling and characterisation.'

Pirates of the Caribbean: The Curse of the Black Pearl not only revived the genre, but also kicked off a groundswell of fascination for all things piratical which resulted in everything from a spate of new books about the seafaring scallywags to a boom in pirate-themed children's (and adults') parties, to pirate dinner shows, not to mention 'I Love Jack Sparrow' stickers plastered on to schoolgirls' binders everywhere.

Clearly, there was a worldwide mandate for more *Pirates*, and Bruckheimer and Verbinski, along with Walt Disney Pictures, decided that just one sequel would not be enough. It made practical sense, economically, to film two follow-ups simultaneously, taking full advantage of locations, sets and availability of its increasingly in-demand stars. It also made sense creatively, because with the characters so well established in the first film, taking them on further voyages was an exciting prospect. 'We were hoping for the success of *The Curse of the Black Pearl* so that we could make more *Pirates* movies,' notes Bruckheimer, 'and when you see the second and third films you'll see that everything relates back to what started everything off in the first. It's a true trilogy.'

'You really need to have some substance behind it,' says Stenson. 'You need to not only deliver the entertainment value, the roller-coaster ride and the laughs, but, if you're going to ask people to stay around for three movies, you have to feel like there's something thematically significant that you're going to explore.'

Certainly, Terry Rossio agrees with that summation: 'Whereas in the first film, the theme-park attraction was a wellspring for ideas, for the second and third films we actually went back to the first movie.'

Ted Elliott agreed. 'There was a richness to the characters that we felt we could explore, but you don't want to just go through the same paces with the characters. You don't want to see them doing the same thing. One of the things we liked about the characters in the first film was that there's a certain moral ambiguity to them, and we wanted to explore that… we wanted to put Jack Sparrow into a situation where he has to do something that, in fact, puts his goals in opposition to Will and Elizabeth's goals. It was all about expanding the characters and taking them in a further direction.

'Much of the basis of the first movie was the romantic story between Will and Elizabeth, and we knew we wanted to get into more of a mature examination of the relationship between the two of them. What happens to Will and Elizabeth after that wildly romantic final kiss with the beautiful sunset at the end of *The Curse of the Black Pearl*?'

Dead Man's Chest also delves deep into the treasure trove of pirate and seagoing lore and mythology, from Davy Jones, he of the famous 'locker', to the legendary Kraken, a sea monster fabled since the 12th century. 'You think of the sea,' Elliott says, 'and there are a lot of supernatural stories you've heard. But nobody had actually done those stories as part of a larger pirate movie or swashbuckler, so there was a wealth of legends to draw from. We touched on some of those in the first movie: there's a line of dialogue in which Will talks about sending himself down to Davy Jones's Locker. So, in *Dead Man's Chest*, we decided to explore who Davy Jones is, and then we brought in another well-known legend of the seas, *The Flying Dutchman*, and combined them together.'

Elliott and Rossio also cleverly utilised one of history's greatest economic and political powers – the East India Trading Company – as a pivotal entity in the plot of *Dead Man's Chest*. Like much else in the *Pirates* movies, historical reality is used as a springboard for fun and fantasy. The real British East India Company was a tool of imperialist domination, economically and politically, from 1600 to its dissolution in 1858, essentially ruling India and spreading its tentacles as far as the Persian Gulf, Southeast Asia and East Asia. Even the most generous contemporary histories describe the East India Company's activities as extraordinarily greedy and inhumane. 'What we like about pirates,' Elliott raves, 'is that they represent freedom. And the East India Company, as a giant multi-national corporation, represents the end of individual freedom. They're defining the world as they want it to be, and there will be a lot of people they're going to leave out. The more dominance they have, the less room there is for people like Captain Jack Sparrow.'

Another person who could enthusiastically explain the movie's attraction was Keira Knightley. Even though she had been happily surprised by the massive success of the first film, she understood why it was so popular. 'We were doing a movie based on a Disney theme-park ride in a genre that hadn't been successful in something like fifty years, but we had Gore Verbinski, whose vision is quite extraordinary, and Johnny Depp, whose portrayal of Jack Sparrow kind of brought the film into a whole new phenomenal world.

'What's nice about this movie is that the characters have evolved. When we first meet Elizabeth at the beginning of the story, she's on the brink of getting married to Will, which falls to pieces because a character named Lord Cutler Beckett comes into the equation, and he wants to annihilate piracy from the world. He's determined to arrest Will for being a pirate and Elizabeth for aiding in the escape of Captain Jack Sparrow. Elizabeth becomes a woman on a mission, and there are some quite nice undertones to her relationship with Will, as well as to Jack Sparrow... which grows into something very interesting.'

Later, of course, when Keira learned that she would be kissing both her leading men on screen, she was simply thrilled. She is still, to this day, the envy of her friends after locking lips with them both. 'I get both of them! My girlfriends were really, really angry. I think I'm hated completely! They were very gentlemanly. Both had Altoids before we started kissing, which is always nice, the sign of a very nice man. The stubble's not great... No, actually I don't remember it being a particular problem!'

Johnny, Keira and Orlando were not the only cast members to return to the *Pirates* set. Once again, Jack Davenport was on board to play a now disgraced British Commodore James Norrington; Jonathan Pryce returned as Elizabeth's aristocratic father, Governor Weatherby Swann, as did Kevin McNally as the often soused sailor Joshamee Gibbs, Lee Arenberg and Mackenzie Crook as the eternally bickering and philosophising piratical best mates Pintel and Ragetti, David Bailie as the silent Cotton, whose parrot does all the talking, and Martin Klebba as the diminutive but tough Marty, unafraid to go up against adversaries three times his size.

For the new roles, Stellan Skarsgård from Bruckheimer's *King Arthur* was recruited to play Bootstrap Bill Turner, Will's

THE SECRET WORLD OF JOHNNY DEPP

long-lost father; Naomie Harris was cast as the soothsayer Tia Dalma, a gypsy queen who has magic powers to see through people; and Tom Hollander accepted the part of Lord Cutler Beckett, who, as head of the East India Trading Company, seeks to forever destroy the age of the pirates.

One of the most challenging roles to fill, however, would be Davy Jones, who is as much sea creature as he is human. Although the final choice of Bill Nighy may have appeared an unconventional one to many, it was obvious to Bruckheimer and Verbinski that he would be perfect. They knew only too well that he would find the humanity beneath the character's beastly veneer.

'Davy Jones is a deeply damaged and isolated individual,' says Nighy. 'He's wounded so deeply that he determines that he will live a kind of semi-life, as long as it means he doesn't have to feel anything any more. And, so, he's torn out the centre of all feeling – his heart – and locks it in a special chest. He also has control of a "pet" as it's sometimes referred to, which is the Kraken – a sea monster which is the likes of which you've never seen before, entirely malevolent, evil and powerful beyond expression. If you possess Davy Jones's heart, you control not only him, but the Kraken as well, which in effect gives you control of the oceans.'

Nighy's primary challenge would be that, because of Davy Jones's astonishing physical appearance, he would be acting throughout the film in what resembles a grey tracksuit and matching cap with reference marks for computer wizards, who would embellish it with the amazing details as imagined by Gore Verbinski and famed conceptual artist Mark 'Crash' McCreery. But Nighy was game to take it on. 'The first movie was not only successful, but is actually beloved, and has entered the language in a way that I think few movies do. To be part of this was a very satisfying notion. As for playing a character which will be physically embellished by computer wizardry, as an actor you use your imagination. The same things are required of you, generally speaking.'

Even if nobody could visualise Nighy as Davy Jones, there was no doubt about Keith Richards. However, the *Pirates* set descended into chaos when the legendary Rolling Stones guitarist shot his long-awaited cameo as Johnny's father for the third movie.

But the most surprising casting choice of all was neither man, woman nor beast, but the 169-foot, full-rig HMS *Bounty*, which in *Dead Man's Chest* was seen as the *Edinburgh Trader*. The *Bounty*, like its real-life namesake, has had an extraordinary history of its own. She was built for Metro-Goldwyn-Mayer's 1962 version of *Mutiny on the Bounty*, which starred Marlon Brando, Trevor Howard and Richard Harris, the first ship ever built from the keel up specifically for a motion picture.

Construction of the *Bounty* began in Lunenburg, Nova Scotia, in February 1960, and took seven months and more than 400,000 board feet of lumber in the Smith and Rhuland Shipyard, before it sailed for Tahiti and the production of the blockbuster feature. Although the historical *Bounty* was 85 feet long, its cinematic reconstruction was 118 feet in length to allow the cameras more free movement during shooting, and her total height from deck to the top of the mainmast is 103 feet. For *Mutiny on the Bounty*, the ship made the 7,327-mile voyage from Lunenburg to Tahiti via the Panama Canal in 33 sailing days. Forty-three years later, the *Bounty*, under Captain Robin R Walbridge, would be required to sail a mere 2,096 statue miles (1,821 nautical miles) in 14 days from Bayou La Batre to St Vincent, where she would be refitted and repainted as the *Edinburgh Trader*.

But what is perhaps most interesting of all about any of the movies is that, when news hit that Johnny was going to make the first *Pirates*, the buzz around Hollywood was that he must be broke, and that he had finally sold out. Not that Johnny was concerned or worried. 'Never, not once, and I don't know why, because one would think that I would have. I suppose it's because I feel like I have a voice. The idea of commercial success never bothered me necessarily. What bothered me was striving for that, and lying to get that. If I was going to do something, it had to be on my terms, not because I'm some hideous control freak, but because I don't want to live a lie. You really don't want to look back on your life and go, "I was a complete fraud."'

It's probably true to say that no one in Hollywood has worked harder at *not* being a movie star than Johnny Depp has, and yet he has evolved into one of the most adored actors of his generation, not in spite of that persistence, but because of it. *Pirates of the Caribbean: The Curse of the Black Pearl* may have grossed $653 million worldwide, making Johnny a $20 million earner and winning him an Oscar nomination, but he still seems an unlikely addition to the A-list. Top-tier stars, even those who are great actors, stay on top by being true to their personas. They're more than actors. They're brands. Johnny is almost pathologically unpredictable. But he is never the same. 'Nobody is sick of Johnny Depp,' says his *Cry Baby* director John Waters.

Tim Burton agrees. 'He's always been true to who he is. He's never been ruled by money, or by what people think he should or shouldn't do. Maybe it's just in America, but it seems that, if you're passionate about something, it freaks people out. You're considered bizarre or eccentric. To me, it just means you know who you are.'

It wasn't that long ago that Johnny got himself a reputation for being outre and unbankable. 'Oh, yeah,' Johnny laughs. 'That guy can't open a film. He does all those weird art movies. He works with directors whose names we can't pronounce. But there are worse things they could say.'

If *Pirates of the Caribbean: The Curse of the Black Pearl* changed all that, then *Dead Man's Chest* would continue with the path Johnny now seemed to be treading. The sequel ended up as the highest-grossing movie of the summer 2006. And, to many, it delivered its promise to be a welcome blast of sunshine in a season when *The Da Vinci Code* proved a joyless blockbuster.

The question on everyone's lips now is will Johnny, after three *Pirates* movies, all as successful as each other, be able to let go of Captain Jack? It seems not just yet. 'He's a blast to play. I'll be in a deep, dark depression saying goodbye to him. I'll keep the costume and just prance around the house, and entertain the kids.'

Or, as one journalist wondered, as did perhaps the rest of the world, in *Pirates 4, 5* and *6*? 'If they had a good script,' Johnny says, 'why not? I mean, at a certain point, the madness must stop, but, for the moment, I can't say that he's done.'

Nor was he done with his working partnership with Tim Burton. As always, Johnny jumps at the chance whenever there is an opportunity to work with him. Soon after

Pirates of the Caribbean had resumed filming for its third outing, DreamWorks Studios confirmed that *Sweeney Todd: The Demon Barber of Fleet Street*, based on the award-winning Stephen Sondheim musical thriller, would be directed by Burton and star Johnny in the title role, as Benjamin Barker, a man unjustly imprisoned by a lecherous judge, played by Alan Rickman. Barker returns as London barber Sweeney Todd and exacts revenge. The film was scheduled to go before cameras at Pinewood Studios in February 2007, marking the sixth collaboration between Johnny and Burton.

To some, especially the sceptics in Hollywood and Broadway, it seemed a risky choice for Johnny to take on as a role. After all, his only musical background was as a guitarist, not a vocalist, so perhaps it was not surprising that the pundits remained leery about the whole idea. To start with it seemed a preposterous notion as no one was quite sure whether Johnny could sing or not, and even if he could, would he be able to do it well enough to carry the picture? But Burton had no doubts whatsoever that Johnny was absolutely the right person to make it work. 'I saw him so clearly as Sweeney Todd, ' he admitted. 'And I know, he wouldn't just do anything with me just to do it. That's all I needed and I just knew he could. It was just a feeling I had that he could do it.'

It probably didn't help that the story of *Sweeney Todd* had been the inspiration for many theatrical shows, as well as a number of films for both cinema and television, the most recent outing being the BBC production in 2006 starring Ray Winstone. Interestingly enough, it was not until Christopher Bond's 1973 stage play that audiences were first introduced to the Barker/Turpin revenge plot that is now considered part and parcel of Sweeney's legend. Then, in 1979, using Bond's play as his template, Stephen Sondheim, the legendary American lyricist and composer – one of a very select group to have won an Academy Award, a Tony, an Emmy, a Grammy and a Pulitzer Prize – brought the story of *Sweeney Todd* to a wider audience, with his and Hugh Wheeler's acclaimed stage musical, *Sweeney Todd: The Demon Barber of Fleet Street*.

Debuting on Broadway on March 1, 1979, and starring Len Cariou as Sweeney Todd and Angela Lansbury as Mrs. Lovett, Sondheim's *Sweeney Todd: The Demon Barber of Fleet Street* was quite unlike anything then seen on stage. Bloody and terrifying, with a score inspired by the work of legendary soundtrack composer Bernard Herrmann, best known for his work on Alfred Hitchcock's *Psycho* and *The Birds*, it initially startled audiences, but quickly became recognized as Sondheim's masterpiece, with the production swiftly transferring to London and later being revived on Broadway in 1989 and 2005.

Of course, there are those who claimed that Sweeney Todd really did exist and how he was responsible for 160 murders in 18th century London. But it's more widely accepted that he was a fictional creation who first came to prominence in a story called *The String Of Pearls: A Romance*, written by Thomas Peckett Prest and published in *The People's Periodical* in November 1846. According to legend, Todd would cut his customers' throats while they sat in his barber's chair, then send their bloody corpses down a chute into the cellar below, where they were chopped up and used as the filling for meat pies by his accomplice in crime, the widowed baker Mrs. Nellie Lovett – pies that were then sold to an unsuspecting public. Pretty soon, Todd's notoriety was rivalling that of another infamous 19th-century London serial killer – Jack the Ripper.

But more than that, according to Sondheim, it has endured for 150 years because it's a really good story. 'It's a very gripping tale. It's a story about revenge and how revenge eats itself up.' So much so, was Sondheim's passion for the story that he turned the story into an acclaimed musical, which in turn, also became the reason that Burton wanted to turn it into a film. 'In that sense it's a tragedy in the classic tradition about someone who goes out for revenge and ends up destroying himself.'

Burton himself had seen Sondheim's stage version in London when he was a student there. 'I'm not a big musical fan, but I loved it,' he recalls. 'I didn't know anything about Stephen Sondheim. The poster just looked kind of cool, kind of interesting. It's like an old horror movie but the music is such an interesting juxtaposition, being very beautiful while the imagery is kind of old horror movie. And it was interesting to see something bloody on stage, too. I went to see it twice because I liked it so much.'

Indeed, he liked it so much that years later, in 2001, long before he was even attached to direct the film, while he was visiting Johnny at his home in the south of France, he gave him a copy of the Angela Lansbury stage production on CD, and told him to give it a listen. Five or six years after that, he asked Johnny what was now on everyone's lips, could he sing? Johnny had no idea but he was willing to give it a try to find out.

But then again, Johnny can't ever remember singing a complete song from beginning to end. Even when he was playing with The Kids in the 1980s, he was never the vocalist of the band. No, he laughs, 'I was always the guy who would come in and sing the harmony, very quickly. It would be all of like three seconds and then I was out, and I could find my way back to the dark and continue playing guitar. So I had never sang a song.' All the same, he told Burton, he would go into former bandmate, Bruce Witkin's studio in Los Angeles, to investigate, and as he put it, 'try and sing the songs,' and if he was close, then he would talk to Burton about it, and if he wasn't, then he would simply tell him that he couldn't do it, that it would just be impossible for him to do the film.

Witkins recorded Johnny singing *My Friends*, which turned out to be the first song he had ever sang in his life. 'It was pretty weird and scary,' he confessed. But he trusted Witkins to be honest enough to deliver a verdict on whether he thought he could sing or not. Witkins remembers the moment well. He asked Johnny if he wanted the good news or the bad news? 'Well, give me the bad news.' And Witkins did exactly that. 'I told him that you're going to have to do this.'

If Witkins was impressed with Johnny's singing voice, then producer Richard D Zanuck would be over the moon the first time he heard him sing. 'I was in my office on the phone, Tim bursts in and lays down a little cassette player and his headphones and he walks out. So I got off the phone, put them on, and listened to Johnny sing for the first time. I went into Tim's office, and we both just stared at each other with great relief. We had the biggest smiles because we knew we had a great voice with Johnny, and we knew he could really pull this off.'

Not only that, Zanuck continues, 'but we knew Johnny could play Sweeney Todd as only Johnny can. Talk about a risk taker. The bigger the risks, the more attractive a role is to Johnny. He's built his whole career on pictures and roles that most actors have turned down or would turn down. He's the master of disguise. He's the master of doing something unique every time out. He has a different look, a different personality, and in this case, he'll have a voice that people will be absolutely astounded by.'

Johnny's co-star Helena Bonham Carter agrees: 'I've always admired Johnny because of his choices as an actor, and because he's always done things according to his own lights. He's never done anything according to any sort of pattern or formula or to create a career, or because he was relying on his looks. I think, in a funny way, we're a bit similar, in that we don't have much respect for what we look like, we rather like camouflaging and getting away from ourselves.'

It was something that Zanuck also admired, not just with Johnny but also with Burton. He also commented on how, when they worked together, they were like any good team with an almost unspoken way of doing things. 'Johnny looks to Tim for guidance and Tim looks to Johnny for taking what he has outlined and pushing it a little further. They really love each other and would do anything for each other. It's a deep friendship, and they're both lovely people, fun to work with and hard-working. And they're both at the top of their game. So the combination is wonderful in terms of freshness and inventiveness.'

Certainly, says Burton, 'Every time Johnny and I work together we try to do something different. And singing for a whole movie is not something we're used to. You never just want to feel like, "Okay, that was easy. What's next?" Johnny and I are always wanting to stretch ourselves, and this was a perfect outlet for that.'

And if no one believed that Johnny could sing, Bonham Carter was adamant that he could deliver a song with the best of them. 'It's very sexy. And it's very sexy singing, and it sounds like him, that's what's exciting. He really sings from the gut, and it's a very emotional role. So it's very naked and very sexy and very touching and brave and beautiful, very beautiful, and soulful.' Certainly continues Burton, 'Johnny's got a nice timbre to his voice. It's coming from within and that's what's so great about it.'

Not so great, however was the day filming had to be halted when Johnny's daughter, Lily-Rose, quite suddenly and quite unexpectdely, fell gravely ill. She was rushed to Great Ormond Street Hospital for Children with suspected blood poisoning just twenty-three days after the project had begun.

CHAPTER 18

'TO SAY IT WAS THE DARKEST MOMENT,
THAT'S NOTHING. IT DOESN'T COME CLOSE TO
DESCRIBING IT. WORDS ARE SO SMALL. NOW EVERY
SINGLE MILLISECOND IS A MINI-CELEBRATION.
EVERY TIME WE GET TO BREATHE IN AND EXHALE
IS A HUGE VICTORY.'

CHICAGO BLUES

Nine days after Lily-Rose fell seriously ill, and she was discharged from hospital. Johnny and Vanessa took her back to the London hotel where they had set up home while he filmed *Sweeney Todd* at Pinewood. As one hotel onlooker observed, when they arrived from Great Ormond Street, 'Johnny carefully lifted her from the car, held her close and carried her in. He looked exhausted and ill with worry.' Not surprising when you consider that his daughter was lucky to have survived what has since been described as a very serious medical condition. It was, said friends and colleagues, 'certainly touch and go for while.'

Despite initial reports that Lily-Rose had suffered blood poisoning that spread through her body to vital organs, it turned out that it was not blood poisoning after all, but a bout of the lethal E coli virus, that caused one of her kidneys to shut down and placed her on the critically ill list. She became even more of a concern when she did not respond to treatment. According to most medical journals E coli is a type of food poisoning that is commonly caused by improperly cooked meat, unpasteurised milk or water contamination. But certain strains can get into the blood, causing a rare but very serious infection. It is a bacterium which normally lives inside the intestines, where it helps break down and digest food. It has up to a 50 per cent mortality rate in the elderly and children under five, and can also lead to long-term kidney and sight problems. And it was that 'very serious infection' which knocked Lily-Rose for six.

Facing their darkest hours, days and nights, Johnny and Vanessa kept a round-the-clock bedside vigil until their seven-year-old daughter pulled through and was well enough to go home. 'It gave us a great scare,' Johnny recalls. 'What got us through this wasn't the strength of Vanessa or me, but our daughter and her incredible ability to make us feel okay even though she was very unwell. She was super-strong. It was a very bumpy patch, but she has come through it beautifully and unscathed, and she is now as healthy as she always was. She is wonderful. It was a reminder to us of how lucky we are to be able to breathe, walk, talk, think and surround ourselves with people we love.'

It was something that Johnny's Los Angeles spokesperson, Robin Baum, confirmed. 'We are happy to report that their daughter is doing much better. The family greatly appreciates the continued support and respect of their privacy.' The respect that Baum was referring to was the fact that the press had refused to reveal details about

Lily-Rose's medical condition, or the location of the hospital where she was being treated.

Johnny and Vanessa were grateful. It would, understandably, be some months before Johnny could bring himself to speak publicly about the pain that had affected him and Vanessa so much, and which at one stage had even threatened his departure from the set of *Sweeney Todd*. He even called Tim Burton to tell him that he should perhaps recast. 'It was a very bumpy patch,' says Johnny. 'To say it was the darkest moment, that's nothing. It doesn't come close to describing it. Words are so small. Now every single millisecond is a mini-celebration. Every time we get to breathe in and exhale is a huge victory. She pulled through beautifully, perfectly, with no lasting anything.'

The cast and crew at Pinewood were also ecstatic to hear the news. A spokesman said: 'We adjusted the schedule to accommodate Johnny's needs at this moment. We understand that Lily-Rose is improving. Obviously, everybody at the studio is certainly with them in their good spirits.' Not that Johnny expected what he had done out of love to be turned into something heroic. As one journalist remarked, quite ironically, 'Isn't it interesting how when Johnny Depp demonstrates he's a devoted and thoughtful dad, the impossible happens, he gets even hotter!'

To show his appreciation for the 'wonderful care and treatment' the medical staff provided to his family, less than nine months later Johnny made an unannounced visit to Great Ormond Street Hospital to donate £1million to their fundraising drive. They needed to raise £170million in five years as part of a redevelopment and expansion programme. Even then, Johnny was still describing the ordeal over his daughter's illness as 'the most frightening thing we have ever been through.' Disney, the studio behind Johnny's *Pirates of the Caribbean* films, also donated £10million. And if that was not enough, Johnny had already spent time at the hospital some months earlier reading bedtime stories to patients while dressed as Captain Jack Sparrow. It was, all enthused, a remarkably gracious thing for him to do.

Once Johnny and Vanessa were given the all-clear about Lily-Rose's health, he dived straight back into work. He was only too aware that the production of *Sweeney Todd* was now behind schedule, and that he had to get back to Pinewood as quickly as he could to complete the filming, which in the end, wrapped, just in time, for him to cut into the promotion for the third *Pirates* outing that was due to open worldwide on Memorial Day weekend, the traditional start to the U.S. summer movie season.

Pirates of the Caribbean: At World's End had its world premiere at Disneyland on May 19, 2007. Thousands of fans lined Main Street to watch Johnny and his colleagues walk the red carpet. Like its predecessor, *At World's End* brought moviegoers to the box office in their droves and in no time whatsoever, it had become the top-grossing film in the world for its year of release, earning more than $961 million at the box-office. Not only that, it went onto to become the fifth highest-grossing film of all time. Critical reaction was mixed at best, but the general consensus was that it was far too complicated to follow. Just two weeks earlier, the debut of *Spiderman 3* with its biggest movie opening ever for the month of May was promptly broken when *World's End* burst onto 4,362 screens across America.

Not long after *World's End* had opened, there was talk of

a fourth sequel. Obviously, Johnny admits, virtually no cinema's perfect. 'Pirates One had its own thing, Two and Three, I suppose, had their own thing, and it got a little confusing here and there in the story, not that I've seen the movies, but I hear tell,' he laughs. 'I think, for me, because I love the character so much and I enjoy playing the character so much and people seem to like it, if there's an opportunity to try again, you know, it's like going up to bat. You want to get back out there and try and try and try and see what you can do. I enjoy playing Captain Jack very much.'

Having got over one hurdle, Johnny was to soon face another. The news of Heath Ledger's tragic and untimely death in New York from a drug overdose in January 2008, just one month after *Sweeney Todd* had been released, left Johnny's old ally, Terry Gilliam, in a quandry and without a star for his then latest film in production, *The Imaginarium of Doctor Parnassus*. In fact Gilliam was presiding over concept art when he was informed by phone that Ledger had died. His initial thought, after getting over the shock and sadness of Ledger's premature departure was that the film was over, and like some of his previous casulaties, would be abandoned and shut down, and no one would ever get to see Ledger's final work. As expected, the production was suspended indefinitely.

Gilliam, however, was not too concerned. He was still determined to salvage his film somehow, and one consideration he thought of was to use computer-generated imagery to make Ledger's character magically change his appearance, perhaps into another character, in order to keep his final work in the film, and, if he could use the same techniques that had been so succesfully used in the making of Brad Pitt's *The Curious Case of Benjamin Button*, then he could continue with his film and dedicate it to Ledger.

Young, cocksure, handsome and absurdly talented, Ledger was one of Australia's most successful exports to shoot to prominence with his first Hollywood film *10 Things I Hate About You.* With huge charisma and smouldering looks lighting up the screen in a series of subsequent films, Ledger quickly established himself as one of Hollywood's brightest new stars of the 1990s. It wasn't until his award-winning and controversial role as Ennis Del Mar in *Brokeback Mountain*, however, that he cemented his place in the upper echelons of Young Hollywood. In fact, he was one of the youngest stars ever to be nominated for an Oscar. With the world at his feet and a film-stealing turn in the Batman movie, *The Dark Knight*, Gilliam wasn't the only one to share in the global shock and disbelief that he had been found dead from an accidential overdose of prescription drugs. But then again, it didn't seem an unusual, even if tragic, end to a young life. By all accounts it seems to be a growing problem among young celebrities in Hollywood these days. Brittany Murphy's untimely death, almost two years later, in December 2009, aged 32, also from an accidental overdose, was another to have the same global shock and disbelief that Ledger's death had caused. And it didn't take long for the question to be asked. 'Did Murphy's death echo the same kind of tragedy that took the life of Ledger?' It appeared that it did.

In many ways, the one piece of luck that Gilliam had during the making of *Imaginarium* was that he had shot all of the "real world" scenes before Ledger died. So when Ledger's character of Tony steps through the magic mirror into a fantasy world he is transformed, which would allow other actors to take over the role at various stages of Tony's life. Although it was considered a bold and risky way to salvage a project, what else could he do? The question, of course was, would the shifts between Ledger and the other actors feel natural or would they feel forced? According to Gilliam, when the transition happens in the finished film, it was done so smoothly that a sound mixer who worked on the film assumed it was always intended to be that way. It was just what Gilliam wanted to hear.

His first thought was to call Johnny to see if he would be interested in playing Ledger's character in certain scenes, and if he did, he would then ask Colin Farrell and Jude Law if they would also be interested in taking on the other transformatioins of Ledger's character. He had already turned down Tom Cruise, who had expressed interest in being involved, but Gilliam didn't really want him in the film, even though he was an A-list name. Cruise had never been a close friend of Ledger, and as Gilliam wanted to keep it to family, people who were friends with Ledger, there was no point in having him in it. Neither was he interested in all the other people offering to come and help, none of whom knew Ledger either. 'It had to be in the family somehow, I don't know why, but that was my attitude to it.' And of course, if he wanted to change the credits from 'A Terry Gilliam Film' to 'A Film From Heath Ledger And Friends,' then he was right.

Gilliam's first choice was always going to be Johnny. The fact that they were close friends, had worked together in the past, and that Ledger had previously been compared to Johnny on several occasions, made Johnny an ideal choice.

And of course, Johnny jumped at the chance and said he would love to do it. As he himself put it, 'I love Terry and I'd do, personally, anything the guy wants to do.' Farrell and Law also jumped at the opportunity to pay tribute to the friend they had just lost. It probably helped that Law had at one time been considered for the role Ledger had taken. And like Farrell, he was also a friend of Ledger's, so as far as Gilliam was concerned, it was perfect casting.

The greatest challenge, however, was that Gilliam knew Johnny's time was at a premium, and his participation in the film was probably going to be the most difficult one to work out due to the obligation that he had already made to Michael Mann's *Public Enemies*. In the end, though, Gilliam was able to grab all of one day and three hours of Johnny's time, and so, Johnny became the first one to film his scenes, which all had to be done in one take if Gilliam's plan was to work.

'That's why I put Johnny in first position because number one, he was going to be the most difficult to get any time with, and number two, I just thought if it works with the transition to Johnny and if the audience goes for it, they'll follow the next two. And that's exactly how it works. That's what's funny, when Johnny appears, so many people think it's Heath! And it's a trick: Johnny's not doing anything. He looks like Johnny.'

The film tells the story Dr. Parnassus, played by Christopher Plummer, a thousand-year-old traveling showman who has the extraordinary gift of inspiring the imaginations of others. Helped by his travelling theatre troupe, including his sarcastic and cynical sidekick Percy (played by Verne Troyer) and versatile young player Anton

(Andrew Garfield), Parnassus offers audience members the chance to transcend mundane reality by passing through a magical mirror into a fantastic universe of limitless imagination.

However, Parnassus' magic comes at a price. For centuries he's been gambling with the Devil, Mr Nick, played by Tom Waits, who is coming to collect his prize for which he will have Parnassus's precious daughter, Valentina (Lily Cole), on her upcoming 16th birthday. Oblivious to her rapidly approaching fate, Valentina falls for Tony (Ledger), a charming outsider with motives of his own. In order to save his daughter and redeem himself, Parnassus makes one final bet with Mr Nick, which sends Tony, during his several visits to the world beyond the mirror on a ride of twists and turns.

The winner of Valentina will be determined by whoever seduces the first five souls. Enlisting a series of wild, comical and compelling characters in his journey, Dr Parnassus promises his daughter's hand in marriage to the man that helps him win. In this captivating, explosive and wonderfully imaginative race against time, Dr Parnassus must fight to save his daughter in a never-ending landscape of surreal obstacles – and undo the mistakes of his past once and for all.

For some time, the press would refer to Gilliam's project as nothing more than another indulgent piece by its film maker. But following its successful premiere at Cannes, the film was given a limited release in Britain in October 2009, and in the US, a nationwide release on Christmas Day. With two Academy Award nominations for Best Art Direction and Costume Design the following year, it could hardly be called indulgent.

In fact, Johnny considered it a masterpiece. 'Maestro Gilliam has made a sublime film,' he raved. 'Wonderfully enchanting and beautiful, *The Imaginarium of Doctor Parnassus* is a uniquely ingenious, captivating creation; by turns wild, thrilling and hilarious in all its crazed, dilapidated majesty. Pure Gilliam magic! And it was an honour to represent Heath. He was the only player out there breathing heavy down the back of every established actor's neck with a thundering and ungovernable talent that came up on you quick, hissing rather mischievously with that cheeky grin, "Hey...get out of my way, boys, I'm coming through..." and does he ever!!! Heath is a marvel, Christopher Plummer beyond anything he's ever done, Tom Waits as the Devil is a God, Lily Cole and Andrew Garfield, the very foundation, are spectacular, Verne Troyer simply kicks ass and as for my other cohorts, Colin Farrell and Jude Law, they most certainly did Master Ledger very proud, I salute them. Though the circumstances of my involvement are extremely heart-rending and unbelievably sad, I feel privileged to have been asked aboard to stand in on behalf of dear Heath.'

No sooner had Johnny finished filming his footage for Gilliam, than he was back in Chicago on the set of *Public Enemies*, the story of the fast and furious life of American gangster, John Dillinger. Dubbed as a man whose criminal exploits captivated a nation besieged by financial hardship, he was a mythic figure who robbed the banks that had impoverished them and outsmarted the authorities who had failed to remedy their hard times. If anything, Dillinger inspired the first nationwide war on crime, led a band of accomplished armed robbers on a cascade of dazzling heists and improbable breakouts, and whose dashing manner and charisma entranced not only a special woman, but an entire country.

Strangely enough, though, *Public Enemies* was one those projects that had been doing the Hollywood rounds close to a decade. It started off like quite a few ideas do, when someone writes an article or a book and has a chance to sell it to Hollywood. If the writer is lucky, he or she will get a few weeks of dinner-table gossip out of it, and then wait. And wait. And wait. And then after a year or two the whole thing melts into nothingness. That is what happened to *Vanity Fair* correspondent Bryan Burroughs, or so he thought.

It was in 1999 when Burroughs first stumbled upon the idea of a project tracking John Dillinger and Baby Face Nelson and all the major Depression-era bank robbers. He thought the subject was too big to be a single book, so instead, with a friend's help, he pitched the idea as a mini-series to HBO. To his amazement, they bought it. With the stroke of a pen, Burroughs recalls, 'I found myself not only a screenwriter but an executive producer, along with Robert DeNiro's Tribeca Films, of what was being billed as a major television event. I had no idea what to do. I didn't know the first thing about screenwriting. The only thing I knew about television was that *Law & Order* aired on Wednesdays at ten. Still, I plunged forward, buying up a stack of screenwriting texts and started research on Dillinger and Bonnie and Clyde and their peers. About six months in, I realised the subject might indeed fit into one book, so I signed a book contract as well.'

Needless to say, the book work went much better than the screenwriting. Burroughs suspected that his scripts were not that good. In fact he considered them to be pretty awful. To overcome the problem that Burroughs was experiencing, HBO and Tribeca recruited one screenwriter, then another, to take over the writing, while Burroughs himself dived headlong into book work. It took another year or two, but in time, the whole TV project eventually and quietly died.

By the summer of 2004, *Public Enemies* the book was set to be published. Burroughs revealed: 'And I did something I'd never tried. I asked HBO to return the movie rights. To my surprise, they agreed. And a few weeks after the book came out, the rights were promptly re-sold to production companies representing Michael Mann and Leonardo DiCaprio. DiCaprio, I gathered, was interested in playing Dillinger. But after one meeting with their representatives, I heard practically nothing for three years. When I thought about the project at all, I figured the whole thing had died for a second time.

'Then, out of the blue, I came into my office in January 2008 to find a friend had e-mailed me the front page of *Variety*. One of the lead stories reported that Johnny Depp had entered into talks with Mann to play Dillinger. DiCaprio had apparently dropped out, and that the movie project was not only still alive, it was about to be "greenlighted" by Universal. It took a few weeks for it to hit me: After eight long years, it was really happening.' He simply could not believe it, and who better than to have Johnny Depp and Michael Mann make it work.

At that time, Mann was one of cinema's most compelling filmmakers, and his level of artistry has created an indelible influence on audiences and critics alike. From

Thief, *Manhunter*, *Ali* and *Heat* to *The Last of the Mohicans* and *The Insider*, as well as *Collateral* and *Miami Vice*, his lasting dramas have brought to the screen a series of tough, iconic figures embodied by the most commanding actors of our time.

Like Burroughs, Mann had also written about the era, not specifically about Dillinger, and not for a book, but a screenplay, about the famed train and bank robber Alvin Karpis, but the real appeal, confesses Mann, was always Dillinger. 'He was probably the best bank robber in American history, even though he only lasted thirteen months. He was paroled in May of 1933, and by July the following year, he was dead.' It was from going through countless essays, books, songs and films about the Great Depression that had got Mann so stirred up and so intrigued that it created his huge interest to examine a turbulent era through the experience of a criminal who became a folk hero for a generation. For Americans in the early 1930s, who watched their life savings vanish and became jobless and hungry, they found a hero in a man who robbed and challenged the banks that caused the collapse, and the government, that could not fix it.

Johnny too was fascinated. In fact, he had been since he was a little kid. 'There was a long period where I was fascinated with Dillinger. No particular explanation why, I just was; he struck my fancy somehow. But looking back on that initial interest and the fact that it's carried through for the majority of my life, it was his character. It was who he was as a man...back at a time when men were really men. He was, for good or ill, exactly who he was, without any compromise whatsoever. I think Dillinger had some idea of what he was doing. I believe he had found himself and was at peace with the fact that it wasn't going to be a very long ride...but it was going to be a significant one.'

Not only that, Johnny continues, 'but I had read books on him... and aside from all the research I had to do, more of it had to do with an instinct and understanding of the man. I related to John Dillinger like he was a relative. I felt he was of the same blood. He reminded me of my stepdad and very much of my grandfather. He seemed to be one of those guys with absolutely no bull whatsoever, who lived at a time when a man was a man.'

Mann agreed. 'Deep in the core of Johnny, there's a toughness. When we started talking about it, he said that he had been interested in Dillinger for a long time and that Dillinger reminded him of some people from his past. He had Dillinger in him; that's something I sensed. Everybody has these dark currents inside of us, but to be able to reach down in a movie and plumb those depths and bring that up...well, that's courageous.'

It probably helped both star and director that they had decided to film in some of the actual locations where the story took place, like the Crown Point Jail, Little Bohemia and the Biograph Theatre, which in turn, provided Johnny the chance to acquaint himself with Dillinger's actual clothing and personal articles. On top of that he could also hang out in some of the very haunts frequented by the 'Gentleman Bandit' and handle weaponry the man himself had used.

While no time frame in Dillinger's life could be considered particularly ordinary, Mann was primarily interested in making a film of the last fourteen months of

Dillinger's life, to tell the story of how he became one of the most famous Americans of the 20th century, and how, along with his antoganists Melvin Purvis, the under-analysed G-man, played by Christian Bale and J Edgar Hoover (Billy Crudup), all contributed to playing major roles in American history.

In the end, the film focused on the period soon after Dillnger was released from prison until late June 1934, the time span in which Dillinger embarked upon a whirlwind bank-robbing spree across the Midwest that attracted fervent nationwide attention, especially from J Edgar Hoover and his nascent Bureau of Investigation. To track and capture Dillinger, Hoover assigned a young, square-jawed agent named Melvin Purvis, whose profile actually inspired cartoonist Chester Gould in creating the look for Dick Tracy. But Dillinger and his men proved to be much more difficult to track down and catch than the FBI agents had first thought.

As they honed their techniques, Dillinger and his crew used a number of strengths to their advantage: a hardness hewn by years in prisons that were as lawless as they, the latest in automatic weaponry, a fragmented public safety system that had not yet been nationalized, state-of-the-art Ford V8 getaway cars and the knack for riding the wave of anti-banking sentiment from the very public whose banks they plundered. While they could easily argue with his methods, few who saw the newsreels during Saturday matinees would disagree that someone was finally 'sticking it to the fat cats' who they felt had destroyed their lives.

Time and again, the outlaw embarrassed government at every level and escaped from seemingly impossible situations, including a breakout of his crew from Indiana State Prison in September 1933, an escape from the Lake County Jail in Crown Point, Indiana, in March 1934 and an evasion of Purvis at the Little Bohemia travel lodge in northern Wisconsin in April 1934. And while his men never hesitated in the use of violence, the often chivalrous Dillinger could be counted upon to give money back to citizens during a bank robbery and not curse in front of female hostages.

When it comes to the law and lawless, Mann understands and appreciates that truth is stranger than fiction. The story of Dillinger and his pursuers was just the inspiration he was looking for. 'Their mobility and use of technology made them almost invincible. This was happening at a time when massive forces conspired against Dillinger: what Hoover built with the FBI – the first national police force, the first interstate crime bill, the use of very progressive, modern technology and data management. They were doing what is routine in law enforcement now, but what had never been done before in this country.'

Battling a doubtful Congress about the efficacy of his newly formed FBI, Hoover grew furious that Dillinger was becoming a folk hero to American citizens, while his schooled and polished agents were flubbing cases. Many of his colleagues saw the head of the bureau as an inexperienced, puffed-up suit and didn't trust his methodology. In a frustrated effort to escalate the pursuit by Purvis and his agents, Hoover enlisted the aid of a Western lawman, Special Agent Charles Winstead, and two of his associates to track Dillinger down, once and for all. That, coupled with such orders to arrest relatives,

girlfriends and associates of the criminals in the FBI's efforts
to get tough on crime, the idea seemed to be paying off.

While eluding the law, the bank robber had traveled
across the country with girlfriend Billie Frechette (Marion
Coutillard), spending money in lavish quantities and
rubbing elbows with the elite of Florida. Eventually,
Dillinger's luck ran out at the Biograph Theater in Chicago
on July 22, 1934. As he watched Clark Gable in *Manhattan
Melodrama* end, and he left the movie theatre, law
enforcement officials, under the direction of Agent Purvis
and with the help of a Dillinger traitor called the 'Lady in
Red' put him to rest with a slew of bullets.

Devastated fans of the gangster dipped handkerchiefs in
the pool left by his blood, and thousands lined up at the
morgue to view his body. From curious onlookers to
lawmen, everyone wanted a piece of the legacy. Dillinger's
primary antagonist, Melvin Purvis, received the lion's share
of the credit. And none were more unnerved by Purvis'
accolades in the celebration of Dillinger's demise than J
Edgar Hoover. Dillinger was so famous that when he was
killed, Purvis became 'The Man Who Shot John Dillinger,'
even though he was not the man who pulled the trigger. As
a result, Hoover started to resent the fame and acclaim that
Melvin Purvis, G-man, had in the United States and
drummed him out of the FBI.

Three-quarters of a century later, Dillinger's status as a
legendary criminal is cemented. From the classic image of
his crooked smirk as he draped his arm around one of his
admiring captors, to his status as one of Chicago's most
famous residents, the dapper Dillinger remains iconic. And
no one would be more inspired by him than Johnny who

grew up less than 160 miles from Dillinger's boyhood home of Mooresville in Indiana.

Perhaps, one of the most intriguing facts about Dillinger and his gang is that he was able to maneuver so easily with such heavy weaponry. It was something Johnny would have to make look as natural and realistic as he could for the film. As producer Kevin Misher explains: 'If you look at the guns that Dillinger and his gang were carrying around, those Tommy guns with big drums, they were very, very heavy. Some were about 80 or 90 pounds in weight. And they're holding onto the sideboards of cars while they're hightailing it out of town after robbing a bank.'

Although Johnny had previously trained in the use of weaponry for other films, he soon realised that the shooting techniques needed for *Public Enemies* was going to be a completely different ball game. Of the several FBI agents that were recruited to help out with the film was weaponry expert, Dale Shelton. As he points out, 'You have to remember that during that time period, when you were shooting with a handgun, you would use one hand only. It wasn't even thought of to use two hands. That didn't occur until the 1940s, when it was decided that it was a much more stable shooting platform to use two hands instead of one. In addition, your stance was completely different. It was more of a traditional bullseye-type stance, more of a target-shooter-type stance. That, as all tactics have, has evolved over the years.'

For much of the film, Johnny was carrying a 1921 Thompson submachine gun and a couple of .45s, 'So yes, I had to do a lot of preparation. I've been shooting guns since I was about five or six, so I had a pretty strong advantage in that area. Primarily, I was firing the Thompson and a couple of .45s, and when you've got a beast like that strapped to you and you're emptying magazines, a 50-round drum, it's a good feeling.'

Although the film was praised for its attention to period detail and general accuracy, according to most historians and experts, it took significant creative license with well-known facts. For instance, Purvis and Dillinger never met each other, hence the scene depicting Purvis and Dillinger conversing with each other in a Tucson jail never happened. However, witnesses did verify that Dillinger looked directly at Purvis as he left the Biograph Theatre the night he was killed, and perhaps surprisingly, he did not turn to confront an FBI agent shortly before he was killed. Nor did he issue dying words to Agent Winstead. Of the five shots fired by three agents, four of the five struck their target. One of these, a .45 caliber bullet had shattered his cervical spine, passed through his lower brain, and exited through his face. This would have made simple speech, let alone eloquent last words, impossible.

Even so, and despite working with incidents drawn from Burroughs's *Public Enemies: America's Greatest Crime Wave and the Birth of the FBI: 1933–34*, most critcics thought Mann's film emerged as something surprising, fascinating and technically dazzling, and most thought that Johnny's performace as Dillinger was something else. One of those reviews was Manohla Dargis's write-up in the *New York Times* in July 2009, just a few weeks after the film had been released.

'When not in pirate drag,' raved Dargis, 'Mr. Depp can be a recessive, even inscrutable screen presence, which is crucial to his strengths and performative limits. He's a cool cat, to be sure: veiled and often most memorable when he's staring into space while the camera soaks in his subdued but potent physical charms. He might have made a great silent star, as earlier roles suggest. Part of his initial appeal was that he seemed almost Garboesque in a movie world that increasingly makes no room for sacred idols. Very few contemporary actors can wear a fedora as persuasively, but the performance sneaks up on you, inching into your system scene by scene.'

And certainly, that was true.

CHAPTER 19

'THE COMBINATION OF BEING ABLE TO PLAY
THE MAD HATTER AND TAKE WHAT LEWIS CARROLL
HAS DONE AND WHAT TIM'S VISION IS, AND THEN
THROW YOUR OWN STUFF IN THERE...
IT'S A DREAM COME TRUE.'

MAD AS A HATTER

When Johnny announced he intended to follow *Public Enemies* with a role in Tim Burton's next film, *Alice in Wonderland*, no-one was surprised to hear that they were reuniting for their seventh collaboration together in twenty years. But what was it about working with Burton that attracted him to return to work with Burton time after time, or at least more than any other actor and director has in the past? When asked about it, Johnny couldn't quite put his finger on it either. He reasoned away his voracious appetite to constantly link up with Burton by explaining how each time was a new experience, like the first time they worked together on *Edward Scissorhands*. 'The initial thing for me is to come up with a character. Even though there's a certain amount of pressure where I go, "Jesus, will this be the one where I disappoint him?" I try really hard not to, especially early on, to come up with something that's very different, that he hasn't experienced before, and that we haven't experienced together before, and that will stimulate him and inspire him to make choices based on that character.' To sum up, he said 'I try not to embarrass him!'

Not that he had, and nor was he about to. If anything, he couldn't wait to work with Burton again, and help his favourite director put his own new spin on such a timeless classic. Originally published in 1865, Lewis Carroll's *Alice's Adventures in Wonderland* changed forever the course of children's literature 'It's so much a part of the culture,' Burton reflects of Carroll's tale that has inspired numerous stage, television and film adaptations. 'So whether you've read the story or not, you'll know certain images or have certain ideas about it. It's such a popular story.'

Johnny would be playing the Mad Hatter, and it was in many ways, a far cry from any role Johnny had played in the past! But that, he said, was a bonus. 'It was a real challenge to find something different, to define the Mad Hatter in terms of cinema. One of the things Tim and I talked about early on, was the idea that he would be so pure, in the sense that you see, instantly, what he's feeling – so much, so that his clothes, his skin, his hair, everything, reflects his emotion. So when he's beaming, you get this kind of bright effect and everything comes to life, like a flower blooming, very, very quickly. He's like a mood ring. His emotions are very close to the surface.'

Producer Richard Zanuck was grateful. 'He has an ability for transformation that is fabulous. There's no one who can do these crazy, offbeat, eccentric characters like Johnny can. He has a way of being funny and crazy, yet poignant. He's one of the world's great actors; he takes bigger chances than any other male star.'

Indeed, as Johnny developed the character, he discovered that the hatters of the period often suffered from mercury poisoning. 'The term, "mad as a hatter" actually came from real hatters when they were making these sort of beautiful beaver-pelt top hats. The glue they used had very high mercury content. It would stain their hands; they'd go goofy from the mercury and go nuts.' If anything, he felt his character's entire body, not just his mind, would be affected by the mercury poisoning, and painted a watercolour of the Hatter with orange hair, a clown-like face, and green eyes of different size. 'I just knew what he looked like for some reason,' he says of the Hatter's final look. 'When I went into the makeup trailer the process just sort of happened. It's very rare that everything works so quickly. The only time I'd ever had that happen on that level was with Captain Jack.'

Johnny's identification with his character was further enhanced when he worked out that the Hatter would have had several distinct personalities and accents. 'It seemed to me also that because he would be so hyper-sensitive, he would need to travel into another state, another personality, to be able to survive, which kicks in when he is threatened or when he's in danger. I thought it would be like experiencing a kinder form of personality disorder in a way.'

In designing the Hatter's costume, costume designer Colleen Atwood began, unsurprisingly, with his hat. 'The hat's based on a real hat shape of the period. It's just exaggerated and stretched out. I found this leather in Italy that was laser-cut in a weird pattern that looked like it had been burnt, just by chance, and I said, "Oh, the Hat could be made out of this stuff," and then I had it made by a milliner in London who's a great hat maker.'

Atwood had first met Johnny on the set of *Edward Scissorhands*. The pair have worked together many times since. 'As a costume designer, there's nothing quite like working with Johnny,' she says enthusiastically. 'First of all, he's a very generous artist and he brings a lot to everything. He has a great sense of play. He knows how to wear clothes in a very special way. We started playing around with who the Hatter was. Every time Johnny and I hooked up, he took it to another place. We kept pushing it. We talked about him having all the tools of his trade apparent, so they aren't just on a shelf but part of his costume. So he's got his thimbles and his pincushion ring. All these things help make the Hatter otherworldly and magical, but still real, in a sense.'

As far as Johnny is concerned, 'Clothes are the shell of the character, a first, major step to seeing how the guy behaves and moves. Colleen has always been incredible with that kind of thing. She thinks like the character, and finds his outer skin.' One of Johnny's early ideas for the Hatter was that his clothes would change colour depending on the character's mood. 'When I mentioned the idea of mood clothing, Colleen went crazy for it. She started immediately building all these cool things, like a bow tie that has a kind of mechanism in it.'

It probably helped that Johnny was such a huge fan of the book even if he couldn't quite place when the book or the story first came into his life. As he told journalists at a press conference for the film, it must have been around when he was about five years old because that is when he vaguely recalls reading several versions of it. 'I always knew the characters. Everyone knows the characters, and they're very well-defined characters, which I always thought was fascinating. Most people who haven't read the book definitely know the characters and reference them. Ironically, it was only maybe a year prior to Tim calling, I had gone back and re-read *Alice in Wonderland* and *Through The Looking Glass*, and what I took away from it was these very strange, little cryptic nuggets that he'd thrown in there, and I was really intrigued by them and became fascinated by them because they were asking questions that couldn't be answered, or were making statements that you couldn't quite understand, like "I'm investigating things that begin with the letter M." That took me through a whole stratosphere of possibilities, and I did a little research and discovered that the M is mercury. And then there was, "Why is a raven like a writing desk?" Those things just became so important to the character. If I read the book again today, I'd find 100 other things that I missed last time. It's a constantly changing book. And it's such a beast in terms of invention, of literary achievement. It's as brilliant and as fresh and as new and as interesting today as it was then.'

Certainly that is how screenwriter Linda Woolverton thinks of it. 'Lewis Carroll had a remarkable mind and these books just transcend time and place. The characters are all so wild and funny, and there's a little bit of us in all of them: The Red Queen, in her rages; Alice's wonder at everything she sees around her; and The Hatter's tragedy. It makes for great cinema.'

With the success of *Alice*, Carroll (the pen name for

Reverend Charles Lutwidge Dodgson, a lecturer in mathematics at Christchurch University in Oxford, England) became the leading children's author of his day, and he followed it six years later with *Through The Looking-Glass, and What Alice Found There*, which was even more popular than its predecessor. Today, both books tend to be published together under the title *Alice in Wonderland*, and their continued influence can be seen in everything from music videos to films, comic books to computer games, opera to art.

As any film or book buff would confirn, as co-star Anne Hathaway did during a break playing the the White Queen, it's one of the reasons why Lewis Carroll's characters work so well in cinema. They're wildly imaginative and there's no one way to interpret them, because Lewis Carroll played around with words and concepts, and because the characters appeal to the imagination, there are as many interpretations as there are imaginations in the world. It depends on what your take is.

Yes, agrees Burton. 'That's why all those great stories stay around because they tap into the things that people probably aren't even aware of on a conscious level. There's definitely something about those images. That's why there have been so many versions of it. It somehow taps a subconscious thing. As a movie, it's always been about a passive little girl wandering around a series of adventures with weird characters. There's never any kind of gravity to it. The attempt with this was to take the idea of those stories and shape them into something that's not literal from the book but keeps the spirit of it.'

Like Burton, Johnny truly believed that Carroll would be

ecstatic because the movie is done with such respect and is rooted deeply in the original material. 'This story by Carroll, along with the characters, under Tim Burton's vision is a real treat.'

Part of that treat was how Burton incorporated characters, story elements and central themes from Carroll's books, and takes the stories to new heights, so to speak, by featuring a grown-up Alice as she returns to the place she visited as a child. When Woolverton had pitched the idea to producers Joe Roth and Suzanne and Jennifer Todd, they were bowled over. 'Linda came up with a great idea,' says Roth. 'It all hangs together, kind of a political allegory – those residents down there are not just crazy, they're actually revolutionaries. So it just struck me right on every single level, and Disney seemed like the right place to take it. And there was only one choice of director, Tim Burton, and low and behold, he wanted to do it.'

They gave Burton a script and they said 3D, recalls Burton. 'And even before I read it. I thought that's intriguing, and what I liked about Linda's script was she made it a story, gave it a shape for a movie that's not necessarily the book. So all those elements seemed good to me.' According to Linda, that is exactly how she had visualised it. The story takes place when Alice is 19, and she's about to enter into a marriage she's not sure about. Time has passed. The Red Queen rules the whole land. It's under her thumb. And the people of Underland need Alice.

Underland, Woolverton contnues, is the same fantastical land that Alice visited as a child. 'But she misheard the word "Underland" and thought they said, "Wonderland." Now as a girl on the cusp of adulthood, when Alice goes back there, she discovers that the real name of the world is Underland.'

Much of what appealed to Burton about the script was that it centered on an Alice who, at 19, is substantially older than in Carroll's books, yet feels very real and identifiable. 'What I liked about this take on the story is Alice is at an age where you're between a kid and an adult, when you're crossing over as a person. A lot of young people with old souls aren't so popular in their own culture and their own time. Alice is somebody who doesn't quite fit into that Victorian structure and society. She's more internal.'

For Alice Kingsleigh (Mia Wasikowska), life is about to take a turn for the unexpected. Hamish, the worthy but dull son of Lord and Lady Ascot, proposes to Alice during a Victorian garden party thrown in their honour. She flees without giving an answer, heading off after a rabbit she's spotted running across the lawn; the rabbit, of course, is wearing a waistcoat and pocket watch. Following the White Rabbit (Michael Sheen) across a meadow, Alice watches as he disappears into a rabbit hole, and suddenly finds herself falling down after him, tumbling through a strange, dreamlike passage before landing in a round hall with many doors. She discovers a bottle labeled "Drink Me" – its contents shrink her, and a cake with the words "Eat Me" iced on top; it makes her grow. Alice eventually finds her way through a door into the wondrous and fantastical world called Underland – the same place she visited as a young girl, although she has no memory of her previous adventures there, except in her dreams.

Underland is a part of the earth, but it lies somewhere far beneath our world. And the only way to get there is to fall down a rabbit hole. There she meets a menagerie of colorful characters, including a swashbuckling Dormouse (Barbara Windsor), an off-his-rocker Mad Hatter, a grinning Cheshire Cat (Stephen Fry), a wise caterpillar called Absolem (Alan Rickman), a beautiful White Queen (Hathaway) and her spiteful older sister, the Red Queen (Helena Bonham Carter), who happens to be the petulant ruler of Underland.

According to Woolverton, Underland has come upon hard times since the malevolent Red Queen has taken over the throne. It is, however, a truly wonderful land, which might explain why the girl who mistook it for "Wonderland" has been called upon to help return it to its glory. But, says Woolverton, 'Underland has always been Underland since the beginning, no matter who sits on the throne. It will remain Underland until the end.'

What Linda has done is fashion a story with an emotional context for the film's events to occur, remarked Bonham Carter. 'In this, there's a point to the whole story and a journey for Alice. In the beginning, Alice is very awkward and uncomfortable in her skin, so her experience in Underland is about reconnecting with herself and finding she has the strength to be more self-assured in figuring out what she wants.'

Producer Suzanne Todd couldn't help wondering if Tim Burton is, in his own way, becoming a modern-day Walt Disney. She thought he was. 'There's no one else like him. And Alice really spoke to Tim. The idea of Alice and her journey, going someplace else to find out who she really is.'

No one argued with that summation. For a fabulist filmmaker renowned for creating fantastical and breathtakingly elaborate worlds, Carroll's rich tapestry of characters and their magical world afforded Burton ample opportunity to run wild with his imagination, putting his own, indelible stamp on the material. 'The combination of the 135-year-old best seller, *Alice in Wonderland*, Tim Burton, Johnny Depp, Disney and 3D promised to make this an irresistible and "must see" movie event,' affirmed Zanuck.

Using a mixture of visual effects techniques, including actors shot against green screen, all CGI characters, as well as 3D, *Alice in Wonderland* promised to showcase Burton's vision in a unique, richly detailed way. Ken Ralston, senior visual effects supervisor on the film, says it was a challenge deciding how to tackle the director's vision. Ultimately, says Ralston, they decided to 'blend a lot of different types of techniques into something that would give us a very unique look for the movie. And it was really based on what it should be based on, what the environments needed to be to best tell the story, what the characters would look like to best tell the story. 'I think the film provides a very visceral, exciting, almost tactile experience in the 3D thing that's happening within these weird worlds. I want to put audiences right in the middle of this strangeness and just let it happen, you know, let these characters take them on this journey which I think will be really fun.'

Ralston, of course, was the perfect choice. One of the founding members of George Lucas's Industrial, Light & Magic, Ralston is a visual effects legend, having worked on the original *Star Wars*, *Who Framed Roger Rabbit?*, *Back to the Future*, *Forrest Gump*, *The Polar Express* and *Beowulf*, winning four Oscars for his pioneering work.

While the live-action sequences involving Alice in the

real world that bookend the film were shot on location in Cornwall in England, all the scenes that take place in Underland itself were shot on green-screen stages at Culver City Studios in Los Angeles, with all its environs created entirely digitally in post-production. 'This is a very unique project,' said visual effects producer Tom Peitzman. 'I've been in visual effects for a long time and to have a film like this, where you're throwing so many different disciplines into one project, makes it that much more fun and unique.'

For instance, for the Hatter, Ralston's team increased the size of Johnny's eyes. 'If you go too far, it looks cartoony,' explains Peitzman. 'If you don't do enough, it's like you didn't do anything. The team had some fun with the Hatter's mood changes, which were reflected quite literally in his appearance. 'Sometimes it'll be very subtle. If he's in a more melancholy mood, it may be a little dark or a little gray. Whereas if he's suddenly happy, you'll see vibrancy come into the clothing. Or you may see his bow tie go up, almost like a smile. We were trying to do things that were very subtle, so they're not drawing attention to themselves, but will give his whole character this unique, fun persona.'

Alice in Wonderland was released in the Spring of 2010 in both America and Britain. It was a lavish production that filled all the criteria for a blockbuster movie from the moment it opened, and rapidly became both a critical and box office smash. *Variety*'s Todd McCarthy praised it for its 'moments of delight, humor and bedazzlement'. His was only one of many effusive reviews. Michael Rechtshaffen writing in the *Hollywood Reporter* said: 'Burton has delivered a subversively witty, brilliantly cast, whimsically appointed dazzler that also manages to hit all the emotionally satisfying marks.' He also raved over the film's computer-generated imagery, saying, 'Ultimately, it's the visual landscape that makes Alice's newest adventure so wondrous, as technology has finally been able to catch up with Burton's endlessly fertile imagination.'

With an opening as the number one film in North America, it took a more-than-respectable $41 million gross, and set a new record for an opening day in March, and quickly became the biggest weekend opener since *300* three years earlier, taking an overall $116 million in the first three days of its opening. It also became the sixth highest grossing weekend opening of all time, and the highest opening weekend for a non-sequel, taking the record from *Spiderman*. And on top of that, it broke the previous IMAX record held by *Avatar* on 188 of the large format screens.

But it was not all good news. One month before its British release three major UK cinema chains, Odeon, Vue and Cineworld, planned to boycott the film because of a reduction of the interval time between cinema and DVD release, which was reduced from the usual seventeen weeks to twelve. Then one week after the announcement was made, Cineworld, chose not to boycott it after all, but to play it on over 150 screens. Cineworld's chief executive Steve Wiener told reporters that 'as leaders in 3D, we did not want the public to miss out on such a visual spectacle. As the success of *Avatar* has shown, there is currently a huge appetite for the 3D experience.' Shortly after, the Vue cinema chain also reached an agreement with Disney, but Odeon had still chosen to boycott it in Britain, Ireland and Italy. They finally relented on February 25, when they claimed they had reached an agreement and had decided to show the film from March 5 onwards in both Disney Digital 3D and IMAX 3D, as well as at regular theatres.

By the time *Alice in Wonderland* was out playing across screens in both the UK and the US , Johnny was again being tentatively linked with the portrayal of former KGB officer Russian agent Alexander Litvinenko, who was poisoned in London in 2006, in the feature adaptation of the unpublished book *Sasha's Story: The Life and Death of a Russian Spy*. Johnny's production company Infinitum Nihil and Warner Bros optioned the book currently being written by *New York Times* London bureau chief Alan Cowell. The project will examine Litvinenko's life and claims that his death, which is still under investigation, was ordered by Russian president Vladimir Putin.

But then again, Johnny has often been linked to projects that have ultimately come to nothing. But one that was more than a rumour was Indian director Mira Nair's latest film *Shantaram*, to which Johnny appears to have been attached for ages. The buzz around Hollywood is that it has 'prestigious Oscar chaser' written all over it. It's the story of an Australian heroin addict who escapes from prison and heads to Bombay, where he poses as a doctor, a course of action that leads to counterfeiting, gun running, smuggling and really small hard-to-read squiggly handwriting. It's based partially on a true story, which gives *Shantaram* another notch on the potential Oscar meter!

Although *Sasha's Story* and *Shanataram* still have to go before the camera, one has to wonder when Johnny will find the time to do them. One month before *Alice* hit the screens, he was filming *The Tourist* in Venice with Angelina Jolie. Not that Vanessa was very happy about it, which considering Johnny had been touted for the role since the summer of 2009, it seemed strange that it took her almost eight months to object to his involvement with the film. It appeared that the problem lay with the passionate sex scenes that the script demanded. In fact, she was so concerned that she allegedly, ordered Johnny to find another gig after hearing about the shoots with Jolie, who famously fell in love with co-star Brad Pitt, while shooting *Mr & Mrs Smith* together. Although Johnny would have received the script for the movie several months before filming began, according to sources, Paradis had only just found out that there was a long and intense love scene between Johnny and Jolie in the movie, in which Jolie plays an Interpol agent who seduces a tourist.

According to a draft of the screenplay that *US* magazine had got sight of, Johnny's character Frank Taylor will approach Jolie's character, Interpol agent Cara Mason, when she is naked in the shower. 'Walking in, he lifts Cara against the glass, clutching at her slithery body, kissing her frantically. She kisses him back with ardour, wrapping her dripping legs around his back. Cara later turns abruptly to Frank and presses her body against his. He's taken by surprise but willingly responds to her advance, wrapping his arms around her back. They exchange a long, passionate kiss.' It was that description in the script that apparently got Paradis all hot and bothered. Perhaps she was only too aware that Jolie had, on several occasions, ended up with her leading man even though the leading man may have been spoken for. In Pitt's case, he was married to Jennifer Aniston, and of course, years earlier, she started dating Billy Bob Thornton while he was said to have been engaged to

Laura Dern. Much the same as when she was making _Taking Lives_ with Oliver Martinez and was rumoured to have had a fling with the French heartthrob even though he was reportedly engaged to Kylie Minogue.

Although there were reports that Johnny was trying to get out of the movie, according to information listed on the Internet Movie Database, it doesn't look like he has. There was, at one time, talk of replacing him with either Pitt or Leonardo DiCaprio, but nothing seems to have come of it. Beside, if Johnny had left the movie, surely it would have been headline news, so one has to presume that the story of Paradis's concerns is nothing more than idle gossip. But then again, with Jolie's reputation as the world's most seductive star, both on and off-screen, and the departure of Charlize Theron and Sam Worthington from the cast, one has to wonder.

Not that Johnny would have been worried. He was already committed to another three film projects, one of which would be another outing with Burton. But that would have to wait until after he had completed the filming of Jerry Bruckheimer's remake of _The Lone Ranger_, with Johnny playing Tonto, the hero's Native American sidekick, who in the original television series, was as much the star as the Lone Ranger himself. And after that he would be reprising his most famous role as Captain Jack for the fourth _Pirates_ film, again for Bruckheimer and Disney, alongside Ian McShane and Penelope Cruz.

For many journalists, though, the Burton project sounded like the most exciting, simply because vampires were back in vogue. Long before Lestat, Angel and Edward Cullen stalked the screen, there was Barnabas Collins, a 175-year-old vampire who stalked the town of Collinsport, Maine pining for his lost love. Originally, the character of Barnabas, played by Jonathan Frid, was only intended for a 13-week story arc on the television series, *Dark Shadows*, but he caused such a sensation with viewers he became the lead character for the next four years. The show spawned two movies in the early 70s, a revived series in 1991, and a pilot that was not picked up for a series in 2004.

Johnny would be playing Barnabas, a role he says, has been a lifelong dream for him. He simply adored the show as a child: 'Yes, I was obsessed with Barnabas Collins. I have photographs of me holding Barnabas Collins posters when I was five or six.' By all accounts he had been pursuing the movie adaptation for years, buying the remake rights through his production company, Infinitum-Nihil.

If there was any concern about it at all, it would be the timing of its release. If it hit theatres in 2011, it could well be up against the final *Twilight* saga, *Breaking Dawn*. And of course, if it was delayed to the following year, audiences might be over their vampire addiction. Vampires may no longer be hot. Still, it seems that if anyone was going to be able to create a dark, atmospheric, and a truly entrancing vampire tale, it would have to be Johnny Depp and Tim Burton.

So, as always, the immediate future for Johnny sounds promising, doesn't it? And, although frequently traumatised and trapped by his own past, his childhood and emotional ups-and-downs, he admits: 'For many years I was confused about all sorts of things: life, growing up and not knowing what was right or wrong, but now, because Vanessa and my children have taught me, the only thing that matters in life is being a good parent. Fatherhood gave me real strength. It also put everything into perspective and made everything make sense. For years, everyone kept saying that I was living for my work and my career. I heard, "Your life is about playing these damaged characters."'

But, as a dad, he continues, 'You get those moments where it's eight in the morning and your kid wants candy. You're like, "Uh, it's not really a good idea." But then I'm like, "All right, maybe you can have a little bit of candy." I guess I'm the softie. I'm the weak one. Vanessa is the woman so she's infinitely stronger. Women rule, you know. Men are quivering wrecks. That's just how it is.'

Despite rumours that he and Vanessa were about to tie the knot in the summer of 2007, at their South of France villa in Plan da la Tour, Johnny is not that concerned. 'We've been together for eight years and have two kids. We're married in our hearts. We just haven't done the entire "I shall, I will" thing. It doesn't matter to us.'

After all the turbulence the public have seen him go through, who would have thought that Johnny Depp would have ever quit fighting the personal and professional demons he seemed to have been plagued with for years, but it appears he has. 'I think everything happened the way it was meant to happen, but I don't know why,' he says. 'I remember every bump in the road, and I still don't know how I got here. But who am I to ask why? The fact is, this is where I am. So I enjoy it, salute it, and keep moving forward. None of it makes any sense to me, but then, why should it?'

NOTES

The following information on the making of Pirates of the Caribbean: Dead Man's Chest *has been compiled to complete any references that are not included in that chapter (17).*

1. *The Black Pearl* is the only ship in the *Pirates of the Caribbean: Dead Man's Chest* and its sequel which operate under power. All others, except for the *Interceptor* from the first movie, are built atop other ships such as barges with only the portions seen by the cameras completed.

2. Stay after the credits for an additional scene.

3. The movie was shot back-to-back with *Pirates of the Caribbean: At World's End* (2007).

4. Rolling Stone Keith Richards was set to make a cameo appearance as the father of Captain Jack Sparrow, but Richards had to pull out of the project due to his commitment with the Rolling Stones world tour. Johnny Depp had previously said that his performance as Jack Sparrow was based on Richards

5. Keira Knightley had to wear hair extensions because she had cut her hair short for her role in *Domino* (2005).

6. The gigantic wheel upon which the sword fight between Sparrow, Turner and Norrington takes place weighed 1,800 pounds and stood at 18 feet tall.

7. For the film's release, the Walt Disney Company redesigned the Pirates of the Caribbean rides in Walt Disney World and Disneyland to feature captain Jack Sparrow and Barbossa, as well as an appearance by the films' supernatural character Davy Jones, as part of the attraction which will begin on the film's opening day.

8. While the script for the second movie was being written, Keira Knightley suggested the scene between Jack and Elizabeth where Jack is handcuffed to the ship.

9. Gore Verbinski did not tell the cast what was to happen with the bone cage. He wanted to get their natural reactions when it swung from side to side.

10. In June 2006, *The Flying Dutchman* set ship was towed to Castaway Cay, Disney Cruise Line's private island, where it was displayed in promotion release of the movies.

11. Davy Jones and his 18-member crew of *The Flying Dutchman* were entirely computer-generated, except for Bootstrap Bill. Bill Nighy wore a dark-grey motion-capture suit with dozens of reference marks on his face and body while performing. ILM has refined the motion-capture system so that only two cameras were needed, compared with at least 16 in the past.

12. The music played during the pub brawl on Tortuga was not composed for the movie. It is a traditional piece called 'Fisher's Hornpipe'.

13. The conch-man spoke Cantonese after his head was cut off.

14. When the word 'Tortuga' is set on fire on the deck, it is written in the trademark Disney font.

15. The shack by the river as the crew go to see Tia Dalma is identical to the shack on the far side of the river across from the boarding dock of the Magic Kingdom's 'Jungle Cruise' ride in Orlando, Florida.

16. The pirate musical 'band' that was playing in the inn at Tortuga are also from the ride. Notice the one playing the accordion.

17. Tia Dalma's swamp is a recreation of the opening bayou scene in the ride in Disneyland complete with fireflies.

18. During filming, the cast and crew had to be evacuated to Los Angeles because of Hurricane Wilma.

19. Earning $135,634,554 domestically in its opening weekend, it was the fastest motion picture to reach $100 million, accomplishing the feat in two days.

20. When Mr Gibbs is enlisting new recruits at the tavern, a bunch of men are pulling a man out of a well, and he slowly spits out water. This is a recreation of a scene in the Pirates of the Caribbean ride at the Walt Disney theme parks.

21. This is the first film to feature Disney's new logo, a computer-generated model of the Magic Kingdom, replacing the blue and white silhouette.

22. Deleted footage of Tortuga from *Pirates of the Caribbean: The Curse of the Black Pearl* (2003) was added to the final cut of this movie.

23. The dice game that Will Turner plays with Davy Jones is called Liar's Dice, a gambling game where each player has to make consecutively higher bids based upon how many of each die they claim are on the table (two threes, four fives, etc.), until a player is called a liar, in which case all the dice are shown and it's seen if the bid is correct. Normally a player only loses a die when caught in a lie and is not out of the game until he has lost all his dice.

24. During the course of the movie, Elizabeth claims to have learned swordsmanship from Will. Later on she pulls a sword stunt hitting two enemies backwards which was actually enacted by Orlando Bloom as Legolas in *Lord of the Rings*.

25. In an interview with CGSociety, Visual Effects Art Director Aaron McBride revealed that, when he was given the task of doing photo-real illustrations of Davy Jones, there was talk that Christopher Walken might be brought on for the role.

26. Johnny Depp's frequent collaborator Tim Burton contributed some of the conceptual designs of several crew members aboard *The Flying Dutchman*.

27. When Will is looking for Captain Jack Sparrow, the last guy he asks tells him about an island where the 'long pork' is very good. 'Long pork' is a euphemism for human flesh.

28. The texture of Davey Jones's skin was made by scanning a dirty coffee cup and applying it to the screen using Photoshop-type software.

29. When the sailors fight over the dress on the ship Elizabeth has stowed away on, they talk about the ghost of a woman who killed herself before her wedding. This is a plot point in the Disney Ride The Haunted Mansion.

FILM GLOSSARY
BY CHARLOTTE RASMUSSEN

The following is a guide to definitions frequently used in the technical and creative side of filmmaking which readers may find useful as a glossary to this book.

Ad lib
From the Latin phrase ad libitum, meaning 'in accordance with desire', this is improvised dialogue where the actors make up what they say in real time on the movie set or on stage. When in the exact situation required by the script the actors (or the director) often discover that the production may benefit from a different dialogue or reaction. This way, the final result is often much improved.

Agent
The manager responsible for the professional business dealings of an actor, director, screenwriter or other artist, an agent typically negotiates the contracts and often has some part in selecting or recommending roles for their client. Professional actors usually have assistants, publicists and other personnel in

addition to this involved in handling their day-to-day schedule and career.

Billing

The placement (or display) of names of actors, directors and producers for a movie in publicity materials, opening (or closing) film credits, and on theatre marquees. A person's status is indicated by the size, relative position and placement of their name. Generally, positions closer to the top, with larger and more prominent letters, designate higher importance and greater box-office draw, and precede people of lesser importance. The most prominent actor that appears first is said to have top billing, followed by second billing, and so forth.

Block-buster

A movie that is a huge financial success: $100 million or more. The gross of a movie is, to some extent, a measure of the popularity and talent of its leading actors and can determine whether or not a sequel is economically worthwhile. Often the term gross profit is mentioned in reference to 'first dollar gross' and this form of compensation entitles an individual to a percentage of every dollar of gross receipts.

Blocking

The rehearsal used to determine the position and movement of the camera, actors and crew during a particular shot or scene.

Blooper

Funny outtakes and mistakes by cast or crew caught on camera. Bloopers are sometimes included in the end-credits of a movie or in the special features section of the final DVD, also known as blooper reels or gag reels. Causes for bloopers are often uncontrollable laughter, props (falling, breaking or failing to work as expected), forgotten lines or sudden incidents such as a bird flying in front of the camera. The term blooper is sometimes also applied to a continuity error, which somehow goes unnoticed (and makes it through) the editing process and is thus released in the final product for viewers to see. However, strictly speaking this is a film error, not a blooper.

Blue screen
Special effects photography in which a subject (an object or a performer) is photographed in front of a uniformly illuminated blue or green screen; during post-production, the coloured screen is optically or electronically eliminated and a new background substituted in its place, allowing images to be combined. Blue is normally used for people (because the human skin has very little blue colour to it) and green for digital shots (the green colour channel retains more detail and requires less light). Other colours may be used depending on what technique is applied. Often used to achieve the effect of a natural environment, such as a forest, beach, prairie, mountain or other landscape in a shot or sequence, but also to create science fiction worlds, or environments that are inaccessible during production.

Boom pole
Operated by a person from the sound department, the boom pole is a special piece of equipment. It is made from a length of light aluminium or carbon fibre that allows precise positioning of the microphone, above or below the actors, just out of the camera's frame.

Box office
Measure of the total amount of money paid by moviegoers to see a movie in theatres.

B-Roll
Cutaway shots used to cover the visual part of an interview or narration. Often made available on the Internet or on DVDs as extra material.

Call bsck
The follow-up after an audition when the actor in question is called back for a more personal meeting, maybe to discuss the script or the character. It gives the director and producers a chance to consider whether the actor is appropriate for the role and to check if there is the necessary chemistry between other members of the cast.

Call sheet
The call sheet details what is being filmed on a particular day, in scene order. It lists the same information to be found in the liner shooting schedule, plus each character name, what extras are needed and what time each actor is to be picked up, when they are required to go into makeup/hair and onto set. Crew and special requirements for each scene are also noted.

Cameo (appearance)
Small part played by a famous actor, who would ordinarily not accept such an insignificant role for little, sometimes even no money. Often big Hollywood stars choose to appear in independent productions to support and perhaps draw attention to the specific movie (theme, co-star or director).

Camera dolly
The camera can be mounted on top of this little moveable car. During shooting it is often placed on tracks to ensure stability.

Cast
The characters physically present in the play or film. These are the roles for which actors will be needed.

CD
First generation of optical media with a storage capacity of up to 700 MB, mostly used for music, data and images, but some CDs are designed specifically for video (such as VCD or SVCD).

CGI
Computer Generated Image: A term denoting computers will be used to generate the full imagery.

Character
Any personified entity appearing in a film or a play.

Composite video
The format of analogue television before combined with audio, composed by three signals called Y (luminance), U and V (both carrying colour information).

Credits
The opening credit is an on-screen text that describes the most important people involved in the making of a movie. End credit is usually a rolling list at the end of the movie, where everybody involved (cast, crew, studio, producers etc.) is named or thanked.

Cutting room
Location where film rolls or tapes are edited by cutting out the unwanted parts.

Dailies
First positive prints made from the negatives photographed on the previous day. Watching the dailies often determines which scenes needs to be re-shot or changed.

Director
In a stage play, the individual responsible for staging (placing in the space or blocking) the actors, sculpting and coordinating their performances, and ensuring they fit with the design elements into a coherent vision of the play. In a musical, there will typically be a separate musical director responsible for the musical elements of the show. In a Dramatists Guild contract, the playwright has approval over the choice of director (and the cast and designers). In film, however, the director carries out the duties of a stage director and has considerably more say-so over the final product. A casting director plays an important part of pre-production in selecting the cast. This usually involves auditions and if hundreds or thousands of candidates come in to perform, special staff are required to be in charge of this process.

Distributor
Organisation responsible for coordinating the distribution of the finished movie to exhibitors, as well as the sale of videos, DVDs, laserdiscs and other media versions of movies.

Dubbing
Dubbing or looping is the process of recording voices to match the exact mouth-movements of the actors on screen. Often used to replace the original language with another (i.e. Spanish voice track over an American movie). Dubbing or ADR (Additional Dialogue Recording or post-synchronisation) is also used to re-record the lines by the same actor, who originally spoke them – often the case when the original sound on set was interrupted by unwanted or uncontrollable noise

such as traffic or is just too un-clear. The actors are then called into a sound studio. While watching the film on video they re-perform their line, which is recorded by a sound technician.

DVD

Short for Digital Versatile Disc or Digital Video Disc. Like a CD, a DVD is an optical media, but has much higher density. There are many different types of DVDs (DVD-R, DVD+R, DVD, DVD-RW, DVD+RW) and they are used for video, audio and data storage. Most DVDs used for movies are 12cm in diameter and their usual sizes are 4.7 GB (single layer) or 8.5 GB (dual layer) – both types can be double-sided. Dual layer DVDs have a semi-transparent layer on top, in which the red laser shines through to reach the layer at the bottom. Switching from one layer to another may cause a noticeable pause in some DVD players. A newer type of high-density disc is the High Definition DVD (HD DVD), which is able to store three times as much data as the standard DVD format. The Blu-ray disc (BD) offers storage capacity up to 25 GB (single layer). Blu-ray format uses a blue-violet laser (with a shorter wavelength than the typical red laser), which enables a Blu-ray disc to be packed more tightly.

Extras

Individuals who appear in a movie where a non-specific, non-speaking character is required, usually as part of a crowd or in the background of a scene. Often family-members of the cast or crew (who may hang around the set anyway) are used.

Feature film

A movie primarily for distribution in theatres, it is at least 60 minutes long or the script at least 90 pages long. As opposed to feature films, these are movies made for TV or produced for video-release only.

Foley
The art of recreating incidental sound effects (such as footsteps) in synchronisation with the visual component of a movie.

Frame
Movies are created by taking a rapid sequence of pictures (frames) of action and by displaying these frames at the same rate at which they were recorded, thus creating an illusion of motion. In the US, film equals 24 frames per second (NTSC) and video equals 30 frames per second (NTSC). In Europe, most film equals 25 frames per second (PAL). In France and fractions of Europe, Africa and the former USSR, another standard called SECAM is used.

Franchise
A media franchise (literature, film, videogame, TV programme) is a property involving characters, settings, trademarks, etc. Media franchises tend to cross over from their original media to other forms (i.e. from books to films). Generally a whole series is made in a particular medium, along with merchandise. Some franchises are planned in advance, others happen by accident because of a sudden profitable success.

Freebie
Promotional samples such as tickets, clothing, gadgets, promotional DVDs, books or whatever the production or distributing company chooses to give away free of charge, maybe in limited amounts. Some may be signed by the cast or are otherwise unique merchandise or bonus material.

Gate
The film gate is an opening in front of the camera where the film is exposed to light. Sometimes the film celluloid can break off, giving débris known as hair that can create a dark line on

the edge of the film frame. Such a hair can only be removed by painting it out digitally in post-production, an annoying, time-consuming and costly affair. Several factors influence the frequency of hairs: environment, humidity, camera position, type of film, etc. When the director feels he has got a particular shot he calls out to the crew to 'check the gate'; a clean shot is replied with 'Gate is good'. Note: this problem does not exist when shooting digitally.

Grip
A trained lighting and rigging technician.

Hook
A term borrowed from song-writing and used to describe a thing (or line) that catches the public's attention and keeps them interested in the flow of a story.

Independent films
Also known as 'Indies', these films are financed by a smaller production company independent of a major film studio. Often they produce small, interesting movies on a low budget, which sometimes get no further than recognition at film festivals and/or are released in a limited number of theatres.

Laserdisc
First type of commercial optical disc (LD) with a common size of 30cm in diameter. 18 and 12 cm discs were also published. Analogue video combined with digital audio. Laserdiscs were recorded in three different formats: CAV, CLV and CAA. Mostly caught on in North America and Japan, only to be quickly replaced by the more popular and smaller DVDs when they were introduced.

Location

The physical site where all or part of a film is produced as opposed to the set or soundstage. If the storyline is based on authentic events, it doesn't necessarily mean the exact same location where the action took place in real life but something similar.

Method acting

Sometimes referred to as 'the method', it is a style of acting formalised by Russian actor and theatre director Konstantin Stanislavsky. The actor interprets the role by drawing from experiences in his own personal life in direct parallel to the character.

Miniatures

Small landscapes, towns or buildings built in miniature (and usually to scale) to make effects that are impossible to achieve otherwise, either because it is too expensive or too dangerous to do so in reality.

Option

Legal agreement to rent the rights to a script for a specific period of time.

Padding

Material added to clothing or shoes to enhance an actor's physical appearance or to protect a stuntman from unnecessary injuries.

Plot

The order of events in a story: the main plot is called A-plot. Typical plot structure includes (a) Beginning/initial situation, (b) Conflict/problem which has to be achieved/solved, (c) Complications to overcome, (d) Climax, (e) Suspense, (f)

Resolution (or not) after the conflict/problem has been solved and (g) Conclusion/end. Simplified, a dramatic structure of a story can be divided into five acts: exposition, rising action, climax (turning point), falling action and resolution (dénouement), meaning unravelling or untying of the plot). This is also known as Freytag's pyramid.

Producer

The person or entity financially responsible for a stage or film production; the chief of a movie production in all matters save the creative efforts of the director, who raises funding, hires key personnel, and arranges distribution. An executive producer is not involved in any technical aspects of the filmmaking process, but is still responsible for the overall production (usually handling business and legal issues). The production company is headed up by a producer, director, actor or writer and is to create general entertainment products such as motion pictures, television shows, infomercials, commercials and multimedia.

Production

Pre-production is the stage during the creation of the movie where the producer gets everything ready to shoot: hiring actors through casting, picking directors and the rest of the crew, making costumes, finding locations, editing the script, constructing sets, doing rehearsals, etc. The production is the actual shooting of the movie (also known as principal photography). In post-production (or simply post), extra scenes or alternative versions are shot. Also includes editing and cutting of the movie, creating CGI special effects, adding sound-effects and composing the music score and generally making promotion (press conferences, trailer shows, billboards, etc.) before the première.

Prop

A prop is any object held, manipulated or carried by a performer during a theatrical performance, on stage or film. For example, stage gun, mock glassware, etc.

Rating

In the USA, The Motion Picture Association of America (MPAA) and the National Association of Theatre Owners (NATO) operate a rating system for movies: G (general audience, all ages admitted), PG (parental guidance suggested, some material may not be suitable for children), PG-13 (parents strongly cautioned, some material may be inappropriate for children under 13), R (restricted, under 17, requires accompanying parent or adult guardian) and NC-17 (no one 17 and under will be admitted). The rating for a particular movie is decided by a board of parents. They also define an informational warning for the particular movie, along with the rating (i.e. for strong language, violence, nudity, drug abuse, etc.). In the UK, the British Board of Film Classification (BBFC) classifies films and videos. The rating system differs from the American system: U (suitable for audiences aged 4 years and over, while movies classified Uc are particularly suitable for pre-school children), PG (general viewing, but some scenes may be unsuitable for young children), 12 (no one younger than 12 may rent or buy the movie; movies classified 12A may not be seen by children younger than 12 in the cinema unless accompanied by an adult), 15 (suitable only for 15 years and over; no one younger may buy, rent or see a movie in a cinema), 18 (suitable only for adults; no one younger may buy, rent or see a movie in a cinema). Movies classified R18 mean a special and legally restricted classification, they are to be shown only in specially licensed cinemas and may only be supplied in licensed shops, never by mail order.

Red carpet

A red carpet is a strip of carpet in the colour red, laid out in front of a building to welcome VIPs such as dignitaries and celebrities to formal events such as premières, special screenings, press conferences, etc.

Region encoding

To avoid the newest movie released in the United States on DVD from being played in other parts of the world before they have even premièred in theatres there, a DVD region locking system is used to control which type of DVDs can be played on DVD players. DVDs are coded for 9 different regions (0–8) and they require a DVD player of the same region to play the DVD. The Blu-ray movie region codes are different from DVDs and there are currently three: A/1, B/2, C/3.

Rehearsal

Preparatory event in music and theatre, this is a form of practice to ensure professionalism and to eliminate mistakes by working on details without performing in public or on camera. At a dress rehearsal the ensemble tries out their wardrobe for the first time and the different outfits and costumes are fitted to match their exact size.

Re-shoot

When it is clear that some scenes don't fit each other very well or the story doesn't come together as intended, it is sometimes necessary to shoot a scene again after principal photography has ended. It may be months after the final wrap when the actors are called back to re-shoot their part.

Scene

Continuous block of storytelling, set in a single location or following a particular character.

Score

Any printed version of a musical arrangement for opera, film or other musical work in notational form, it may include lyrics or supplemental text.

Screening

The showing of a film for test audiences and/or people involved in the making of the movie, often several different cuts of a movie are produced in the process. This is why a DVD sometimes refers to the term 'director's cut' whereas the final version that hits the theatres is a collaboration between the director, editors, producers and the studio executives.

Script

Blueprint or roadmap outlining a movie story through visual descriptions, actions of characters and their dialogue, a lined script is a copy of the shooting script prepared by the script supervisor during production to indicate (via notations and vertical lines drawn directly onto the script pages) exactly what coverage has been shot. The production script is the script prepared and ready to be put into production. A shooting script has changes known as revised pages made to the production script after the initial circulation. These pages are different in colour and incorporated into the shooting script without displacing or rearranging the original, unrevised pages. A method of script submission in which the writer sends the script (without prior contact) to the theatre or production company is called an unsolicited script.

Sequel

A second creative work (book, movie, play) set in the same universe as the first, but later in time. Often employs elements such as characters, settings or plots as the original story. Opposed to prequel that is set before the original story.

Prequels suffer the disadvantage of the audience knowing what the outcome will be.

Set
The physical elements constructed or arranged to create a sense of place. Usually there is a set designer/art director, as well as other professional designers whose job it is to envision any of the following elements: costumes, sets, lights, sounds or properties.

Sitcom
Also known as a situation comedy. In the US it is normally a 30-minute comedic television show revolving around funny situations for the main characters.

Soap opera
Daytime drama. So-called because it airs during the day and was originally sponsored by the makers of laundry detergent in the early days of television.

Soundstage
Large studio area where elaborate sets may be constructed and usually a sound-proof, hangar-like building.

Spoiler
A summary or description relating plot elements not revealed early in the narrative itself. Moreover, because enjoyment of a narrative sometimes depends upon the dramatic tension and suspense, this early revelation of plot elements can 'spoil' the enjoyment otherwise experienced. The term spoiler is often associated with special Internet sites and in newsgroup postings. Usually, the spoiling information is preceded by a warning.

Stills
Static photographs taken from a movie and usually used for advertising purposes.

Storyboard
An organised set of graphics used to illustrate and visualise the sequence of filming. Looks like a comic and is used early in the filming process to experiment and move scenes around. Newer movie-makers often prefer computerised animations.

Stunts
Trained and professional stunt personnel used in dangerous situations to avoid exposing the cast to any risk or for acts requiring special skills (for instance, diving, falling or a car crash). The stunt is carried out by the actor's stunt double, which is not to be confused with a body/photo double (a look-alike used for scenes where the actor isn't required, i.e. shots where the face isn't visible or for scenes involving nudity).

Subtitles
Also known as Closed Captions (CC). 'Closed' meaning they are only visible when activated (i.e. extra features on a DVD) as opposed to 'open' captioning, where all viewers see the captions all the time (i.e. TV programmes). They are used in the following ways: (i) explanatory when foreign languages are used in a movie, (ii) for hearing impaired and (iii) as general translation for viewers not speaking the language in question.

Syndication
In television, individual stations may buy programmes outside of the network system.

Table-read

When the writer (or writing team) is finished with the script, it's time for the table-read. During this process the entire cast of actors, all the writers, producers and anyone else who is interested, gets together and acts out the script. This is very important because it lets the writers finally hear how their words sound spoken out loud. They pay close attention to the audience's reaction and take notes on what works and what doesn't – for example, do people get the jokes and laugh at the right places? Afterwards, the writers (and sometimes producers) discuss the problems and explore ways to improve the script.

Tape marks

Most times the exact spot where the actors are supposed to be standing is marked with tape on the floor (off-camera), since it's important for the cameraman and the rest of the cast to know where everyone is positioned.

Teaser/Trailer

A set of scenes used for promotional purposes, appearing on television and in theatres before other films is called a teaser since it is used to 'tease' the audience and grab their attention. Like the teaser, the trailer is a short, edited montage of selected scenes to be used as an advertisement for the film, a preview of coming attractions. Running times vary from 15 seconds to 3 minutes. Not everything in the trailer will necessarily appear in the final film since the trailer is often produced early in the filming process. A trailer is sometimes used as a selling tool to raise funds for a feature film. Originally it was shown at the end of a film (hence the term 'trailer'), but people left the theatre before seeing it and so it was moved to the beginning.

Trailer

A mobile home for the actors while filming on location or in a studio, it can be a mid-sized RV (recreational vehicle). The trailers may be elaborately equipped with bedroom, bathroom, small kitchen, etc. since the actors sometimes spend a lot of hours there, preparing their work, having meetings, relaxing, spending time with their family or just hanging out and waiting in-between takes. Some trailers are made into schoolrooms, dressing rooms or hair and make-up trailers, where the cast is fixed up before the shoot. For temporary stays, such as on a movie-set, the trailers do not become so personalised as for larger productions, such as on-going television shows where the actors tend to decorate their home-away-from-home.

Two-shot

Close-up camera shot of two people in the foreground, framed from the chest up, and often in dialogue with each other to indicate relationship information. Likewise three-shot, etc.

VHS

The Video Home System is a recording and playing standard for analogue video-cassette recorders (VCR). The recording medium is magnetic tape. Several variations exist (VHS-C, Super-VHS and others), each again dependent on the type of signal (SECAM, PAL or NTSC).

Voice over

Also known as V.O. or off-camera commentary, a speaker narrates the action onscreen.

Wide-angle shot

A shot filmed with a lens that is able to take in a wider field of view (to capture more of the scene's elements or objects) than a regular lens.

Widescreen

Refers to projection systems in which the aspect ratio is wider than the 1.33:1 ratio, which dominated sound film before the 1950s. In the 1950s, many widescreen processes were introduced to combat the growing popularity of television, such as CinemaScope (an anamorphic system), VistaVision (non-anamorphic production technique in which the film is run horizontally through the camera instead of vertically), and Todd-AO and Super Panavision (both used wider-gauge film). Also known as letterboxing.

Wrap

Term used to define the end of shooting, either for the day or the entire production, and short for Wind Roll And Print. Often associated with the wrap party, where cast, crew, producers, studio executives and other associates get together on the last day of filming to celebrate.

FILMOGRAPHY

Nightmare On Elm Street (1984)
Directed by Wes Craven. Screenplay by Wes Craven. Released by New Line Cinema. Cast: John Saxon, Ronee Blakely, Heather Langenkamp, Amada Wyss, Nick Corri, Johnny Depp, Robert Englund.
US Box Office: $25,504,513

Private Resort (1985)
Directed by George Bowers. Screenplay by Gordon Mitchell. Story by Ken Segull and Alann Wenkus and Gordon Mitchell. Released by Tristar Pictures. Cast Rob Morrow, Johnny Depp, Emily Longstreth, Karyn O'Bryan, Hector Elizondon, Dody Goodman, Tony Azito, Hilary Shapiro, Leslie Easterbrook, Michael Bowen, Lisa London.
US Box Office: $331,816

Slow Burn (TV Movie, 1986)
Directed by Matthew Chapman. Screenplay by Matthew Chapman. Cast: Eric Roberts, Beverly D'Angelo, Dennis Lipscomb, Raymond J Barry, Ann Shedeen, Emily Longstreth, Johnny Depp, Henry Gibson, Dan Hedaya.
US Box Office: N/A

Platoon (1986)
Directed by Oliver Stone. Screenplay by Oliver Stone. Released by Orion Pictures. Cast: Tom Berenger, Willem Dafoe, Charlie Sheen, Forest Whitaker, Francesco Quinn, John C. McGinley, Richard Edson, Kevin Dillon, Reggie Johnson, Keith David, Johnny Depp.
US Box Office: $138,530,565

21 Jump Street (TV Pilot Episode 1987)
Directed by Kim Manners. Screenplay by Patrick Hasburgh. Series created by Patrick Hasburgh & Stephen J Cannell. Cast: Johnny Depp, Frederic Forrest, Holly Robinson, Peter DeLuise, Dustin Nguyen.
US Box Office: N/A

21 Jump Street (TV Series 1987–1990)
Screenplay by Patrick Hasburgh. Series created by Patrick Hasburgh & Stephen J Cannell. Regular Cast: Johnny Depp, (Seasons 1-4), Holly Robinson, Peter DeLuise, Dustin Nguyen.
US Box Office: N/A

Cry Baby (1990)
Directed by John Waters. Screenplay by John Waters. Released by Warner Bros. Cast: Johnny Depp, Amy Locane, Susan Tyrell, Polly Bergen, Iggy Pop, Ricki Lake, Traci Lords, Troy Donahue, Mink Stole, Joe Dallesandro, Patricia Hearst, Willem Dafoe.
US Box Office: $8,266,343

Edward Scissorhands (1990)

Directed by Tim Burton. Screenplay by Caroline Thompson, based on a story by Tim Burton and Caroline Thompson. Released by 20th Century Fox. Cast: Johnny Depp, Winona Ryder, Dianne Wiest, Anthony Michael Hall, Kathy Baker, Robert Oliveri, Vincent Price, Alan Arkin.
US Box Office: $56,362,352

Freddy's Dead: The Final Nightmare (1991, Cameo)

Directed by Rachael Talalay. Screenplay by Michael DeLuca, based on a story by Rachal Talalay. Released by New Line Cinema. Cast: Robert Englund, Lisa Zane, Shon Greenblatt, Yaphet Kotto, Tom Arnold, Roseanne Barr, Johnny Depp, Tobe Sexton.
US Box Office: $34,872,033

Arizona Dream (1991)

Directed by Emir Kusturica. Screenplay by David Atkins, based on a story by David Atkins and Emir Kusturica. Released by Warner Bros. Cast: Johnny Depp, Jerry Lewis, Faye Dunaway, Lili Taylor, Vincent Gallo, Michael J Pollard, Sal Jenco, Iggy Pop.
US Box Office: $112,547

Benny & Joon (1993)

Directed by Jeremiah Chechik. Screenplay by Barry Berman, based on a story by Barry Berman and Leslie McNeil. Released by MGM/UA. Cast: Johnny Depp, Mary Stuart Matherson, Aidan Quinn, Julianne Moore, Oliver Platt, CCH Pounder, Dan Hedaya, William H Macy, Noon Orsatti, Dan Kamin.
US Box Office: $23,261,580

What's Eating Gilbert Grape? (1993)

Directed by Lasse Hallstrom. Screenplay by Peter hedges, based on his novel. Released by Paramount Pictures. Cast: Johnny Depp, Juliette Lewis, Mary Steenurgen, Leonardo DiCaprio, John C. Reilly, Darlene Cates, Laura Harrington, Mary Kate Schellhardt, Crispin Glover, Kevin Tighe, Robert B Hedges.
US Box Office: $10,032,765

Ed Wood (1994)

Directed by Tim Burton.Screenplay by Scott Alexander and Larry Karaszewski, based on the book "Nightmare of Ectasy" by Rudolph Grey. Released by Buena Vista. Cast: Johnny Depp, Martin Landau, Sarah Jessica Parker, Patricia Arquette, Jeffrey Jones, , G.D.Spradin, Vincent D'Onofrio, Bill Murray, Lisa Marie, George "The Animal" Steele, Juliet Landau, Conrad Brooks.
US Box Office: $5,869,802

Don Juan DeMarco (1994)

Directed by Jeremy Leven. Screenplay by Jeremy Leven. Released by New Line Cinema. Cast: Johnny Depp, Marlon Brando, Faye Dunaway, Bob Dishy, Geraldine Pailhas, Talisa Soto, Rachel Ticotin, Marita Geraghty, Richard Sarafian, Tresa Hughes, Jo Champa.
US Box Office: $22,150,451

Dead Man (1995)

Directed by Jim Jarmusch. Screenplay by Jim Jarmusch. Released by Miramax. Cast: Johnny Depp, Crispin Glover, John Hurt, John North, Robert Mitchum, Gibby Haynes, Mili Avital, Peter Schrum, Gabriel Byrne, Lance Henriksen, Gary Farmer, Iggy Pop, Alfred Molina.
US Box Office: $1,037,847

Nick of Time (1995)
Directed by John Badham. Screenplay by Patrick Sheane and Ebbe Roe Smith. Released by Paramount. Cast: Johnny Depp, Christopher Walken, Roma Maffia, Charles Dutton, Marsha Mason, Gloria Reuben, Courtney Chase, Bill Smitrovich, G.D. Spradlin.
US Box Office: $8,175,346

Divine Rapture (1995, uncompleted: 20 minutes of footage shot)
Directed by Thom Eberhardt. Screenplay by Thom Eberhardt. Cast: Johnny Depp, Marlon Brando, Debra Winger, John Hurt.
US Box Office: N/A

The Brave (1996)
Directed by Johnny Depp. Screenplay by Johnny Depp, Paul McCudden and D P Depp. Released by Filmax (Spain). Cast: Johnny Depp, Marlon Brando, Marshall Bell, Elpidia Carrillo, Frederic Forrest, Clarence Williams III, Max Perlich, Luis Guzman, Cody Lightning, Nicole Mancera (Marta), Floyd 'Red Crow' Westerman .
US Box Office: N/A

Donnie Brasco (1996)
Directed by Mike Newell. Screenplay by Paul Attanasio, based on "The Book" by Joseph D Pistone. Released by Sony Pictures. Cast: Johnny Depp, Al Pacino, Michael Madsen, Bruno Kirby, James Russo, Anne Heche, Zeljko Ivanek, Gerry Becker, Robert Miano, Brian Taratina.
US Box Office: $41,909,762

Cannes Man (1996, Cameo)
Directed by Richard Martini. Screenplay by Deric Haddad and Richard Martini. Released by Rocket Pictures Home Video. Cast: Seymour Cassel, Francessco Quinn, Rebecca Broussard, Johnny Depp, Treat Williams, Jim Jarmusch, James Brolin, Jon Cryer, Ann Cusak, Benicio Del Toro, Robert Evans, Dennis Hopper.
US Box Office: N/A

LA Without A Map (1998)
Directed by Mika Kaurismaki. Screenplay by Richard Rayner and Mika Kaurismaki based on the novel Los Angeles Without A Map by Richard Rayner. Released by United Media. Cast: David Tennant, Vanessa Shaw, Julie Delpy, Vincent Gallo, Cameron Bancroft, James Le Gros, Saskia Reeves, Steve Huison, Lisa Edelstein, Joe Dallesandro, Jerzy Skolimowsky, Amanda Plummer, Anouk Aimee, Robert Davi, Johnny Depp Montel Hellman.
US Box Office: N/A

Fear and Loathing in Las Vegas (1998)
Directed by Terry Gilliam. Screenplay by Alex Cox and Tod Davies, based on the book Fear and Loathing in Las Vegas by Hunter S Thompson. Released by Universal. Cast: Johnny Depp, Benicio Del Toro, Jake Busey, Gary Busby, Toby Maguire, Christina Ricci, Tim Thomerson, Harry Dean Stanton, Cameron Diaz, Lyle Lovett, Ellen Barkin, James Woods.
US Box Office: $10,680,275

The Astronaut's Wife (1999)
Directed by Rand Ravich. Screenplay by Rand Ravich. Released by New Line Cinema. Cast: Johnny Depp, Charlize Theron, Blair Brown, Nick Cassavetes, Clea Du Vall, Joe Morton, Donna Murphy, Tom Noonan.
US Box Office: $10,672,566

The Ninth Gate (1999)
Directed by Roman Polanski. Screenplay by John Brownjohn and Roman Polanski. Released by Artisan Entertainment. Cast: Johnny Depp, Frank Langella, Lena Olin, James Russo, Emmanuelle Seigner.
US Box Office: $18,661,336

The Source (1999, Cameo)
Directed by Chuck Workman. Written by Chuck Workman. Released by WinStar Cinema. Cast Johnny Depp, Dennis Hooper, John Turturro. Archive Footage Cast: Steve Allen, William F Buckley, William S Burroughs, Neal Cassady, Walter Cronkite, Bob Dylan, Lawrence Ferlinghetti, Allen Ginsberg, Dennis Hooper, Lyndon Johnson, Jack Kerouac, Ken Kesey, Martin Luther King, Timothy Leary.
US Box Office: $360,895

Sleepy Hollow (1999)
Directed by Tim Burton. Screenplay by Andrew Kevin Walker based on the book by Washington Irving. Released by Paramount. Cast: Johnny Depp, Christina Ricci, Casper Van Dien, Michael Gambon, Lisa Marie, Christopher Walken, Miranda Richardson, Jeffrey Jones, Christopher Lee.
US Box Office: $101,071,502

The Man Who Cried (2000)
Directed by Sally Potter. Screenplay by Sally Potter. Released by Universal. Cast: Johnny Depp, Christina Ricci, Cate Blanchett, John Turturro, Harry Dean Stanton, Oleg Yankovsky.
US Box Office: $747,092

Before Night Falls (2000)

Directed by Julian Schnabel. Screenplay by Cunningham O'Keefe based on the memoir by Reynaldo Arenas. Released by Miramax. Cast: Javier Bardem, Olivier Martinez, Andrea Di Stefano, Johnny Depp, Michael Wincott, Olatz Lopez Garmendia, Giovanni Florido, Lola Navarro, Sebastian Silva, Vito Maria Schnabel, Pedro Armendariz Jr, Diego Luna.
US Box Office: $4,242,892

Chocolat (2000)

Directed by Lasse Hallstrom. Screenplay by Robert Nelson Jacobs based on the novel by Joanne Harris. Released by Miramax. Cast: Juliette Binoche, Johnny Depp, Alfred Molina, Carrie-Anne Moss, Aurlien Parent-Koeing, Antonio Gil-Martinez, Lena Olin, John Wood, Hugh O'Conor, Peter Stormare.
US Box Office: $71,509,363

Blow (2000)

Directed by Ted Demme. Screenplay by David McKenna based on the book by Bruce Porter. Released by New Line Cinema. Cast: Johnny Depp, Penelope Cruz, Franka Potemnete, Rachel Griffiths, Paul Reubens, Jordi Molla, Cliff Curtis, Miguel Sandoval, Ethan Suplee, Ray Liotta, Keven Gage, Max Perlich, Jesse James.
US Box Office: $52,990,775

From Hell (2001)

Directed by The Hughes Brothers. Screenplay by Alan Moore and Eddie Campbell. Released by 20th Century Fox. Cast: Johnny Depp, Heather Graham, Ian Holm, Robbie Coltrane, Ian Richardson, Jason Flemyng, Katrin Cartlidge, Terence Harvey, Susan Lynch, Paul Rhys, Lesley Sharp.
US Box Office: 31,602,566

The Man Who Killed Don Quixote (2001, uncompleted: production suspended)
Directed by Terry Gilliam. Screenplay by Terry Gilliam and Tony Grisoni. Cast: Johnny Depp, Jean Rochefort, Vanessa Paradis.
US Box Office: N/A

Lost in La Mancha (2002, Cameo)
Directed by Keith Fulton and Louis Pepe. Screenplay by Keith Fulton and Louis Pepe. Released by Optimum Releasing. Cast: Jeff Bridges (Narrator), Bernard Bouix, Bernard Chaumeil, Rene Cleitman, Johnny Depp, Jose Luis Escolar, Benjamin Frenandez, Pierre Gamet, Terry Gilliam, Tony Grisoni, Vanessa Paradis, Jean Rochefort.
US Box Office: $732,393

Pirates of the Caribbean: The Curse of the Black Pearl (2003)
Directed by Gore Verbinski. Screenplay by Ted Elliott and Terry Rossio. Released by Buena Vista. Cast: Johnny Depp, Orlando Bloom, Keira Knightley, Geoffrey Rush, Jack Davenport, Jonathan Pryce, Lee Arenburg, Damian O'Hare, Giles New, Angus Barnet, David Bailie, Michael Berry Jr, Mackenzie Crook, Kevin McNally.
US Box Office: $305,411,224

Once Upon A Time in Mexico (2003)
Directed by Robert Rodriguez. Screenplay by Robert Rodriguez. Released by Buena Vista International. Cast: Antonio Banderos, Salma Hayek, Johnny Depp, Mickey Rourke, Eva Mendes, Danny Trejo, Enrique Iglesias, Marco Loenardi, Cheech Marin.
US Box Office: $56,330,657

Secret Window (2004)
Directed by David Koepp. Screenplay by Stephen King and David Koepp. Released by Sony Pictures. Cast: Johnny Depp, Kyle Allatt, Maria Bello, Charles Dutton, Gillian Ferrabee, Timothy Hutton, Richard Jutrus, Ving Rhames, John Turturro.
US Box Office: $44,361,036

Finding Neverland (2004)
Directed by Marc Foster. Screenplay by Allan Knee and David Magee. Released by Miramax. Cast: Johnny Depp, Kate Winslet, Julie Christie, Radha Mitchell, Dustin Hoffman, Freddie Highmore, Joe Prospero, Nick Roud, Luke Spill, Ian Hart, Kelly Macdonald, Mackenzie Crook, Jimmy Gardner.
US Box Office: $51,676,606

The Libertine (2004)
Directed by Laurence Dunmore. Screenplay by Stephen Jeffreys. Released by Miramax. Cast: Johnny Depp, Samantha Morton, John Malkovich, Paul Ritter, Stanley Townsend, Francesca Annis, Rosamund Pike, Tom Hollander, Johnny Vegas, Richard Coyle, Hugh Sachs, Tom Burke, Jack Davenport.
US Box Office: $53,337,608

Charlie And The Chocolate Factory (2004)
Directed by Tim Burton. Screenplay by John August. Released by Warner Bros. Cast: Johnny Depp, Jordan Fry, Freddie Highmore, Geoffrey Holder, David Kelly, AnnaSophia Robb, James Arnold Taylor, Philip Wiegratz, Julia Winter.
US Box Office: $206,456,43

Corpse Bride (2005)
Directed by Tim Burton and Mike Johnson. Screenplay by John August, Pamela Pettler and Caroline Thompson. Released by

Warner Bros. Cast: Johnny Depp, Helena Bonham Carter, Emily Watson, Tracy Ullman, Paul Whitehouse, Joanna Lumley, Albert Finney, Richard E Grant, Christopher Lee, Michael Gough, Jane Horrocks, Enn Reitel, Deep Roy, Danny Elfman, Stephen Ballantyne.
US Box Office: $53,337,608

Pirates of the Caribbean: Dead Man's Chest (2006)
Directed by Gore Verbinski. Screenplay by Terry Rossio and Ted Elliot. Released by Buena Vista. Cast: Johnny Depp, Orlando Bloom, Keira Knightley, Naomie Harris, Bill Nighy, Geoffrey Rush, Stellan Skarsgard, Calleigh White, Claudia Adams, Lee Arenberg, Clive Ashborn, Mackenzie Crook, Jack Davenport, Kevin McNally, Joshamee Gibbs, David Ballie, Martin Klebba.
US Box Office: $423,032,628

Pirates of the Caribbean: At World's End (2007)
Directed by Gore Verbinski. Screenplay by Terry Rossio and Ted Elliot. Released by Buena Vista. Cast: Johnny Depp, Orlando Bloom, Keira Knightley, Geoffrey Rush, Jonathan Pryce, Bill Nighy, Yun-Fat Chow, Tom Hallander, Stellan Skarsgard, Kevin McNally, Jack Davenport, Mackenzie Crook, Lee Arenberg, Martin Klebba, Greg Ellis, Reggie Lee, David Bailie, Naomie Harris, Keith Richards.
US Box Office: $309,420,425

Sweeney Todd (2007)
Directed by Tim Burton. Screenplay by John Logan. Released by Universal. Cast: Johnny Depp, Helena Bonham-Carter, Alan Rickman, Timothy Spall, Christopher Lee, Jayne Wisener, Sacha Baron Cohen, Jamie Campbell Bowen, Laura Michelle Kelly, Anthony Head, Peter Bowles.
US Box Office: $52,898,073

Public Enemies (2009)
Directed by Michael Mann. Screenplay by Ronan Bennett and
Anne Biderman. Released by Universal. Cast: Johnny Depp,
Christian Bale, Channing Tatum, Billy Crudup, Stephen Dorff,
LeeLee Sobieski, Marion Cotillard, Stephen Graham,
Giovanni Ribisi, Branka Katic, Bill Camp, Jason Clarke, Rory
Cochran, Stephen Lang, John Ortiz, David Wenham.
US Box Office: $97,104,620

The Imaginarium of Doctor Parnassus (2009)
Directed by Terry Gilliam. Screenplay by Terry Gilliam and
Charles McKeown. Released by Hoyts Distribution. Cast:
Heath Ledger, Johnny Depp, Colin Farrell, Jude Law,
Christopher Plummer, Tom Waits, Verne Troyer, Lily Cole,
Cassandra Sawtell, Andrew Garfield, Paloma Faith, Ryan
Grantham, Simon Day, Richard Riddell, Fraser Aitcheson,
Vitaly Kravchenko, John Snowden, Igor Ingelsman.
US Box Office: $7,555,233

Alice in Wonderland (2010)
Directed by Tim Burton. Screenplay by Linda Woolverton.
Released by Walt Disney Studios. Cast: Johnny Depp, Michael
Sheen, Anne Hathaway, Helena Bonham Carter, Alan Rickman,
Mia Wasikowska, Stephen Fry, Crispin Glover, Christopher
Lee, Timothy Spall, Matt Lucas, Noah Taylor, Eleanor
Tomlinson, Lindsay Duncan, Annalise Basso, Frances de la Tour,
Tim Pigott-Smith, John Hopkins, Jemma Powell, Geraldine
James, Eleanor Gecks .
US Box Office: $265,800,000

MISCELLANEOUS APPEARANCES

1985
Dummies
Student film short made with Sherilyn Fenn for the American
Film Institute

Lady Blue
Cameo in episode: 'Beasts of Prey'

1987
Hotel
Cameo in episode: 'Unfinished Business'

1990
Joey
Concrete Blonde music video

1991
Silent War
Cameo in Aids documentary with Winona Ryder

Tom Petty In Concert
Host for TV Special

Into The Great Wide Open
Tom Petty music video

1992
It's a Shame About Ray
Lemonheads music video

1994
Top of the Pops
Guest guitarist with the Pogues on UK TV music show

Stuff
Producer for John Frusciante music video

That Woman's Got Me Drinking
Shane MacGowan and the Pogues music video (and director)

1995
United States of Poetry
Cameo in television documentary series

1997
Fade In-Out
Guest slide guitarist on Oasis album track

1998
Austin City Music Awards
Live performance with P

Top Secret
Narrator for US television documentary series

Where's It At: The Rolling Stone State of the Union
Interview in US television documentary

What's Eating Johnny Depp
Interview for UK television documentary

1999
The Vicar of Dibley
Cameo in episode: 'Red Nose Day Special'

2000
The Last Ever Fast Show Christmas Special
Cameo in sketch: 'Suits You'

2001
Que fait la vie?
Director for Vanessa Paradis music video

Pourtant
Director for Vanessa Paradis music video

2002
TNT Tribute To Nicholas Cage
Tribute in US TV Special

In Bad Taste: The John Waters Story
Interview in US television documentary

Inside The Actor's Studio
Interview in US television documentary

Iggy Pop In Concert
Guest guitarist at live gig in France

2003
Bravo Profiles: Johnny Depp
Interview in US television documentary

Charlie: The Life and Art of Charles Chaplin
Cameo in US documentary premiered at Boston Film Festival

2005
Johnny Depp on James Dean
Guest presenter on Radio 2 documentary

AWARDS AND NOMINATIONS

GOLDEN GLOBE

1991
Edward Scissorhands
Nominated for Best Comedic Actor

1994
Benny & Joon
Nominated for Best Comedic Actor

1995
Ed Wood
Nominated for Best Comedic Actor

2004
Pirates of the Caribbean: The Curse of the Black Pearl
Nominated for Best Actor, Comedy or Musical

2005
Finding Neverland
Nominated for Best Actor, Drama

2006
Charlie and the Chocolate Factory
Nominated for Best Actor, Musical or Comedy

2007
Pirates of the Caribbean 2: Dead Man's Chest
Nominated for Best Actor, Musical or Comedy

ACADEMY AWARDS

2004
Pirates of the Caribbean: The Curse of the Black Pearl
Nominated for Best Actor in a Leading Role

2005
Finding Neverland
Nominated for Best Actor in a Leading Role

2008
Sweeney Todd: The Demon Barber of Fleet Street
Nominated for Best Actor in a Leading Role

BRITISH ACADEMY FILM AWARDS (BAFTA)

2004
Pirates of the Caribbean: The Curse of the Black Pearl
Nominated for Best Actor in a Leading Role

2005
Finding Neverland
Nominated for Best Actor in a Leading Role

MISCELLANEOUS NOMINATIONS

1990
SHOWEST AWARDS
Nominated for Male Star of Tomorrow
Winner

1994
MTV MOVIE AWARDS
Benny & Joon
Nominated for Best Comedic Performance
Nominated for Best On-Screen Duo with Mary
Stuart Masterson

1996
LONDON CRITICS CIRCLE FILM AWARDS
Ed Wood and *Don Juan DeMarco*
Nominated for Actor of the Year
Winner

1997
CANNES FILM FESTIVAL
The Brave
Nominated for The Golden Camera
Nominated for The Golden Palm

1998
CHLOTRUDIS AWARDS
Donnie Brasco
Nominated for Best Actor

RUSSIAN GUILD OF FILM CRITICS GOLDEN
ARIES AWARD
Fear and Loathing in Las Vegas
Nominated for Best Foreign Actor
Winner

1999
CESAR AWARD
Honorary Cesar for Contribution to the Arts
Winner

STAR ON THE WALK OF FAME
7020 Hollywood Boulevard

2000
GOLDEN SATELLITE AWARDS
Sleepy Hollow
Nominated for Best Performance by an Actor

BLOCKBUSTER ENTERTAINMENT AWARDS
Sleepy Hollow
Nominated for Favourite Actor in a Horror Film
Winner

SATURN AWARDS
Sleepy Hollow
Nominated for Best Actor

2001
SCREEN ACTOR GUILD AWARDS
Chocolat
Nominated for outstanding Performance by the Cast of a Theatrical Motion Picture with Juliette Binoche, Leslie Caron, Judi Dench, Alfred Molina, Carrie-Anne Moss, Hugh O'Conner, Lena Olin, Peter Stormare, John Wood

2002
SATURN AWARDS
From Hell
Nominated for Best Actor

2003
HOLLYWOOD FILM FESTIVAL
Nominated for Actor of the Year
Winner

WASHINGTON DC AREA FILM CRITICS
ASSOCIATION AWARDS
Pirates of the Caribbean: The Curse of the Black Pearl
Nominated for Best Actor

2004
IFTA AUDIENCE AWARDS
Pirates of the Caribbean: The Curse of the Black Pearl
Nominated for Best International Actor
Winner

MTV MOVIE AWARDS
Pirates of the Caribbean: The Curse of the Black Pearl
Nominated for Best Male Performance
Winner
Also Nominated for Best Comedic Performance and Best On-Screen Team (shared with Orlando Bloom)

MTV MOVIE AWARDS, MEXICO
Pirates of the Caribbean: The Curse of the Black Pearl
Nominated for Best Look
Winner

SATURN AWARD
Pirates of the Caribbean: the Curse of the Black Pearl
Nominated for Best Actor

SCREEN ACTOR GUILD AWARDS
Pirates of the Caribbean: The Curse of the Black Pearl
Nominated for Best Actor
Winner

CRITICS CHOICE
Pirates of the Caribbean: The Curse of the Black Pearl
Nominated for Best Actor

EMPIRE FILM AWARDS
Pirates of the Caribbean: The Curse of the Black Pearl
Nominated for Best Actor
Winner

ONLINE FILM CRITICS SOCIETY AWARDS
Pirates of the Caribbean: The Curse of the Black Pearl
Nominated for Best Actor

GOLDEN SATELLITE AWARDS
Pirates of the Caribbean: The Curse of the Black Pearl
Nominated for Best Actor

Once Upon A Time in Mexico
Nominated for Best Actor

TEEN CHOICE AWARD
Pirates of the Caribbean: The Curse of the Black Pearl
Choice Movie Fight/Action Sequence shared with Orlando
Bloom
Winner

Also Nominated for Choice Movie Liar
Winner

PHOENIX FILM CRITICS SOCIETY AWARD
Pirates of the Caribbean: The Curse of the Black Pearl
Nominated for Best Performance by an Actor in a Leading
Role

CHICAGO FILM CRITICS ASSOCIATION AWARDS
Pirates of the Caribbean: The Curse of the Black Pearl
Nominated for Best Actor

2005
IFTA AUDIENCE AWARDS
Charlie and the Chocolate Factory
Nominated for Best International Actor

SATURN AWARD
Finding Neverland
Nominated for Best Actor

LONDON CRITICS CIRCLE FILM AWARDS
Finding Neverland
Nominated for Actor of the Year

EMPIRE FILM AWARDS
Finding Neverland
Nominated for Best Actor

BRITISH INDEPENDENT FILM AWARDS
The Libertine
Nominated for Best Actor

PEOPLE'S CHOICE AWARD
Nominated for Favourite Male Movie Star
Winner

Finding Neverland
Nominated for Favorite On-Screen Chemistry (with Kate Winslet)

CRITICS CHOICE
Finding Neverland
Nominated for Best Actor

GOLDEN SATELLITE AWARDS
Finding Neverland
Nominated for Best Actor

SCREEN ACTORS GUILD AWARDS
Finding Neverland
Nominated for Outstanding Performance by a Cast in a Motion Picture with Julie Christie, Freddie Highmore, Dustin Hoffman, Radha Mitchell, Joe Prospero, Luke Spill, Kate Winslet

Also Nominated for an Outstanding Performance by a Male Actor in a Leading Role

TEEN CHOICE AWARD
Finding Neverland
Nominated for Choice Movie Actor, Drama.

2006
EMPIRE FILM AWARDS
Charlie and the Chocolate Factory
Nominated for Best Actor
Winner

LONDON CRITICS CIRCLE FILM AWARDS
Charlie and the Chocolate Factory

KIDS CHOICE BLIMP AWARDS
Charlie and the Chocolate Factory
Nominated for Favourite Movie Actor

Corpse Bride
Nominated for Favourite Voice from an Animated Feature

NRJ CINE AWARDS
Charlie and the Chocolate Factory
Nominated for Best Look (Meilleur Look)
Winner

TEEN CHOICE AWARD
Charlie and the Chocolate Factory
Nominated for Choice Movie Actor, Comedy
Winner
Pirates of the Caribbean 2: Dead Man's Chest
Nominated for Choie Movie Actor, Drama/Action
Adventure
Winner

PEOPLE'S CHOICE AWARD
Nominated for Favourite Movie Star
Winner

2007
MTV MOVIE AWARDS
Pirates of the Caribbean 2: Dead Man's Chest
Nominated for Best Male Performance
Winner

EMPIRE FILM AWARDS
Pirates of the Caribbean 2: Dead Man's Chest
Nominated for Best Actor

KIDS CHOICE BLIMP AWARDS
Pirates of the Caribbean 2: Dead Man's Chest
Nominated for Favourite Male Movie Star

NATIONAL MOVIE AWARDS
Pirates of the Caribbean 3: At World's End
Nominated for Best Performance by a Male

PEOPLE'S CHOICE AWARD
Pirates of the Caribbean 2: Dead Man's Chest
Nominated for Favourite Male Movie Star
Winner

Nominated for Best Male Action Star
Winner

Nominated for Favourite On-Screen Match Up (with Keira Knightley)
Winner

REMBRANDT AWARDS
Pirates of the Caribbean 2: Dead Man's Chest
Nominated for Best International Actor
Winner

TEEN CHOICE AWARD
Pirates of the Caribbean 3: At World's End
Nominated for Choice Movie Actor, Action Adventure
Winner

2008
MTV MOVIE AWARDS
Pirates of the Caribbean 3: At World's End
Nominated for Best Comedic Performance
Winner

Sweeney Todd: The Demon Barber of Fleet Street
Nominated for Best Villain
Winner

SATURN AWARD
Sweeney Todd: The Demon Barber of Fleet Street
Nominated for Best Actor

CRITICS CHOICE
Sweeney Todd: The Demon Barber of Fleet Street
Nominated for Best Actor

NATIONAL MOVIE AWARDS
Sweeney Todd: The Demon Barber of Fleet Street
Nominated for Best Performance – Male
Winner

PEOPLE'S CHOICE AWARDS
Nominated for Favourite Male Movie Star
Winner
Also nominated for Favourite Male Action Star

KIDS CHOICE BLIMP AWARDS
Pirates of the Caribbean 3: At World's End
Nominated for Favourite Male Movie Star
Winner

REMBRANDT AWARDS
Pirates of the Caribbean 3: At World's End
Nominated for Best International Actor
Winner

TEEN CHOICE AWARD
Sweeney Todd: The Demon Barber of Fleet Street
Nominated for Choice Movie Villain
Winner

2009
SATELLITE AWARDS
Public Enemies
Nominated for Best Actor in a Motion Picture, Drama

TEEN CHOICE AWARDS
Public Enemies
Nominated for Choice Summer Movie Star, Male

BAHAMAS INTERNATIONAL FILM FESTIVAL
Career Achievement Award
Winner

EMPIRE FILM AWARDS
Sweeney Todd: The Demon Barber of Fleet Street
Nominated for Best Actor

2010
PEOPLE'S CHOICE AWARDS
Nominated for Favourite Movie Star
Winner
Also nominated for Favourite Movie Actor of the Decade
Winner